*T*HIS BOOK *is a treasure and a keepsake,*
a family heirloom in the making
to be cherished forever...

and it belongs to:

_____

NAME

_____

ADDRESS

_____

PHONE

GOBLE & SHEA'S
COMPLETE WEDDING PLANNER
FOR THE ORGANIZED & RELAXED BRIDE
© 1989 by Kathleen Goble and Cecily Shea
published by Multnomah Books
a part of the Questar publishing family

Printed in the United States of America
International Standard Book Number: 0-945564-52-X

For information:
QUESTAR PUBLISHERS, INC.
POST OFFICE BOX 1720
SISTERS, OREGON 97759

96 97 98 99 00 01 — 20 19 18 17 16 15 14 13 12 11

GOBLE & SHEA'S
COMPLETE WEDDING PLANNER

FOR THE ORGANIZED
& RELAXED BRIDE

QUESTAR PUBLISHERS, INC.

*W*HILE PLANNING THE WEDDINGS of Cecily and her brother Jeff—two weddings in thirteen days!—we became inundated by the myriad details involved in pulling them off successfully. To add to the mounting details, we were also preparing for the junior high graduation of our twins, Heidi and Chris (which would take place between the two weddings), and at home were hosting my nephew, his wife, and their six-month-old son, who were living with us for three months.

I knew the only way to survive all this (and to really *enjoy* the weddings—which I was determined to do!) —would be to keep organized.

When we consulted available wedding books, the organizational tools suggested were file cards and boxes for the guest list and gift registry, file folders and envelopes for contracts and receipts, and general countdown lists and calendars. But even as we used these tools, things were misplaced, causing wasted time and frazzled nerves as we repeatedly were delayed in putting our fingers on the exact information we were seeking. Even the tools themselves added to the general clutter of wedding apparel, trousseau, gifts, and decorations that began to overflow the house.

Through it all the idea was born for having everything in one location, using *only one tool*—an organizational planner for weddings. For today's busy bride, who often is already actively involved in career and other pursuits, we knew such a tool would be a welcome aid in helping her achieve her wedding day desires with as few hassles as possible.

The result:
        this *COMPLETE WEDDING PLANNER*...just for you!

KATHLEEN GOBLE

Contents

ATTIRE & ATTENDANTS

THE RECEPTION

SERVICES

SPECIAL PARTIES

Family & Bridal Party • Ceremony & Reception Sites • Professional Services • Party Hostesses • Other • Future Home

Our Engagement Keepsake

MY FIANCÉ'S NAME: David, Paul, Jensen

WHERE HE LIVES: We live together at 9405-156 ST
Edmonton, AB

HIS PARENTS' NAMES: Victor and Primrose Jensen

WHERE THEY LIVE: They live at 8620 - 180 ST
Edmonton, AB

WHERE WE WERE WHEN HE ASKED ME TO MARRY HIM: In our basment

WHAT HE SAID TO ME: Baby, Will you marry me?

WHAT I SAID TO HIM: Yes, Yes!

WHAT I WAS WEARING: Sweats, and a T-shirt

WHAT HE WAS WEARING: Jeans and a shint.

WHAT WE WERE DOING: Celebrating Christmas Eve.

HOW WE TOLD MY PARENTS: All parents were there

WHAT WE SAID: N/A

WHAT THEY SAID: Congratulations.

HOW WE TOLD HIS PARENTS: All parents were there.

WHAT WE SAID: _____

_____

WHAT THEY SAID: Congratulations _____

_____

HOW WE TOLD OUR FRIENDS: _____

_____

WHAT WE SAID: _____

_____

_____

WHAT THEY SAID: _____

_____

_____

_____

NEWSPAPER ANNOUNCEMENT: _____

_____

_____

_____

_____

ENGAGEMENT PARTIES: _____

_____

_____

_____

OTHER SPECIAL MEMORIES OF OUR ENGAGEMENT: When Paul asked me to marry him it was Christmas Eve. He had given me my engagement ring as a gift for Christmas. The funny thing was he took our dog's blanket out of our van and wrapped my ring in the dogs blanket the wrapped the blanket to trick me into thinking it was something totally different. It worked!

Introduction

IN RECENT YEARS we've seen a resurgence in popularity of the traditional wedding style. And yet today's couples are not holding to the rigid structure of the past, but are taking the best from the contemporary styles of the 60's and 70's to freshen their traditional weddings.

There's more to planning a traditional wedding than simply collecting something old, something new, something borrowed, and something blue — though this wedding lore could be taken as a bride's first step of organization.

Like every bride, you have a familiarity with weddings and an idea of what you want your own to be like. But how do you personally translate your knowledge of weddings into a workable plan? How do you utilize your time effectively? These are the key questions this book addresses while guiding you in planning the wedding of your dreams.

Let us suggest that you first take a few moments to familiarize yourself with the material presented in this book.

Second, work through the Planning Checklist (page 17), and make a note of the items listed there that are appropriate to your situation. Then incorporate those items into your planning calendars (beginning on page 29).

But above all, remember not to let wedding details overshadow your relationship with your fiance'. Nurturing this relationship now is vitally important to your future happiness, so we recommend that you, as a couple, either participate in premarital counseling or a marriage preparation class (many churches, synagogues, and family counseling centers provide these services). No one wants to think their marriage may end in a divorce, and by attending such a class you lessen the possibility of becoming another divorce statistic.

If at this time you feel you will always have divorce as a way "out" if things don't work, then maybe you're not ready to be married. More than anything else, a high level of commitment to one another is the necessary ingredient in a successful marriage — and that commitment means enduring through the bad times as well as the good.

Also remember to set aside time before the wedding to become better acquainted with the parents of the one you love. Without them, this wouldn't be happening!

Finally— don't take yourself and all this planning too seriously. Instead, take plenty of time …

to relax,

to enjoy each other,

and to grow in love!

PLANNING CHECKLISTS

PLANNING CHECKLISTS

- After you've had the chance to familiarize yourself with the entire book, read through the Planning Checklists and make a note of the items that are appropriate to your situation. Then, incorporate those items into your planning calendars (these begin on page 29).

- Today's grooms are taking a more active role in planning their weddings. So provide your fiancé with a copy of the Groom's Planning Checklist. Having this list will help eliminate any confusion he may feel about the wedding planning process. And by knowing what needs to be done, he'll be able to participate as fully as he desires.

Bride's Planning Checklist

❖ SIX TO TWELVE MONTHS BEFORE ❖

☐ Incorporate items from this Planning Checklist into your COMPLETE WEDDING PLANNER calendar beginning on page 29).

☐ Set a budget for the wedding, working together with those responsible. Use the information on estimated cost percentages on page 98. Record the agreed amounts on Worksheet 1 (page 99).

☐ Complete Worksheet 3 (page 105) with your fiancé to record your choices for the the style (degree of formality) for your wedding; the wedding date and time; and the wedding location.

☐ Select and reserve your ceremony site using Worksheet 5 (page 107). You should also reserve a time now for the wedding rehearsal.

☐ Select and reserve your reception site using Worksheets 14 and 15 (pages137-139).

☐ Coordinate the date and time you've chosen with both the ceremony and reception sites.

☒ Use Worksheet 4 (page 106) as you select the officiant for the wedding ceremony.

☐ If you decide to consult with a wedding coordinator, use Worksheet 8 (page 111) as you meet with various candidates and decide which one to use.

☒ Confirm the wedding and rehearsal times and dates with your officiant and/or wedding coordinator.

☒ Arrange for premarital counseling or marriage preparation classes with your officiant or a family counseling center.

☒ Decide on the approximate number of guests and begin to compile a tentative list.

☒ Select the color scheme for your wedding and reception.

☐ Use the *Wedding Gown Search List* (page 121) and Worksheet 9 (page 122) as you shop for your wedding gown, headpiece, veil, and other accessories.

☒ Soon after setting a wedding date, select your attendants and invite them to participate.

☐ Use the *Bridal Attendants List* (page 127) to record their names, addresses, phone numbers, and clothing sizes.

☐ Select and order your bridal attendants' dresses. Use Worksheet 11 (page 126) to help in this process.

☐ Talk with the mothers about their dresses for the wedding.

❖ Use the worksheets indicated below as you select professionals to provide the following for your special day…

      ❏ *music* (Worksheet 24, page 156)

      ❏ *flowers* (Worksheet 27, page 162)

      ❏ *photography* (Worksheet 29, page 168)

      ❏ *reception catering* (Worksheet 16, page 140)

      ❏ *cake* (Worksheet 19, page 143)

      ❏ *video-taping and audio-taping* (Worksheets 30 and 32, pages 170 and 172)

These professionals often are booked months in advance, so contact them as early as possible.

❏ Register with the Bridal Gift Registry of your favorite store. Use the *Gift Registry* (page 91) as a guide to your selection of possible gift choices.

❖ THREE TO SIX MONTHS BEFORE ❖

❏ Set a deadline no later than three months before the wedding date for your families' completed guest lists.

❏ Use Worksheets 22 and 23 (pages 153-155) as you order the invitations, announcements, enclosures, and other personal stationery and accessories.

❏ Order your groom's ring.

❏ Coordinate the Rehearsal Dinner with the groom's parents.

❏ Provide the Rehearsal Dinner hosts with a list of guests to be invited (use the form on page 200).

❏ Use the guest lists on pages 189-191 when compiling names for Bridal Shower hostesses.

❏ Continue using Worksheet 9 (page 122) as you shop for wedding attire and accessories.

❏ Tell each bridal attendant where their bridal accessories may be purchased.

❏ Coordinate your wardrobe with the trousseau inventory in Worksheet 10 (page 123).

❖ Schedule appointments for your…

      ❏ physical examination   ❏ dental examination   ❏ eye examination

❏ Begin looking for a place to live. If you plan to rent, consult the *Rental Housing Checklist* (page 214).

❏ Use the *Home Furnishings Purchase Plan* (page 218) and Worksheet 50 (*Keep or Toss*, page 220) as you plan and shop for home furnishings.

❏ Discuss honeymoon plans with your fiancé.

❖ TWO MONTHS BEFORE ❖

❖ As gifts arrive, enter descriptions into the gift record of the *Guest List* section, and write thank-you notes. If local custom or family tradition warrants, plan a gift display area in your home.

☐ Address and mail invitations three to five weeks before the wedding.

☐ Buy and wrap your groom's wedding gift.

☐ Buy and wrap your bridal attendants' gifts. Note these gifts on the *Bridal Attendants List* on page 127.

☐ Check on the delivery dates of your gown and the attendants' dresses.

☐ As you decide on the clothes for your honeymoon, use the checklist on page 124.

☐ Plan where to dress on your wedding day.

☐ As you and your fiancé meet with the officiant to plan the order of your wedding ceremony, use Worksheets 6 and 7 (pages 109-110).

☐ Plan your wedding music. To help you, use the list of musical selection ideas on page 245, plus the worksheets and guidelines on pages 156-161.

☐ Finalize plans with the florist. Use the worksheets and other guides on pages 162-167.

☐ Finalize plans with the photographer. Use Worksheet 29 (page 168) and the planning list and guidelines on page 169.

☐ Finalize reception plans with the caterer. Use Worksheets 17 and 18 (pages 141-142), plus the diagrams on page 147.

☐ Finalize plans for the wedding cake with the bakery, using Worksheet 20 (page 144).

☐ Use Worksheet 31 (page 171) to finalize plans for video-taping.

☐ Use Worksheet 33 (page 173) to finalize plans for audio-taping.

☐ Plan the wedding rehearsal with the officiant and/or wedding coordinator. Use the *Rehearsal Information List* on page 115.

☐ Use Worksheet 34 (page 174) as you make lodging or travel plans for out-of-town guests.

☐ To arrange for wedding day transportation for the wedding party, use Worksheets 35 and 36 (pagex 177-178).

☐ Order any rental equipment needed for the wedding and reception. Refer to the *Equipment List* on page 179 for any accessory ideas.

❖ ONE MONTH BEFORE ❖

☐ Have your groom's ring engraved.

☐ Continue writing thank-you notes as gifts arrive.

- [ ] Address your wedding announcements.
- [ ] Make arrangements for the bridal luncheon (or dinner or party) for your bridal attendants. Use the guest list and worksheets on pages 192-194.
- [ ] Write or phone invitations to your attendants for the bridal luncheon.
- [ ] Schedule your formal bridal portrait.
- [ ] Schedule an appointment to have your hair and nails done a day or two before the wedding, with a comb-out on your wedding day.
- [ ] Confirm that your attendants have purchased their wedding accessories.
- [ ] If the attendants' shoes are being dyed to match, have them done at this time.
- [ ] Schedule fittings for your gown.
- [ ] Have each bridal attendant be responsible for making and keeping her own fittings.
- [ ] Start packing your personal belongings for moving.
- [ ] Make plans for the pre-ceremony buffet on the wedding day. Use the guest list and worksheet on pages 195-196.
- [ ] Make any necessary arrangements for after-the-wedding cleanup, return of rental equipment, and transportation of gifts. For assistance, use the *Reception Organizer* on page 148 and Worksheet 37 on page 183.
- [ ] Discuss future financial details with your fiancé.
- [ ] Refer to the *Financial/Legal Checklist* on page 212 for any needed name, address, or beneficiary changes.
- [ ] Use Worksheet 47 (page 211) as you check on your state's marriage requirements.
- [ ] If necessary, have premarital blood tests taken.
- [ ] Go with your fiancé to obtain your marriage license.

❖ TWO WEEKS BEFORE ❖

- [ ] Continue writing thank-you notes.
- [ ] Begin keeping your wedding day clothes in one place. Check them off, using the *Bride's Wedding Day Checklist* on page 125.
- [ ] Pack your clothes for the honeymoon, using the checklist on page 124.
- [ ] Give a copy of the *Bridal Attendants' Guidelines* (page 128) to each attendant.
- [ ] Use Worksheet 48 (page 213) as a guide for writing your wedding announcement, and prepare to have it sent to the newspaper office after the wedding.
- [ ] Have the ceremony programs printed.

- ☐ Obtain a "floater" insurance policy, if necessary, to cover your wedding gifts until you obtain a homeowner's or renter's policy.

- ☐ Arrange for someone to be at your home on the wedding day to answer the phone and keep an eye on things while the family is away.

- ☐ Make arrangements, if necessary, for a policeman or other attendant to direct traffic and parking for the ceremony and reception.

- ☐ Arrange for someone to mail your wedding announcements immediately after the wedding.

- ☐ Send information on guest housing and transportation (see page 175) to your out-of-town guests.

- ☐ Give the list of *Transportation Guidelines for Drivers* (page 176) to those who will be driving out-of-town guests.

❖ *ONE WEEK BEFORE* ❖

- ☐ Keep writing those thank-you notes.

- ☐ Have a final fitting for your wedding gown.

- ☐ Find something to protect your gown—tissue paper, plastic, or a sheet—while transporting it to the ceremony site.

- ❖ Make arrangements for delivery or pickup of…

  - ☐ dresses
  - ☐ wedding cake
  - ☐ beverages
  - ☐ rental equipment, etc.

- ❖ Double-check all plans with phone calls to these people:

  - ☐ coordinator for ceremony site
  - ☐ officiant
  - ☐ musicians
  - ☐ florist
  - ☐ photographer
  - ☐ video operator
  - ☐ audio operator
  - ☐ coordinator for reception site
  - ☐ caterer
  - ☐ cake baker
  - ☐ provider of rental equipment
  - ☐ provider of limo service

- ☐ Check on outdoor automatic lighting and watering schedules for any time conflict with the ceremony or reception.

- ☐ If necessary, make any phone calls to late respondents for the reception head-count.

- ☐ Confirm the number of acceptances with the reception site and caterer.

- ☐ Prepare seating charts or place cards for the reception.

- ☐ Make up an emergency kit—needle, thread, safety pins, bobby pins, tissues, etc.—to be taken to the ceremony site.

- ☐ If any festivities are to be held at your home, arrange to board your pets for the day.

- ❖ Attend your bridal luncheon with your attendants.

❖ *ONE DAY BEFORE* ❖

- ☐ Complete all decorating (have your bridal attendants help).

- ❖ Attend the rehearsal.

- ☐ Give a copy of Worksheet 13 (*Ushers' Assignments*, page 134) to the head usher at the rehearsal.

- ❖ Attend the Rehearsal Dinner.

❖ YOUR WEDDING DAY ❖

- ❖ Bathe slowly.

- ❖ Apply make-up carefully.

- ❖ Dress for the wedding.

- ❖ Close your suitcase.

- ❖ Let someone else check on any last-minute details.

- ❖ Relax.

- ❖ Enjoy every moment.

Groom's Planning Checklist

❖ SIX TO TWELVE MONTHS BEFORE ❖

☐ Determine the wedding budget with your fiancée and your families. Use Worksheet 2 (page 101) as a checklist for your financial responsibilities.

☐ Discuss ceremony and reception sites with your bride-to-be.

☐ Begin compiling a guest list with your family.

☐ With your fiancée, visit the officiant who will perform the ceremony.

☐ With your bride-to-be, take part in premarital counseling or marriage preparation classes.

☐ Select your best man and other attendants and invite them to participate. Write their names and addresses on the *Groom's Attendants List* (page 132).

☐ With your fiancée, discuss preferences for the *Gift Registry* (page 91).

❖ THREE TO SIX MONTHS BEFORE ❖

☐ Purchase your fiancée's engagement and wedding rings.

☐ Complete your guest list and give it to your fiancée no later than three months prior to the wedding.

☐ Decide on the style and color of your wedding attire and accessories (see Worksheet 12, page 129), and order as necessary.

☐ With your family, arrange for the Rehearsal Dinner. To assist you, use Worksheets 44-46 (pages 202-204) and the guest list on page 200.

☐ With your fiancée, begin your search for your new home. (See the checklist on page 214.)

☐ Plan and purchase needed home furnishings. (See the checklists on pages 218-220.)

☐ Discuss honeymoon plans with your fiancée, and use Worksheet 38 (page 184) to begin making arrangements.

☐ If you plan to travel abroad, update passports, visas, and inoculations.

❖ Schedule appointments for your…

  ☐ physical examination   ☐ dental examination   ☐ eye examination

☐ Decide on the attire for the fathers and your attendants, again using Worksheet 12 on page 129.

❖ TWO MONTHS BEFORE ❖

☐ Plan the order of the wedding ceremony with your fiancée and the officiant.

☐ Purchase and wrap your gift for your bride-to-be.

☐ Purchase and wrap your gifts for your attendants.

☐ With your fiancée, make necessary housing and transportation arrangements for out-of-town guests.

☐ Complete your honeymoon plans, and make reservations.

☐ As needed, use Worksheet 49 (page 216) to plan your move into your new home.

❖ ONE MONTH BEFORE ❖

☐ Have your fiancée's wedding ring engraved.

☐ Shop for any wedding or honeymoon attire you need.

☐ Confirm that your best man, ushers, and both fathers have ordered their wedding attire and have scheduled their fittings.

☐ If necessary for the marriage license, have premarital blood tests taken.

☐ Go with your fiancé to obtain your marriage license.

☐ Finalize plans for the Rehearsal Dinner.

☐ Address and mail—or phone—invitations to the Rehearsal Dinner.

☐ If you're giving a Bachelor's Party, make arrangements for it — using the guest list and Worksheets 42 and 43 on pages 197-199.

☐ Discuss future financial details with your fiancée, using the checklist on page 212.

❖ TWO WEEKS BEFORE ❖

☐ Give copies of the *Groom's Attendants Guidelines* (page 133) to the best man and ushers.

☐ Finalize plans for the Bachelor's Party.

☐ Confirm all honeymoon arrangements.

☐ Begin packing to move.

❖ ONE WEEK BEFORE ❖

☐ Schedule a haircut early in the week.

☐ Have a final fitting for your formal wear.

❏ Arrange for your transportation to the ceremony site.

❏ Confirm with your banquet manager the head count for the Rehearsal Dinner.

❏ Confirm with your banquet manager the head count for the Bachelor's Party.

❏ Using the checklist on page 130, begin packing for the honeymoon.

❏ At the Bachelor's Party or the Rehearsal Dinner, give gifts to your attendants.

❖ *ONE DAY BEFORE* ❖

❏ Pick up wedding attire.

❏ Use the checklist on page 131 to set aside clothes for the wedding and afterwards.

❖ Attend the rehearsal.

❖ Attend the Rehearsal Dinner.

❖ *YOUR WEDDING DAY* ❖

❖ Have breakfast with your family.

❖ Shower and dress for the wedding.

❖ Give the wedding ring, marriage license, and the envelope for the officiant to the best man.

❖ Designate someone to take care of any last minute details.

❖ Relax.

❖ Enjoy every moment.

Sun.	Mon.	Tues.	Wed.	Thurs.	Fri.	Sat.
	1	1	1	2	3	4
5	6	7	5	9	10	11
12	13	14	15	16	17	18
19	20	21	22	23	24	25
26	27	28	29	30		

	Sun.	Mon.	Tues.	Wed.	Thurs.	Fri.	Sat.
	1	2	3	4	5	6	7
	8	9	10	11	12	13	14
	15	16	17	18	19	20	21
	22	23	24	25	26	27	28
	29	30	31				

THIS MONTH: FEBUARY

Sat.	Fri.	Thurs.	Wed.	Tues.	Mon.	Sun.
7	6	5	4	3	2	1
14	13	12	11	10	9	8
21	20	19	18	17	16	15
28	27	26	25	24	23	22

	Sat.	Fri.	Thurs.	Wed.	Tues.	Mon.	Sun.
	3	2	1				
	10	9	8	7	6	5	4
	17	16	15	14	13	12	11
	24	23	22	21	20	19	18
	31	30	29	28	27	26	25

THIS MONTH: December

MONTHS TO GO: 7'½

Sun.	Mon.	Tues.	Wed.	Thurs.	Fri.	Sat.
	1	2	3	4	5	6
7	8	9	10	11	12	13
14	15	16	17	18	19	20
21	22	23	24	25	26	27
28	29	30	31			

THIS MONTH:

November

Sat. 1	8	15	22	29
Fri.	7	14	21	28
Thurs.	6	13	20	27
Wed.	5	12	19	26
Tues.	4	11	19	25
Mon.	3	10	17	24	31
Sun.	2	9	16	23	30

THIS MONTH: October

Sat.	4	11	18	25	
Fri.	3	10	17	24	31
Thurs.	2	9	16	23	30
Wed.	1	8	15	22	29
Tues.		7	14	21	28
Mon.		6	13	20	27
Sun.		5	12	19	26

THIS MONTH:

SEPTEMBER

Sat. 6	13	20	27	
Fri. 5	12	19	26	
Thurs. 4	11	18	25	
Wed. 3	10	17	24	
Tues. 2	9	16	23	30
Mon. 1	8	15	22	29
Sun.	7	14	21	28

THIS MONTH: Jul August /97

	Sat.	Fri.	Thurs.	Wed.	Tues.	Mon.	Sun.
	2	1			1		
	9	8	7	6	5	4	3
	16	15	14	13	12	11	10
	23	22	21	20	19	18	17
	30	29	28	27	26	25 / 27	24 / 31

CALENDARS

- Incorporate the appropriate items from your Planning Checklist (pages 17-22) into these calendars.

- Use the monthly calendars early in your planning, when there are fewer details to record. (Nine monthly calendars have been provided for you here.)

- As your list of things to do and remember grows longer during the last weeks before the wedding, you can keep track of them better by switching to the weekly calendars (ten are provided here), and then the daily calendars (there are fourteen here — enough for each day in those final two weeks).

CALENDARS

| Mon. | WEEKS TO GO: | DATE: April 27 |
| | 12 1/2 | |

| Tues. | | DATE: 28 |

| Wed. | | DATE: 29 |

| Thurs. | | DATE: 30 |

| Fri. | | DATE: May 1 |

| Sat. | | DATE: 2 |

| Sun. | | DATE: 3 |

	DATE:
Mon.	4
Tues.	15
Wed.	16
Thurs.	7
Fri.	8
Sat.	9
Sun.	10

	DATE:
Mon.	11
Tues.	12
Wed.	13
Thurs.	14
Fri.	15
Sat.	16
Sun.	17

Mon.	**DATE:** 18
Tues.	**DATE:** 19
Wed.	**DATE:** 20
Thurs.	**DATE:** 21
Fri.	**DATE:** 22
Sat.	**DATE:** 23
Sun.	**DATE:** 24

Mon.

DATE: 25

Tues.

DATE: 26

Wed.

DATE: 27

Thurs.

DATE: 28

Fri.

DATE: 29

Sat.

DATE: 30

Sun.

DATE: 31

	DATE:
Mon.	June 1
Tues.	2
Wed.	3
Thurs.	4
Fri.	5
Sat.	6
Sun.	7

	DATE:
Mon.	8
Tues.	9
Wed.	10
Thurs.	11
Fri.	12
Sat.	13
Sun.	14

	DATE:
Mon.	15
Tues.	16
Wed.	17
Thurs.	18
Fri.	19
Sat.	20
Sun.	21

	DATE:
Mon.	22

	DATE:
Tues.	23

	DATE:
Wed.	24

	DATE:
Thurs.	25

	DATE:
Fri.	26

	DATE:
Sat.	27

	DATE:
Sun.	28

Mon.

DATE: 29

Tues.

DATE: 30

Wed.

DATE: July

Thurs.

DATE: 2

Fri.

DATE: 3

Sat.

DATE:

Sun.

DATE:

TODODAY'S DATE: July 4   DAY OF THE WEEK: Saturday   DAYS TO GO: 14

a.m.

p.m.

notes:

TODODAY'S DATE: July 5   DAY OF THE WEEK: Sunday   DAYS TO GO: 13

a.m.

p.m.

notes:

TODAY'S DATE: July 6   DAY OF THE WEEK: Monday   DAYS TO GO: 12

a.m.

p.m.

notes:

TODAY'S DATE: July 7   DAY OF THE WEEK: Tuesday   DAYS TO GO: 11

a.m.

p.m.

notes:

TODAY'S DATE: July 8   DAY OF THE WEEK: Wendsday   DAYS TO GO: 10

a.m.

p.m.

notes:

TODAY'S DATE: July 9   DAY OF THE WEEK: Thursday   DAYS TO GO: 9

a.m.

p.m.

notes:

TODAY'S DATE: July 10   DAY OF THE WEEK: Friday   DAYS TO GO: 8

a.m.

p.m.

notes:

TODAY'S DATE: July 11   DAY OF THE WEEK: Saterday   DAYS TO GO: 7

a.m.

p.m.

notes:

TODAY'S DATE: July 12   DAY OF THE WEEK: Sunday   DAYS TO GO: 6

a.m.

p.m.

notes:

TODAY'S DATE: July 13   DAY OF THE WEEK: Monday   DAYS TO GO: 5

a.m.

p.m.

notes:

TODAY'S DATE: July 14   DAY OF THE WEEK: Tuesday   DAYS TO GO: 4

a.m.

p.m.

notes:

TODAY'S DATE: July 15/98   DAY OF THE WEEK: Werdsday   DAYS TO GO: 3

a.m.

p.m.

notes:

TODAY'S DATE: July 16/98   DAY OF THE WEEK: Thursday   DAYS TO GO: 2

a.m.

p.m.

notes:

TODAY'S DATE: July 17/98   DAY OF THE WEEK: Friday   DAYS TO GO: 1

a.m.

p.m.

notes:

GUESTS & GIFTS

Guests & Gifts

- You can use the main *Guest List* as a checklist for sending wedding and reception invitations, as well as announcements. You can also use it to record:

    * the responses of your guests (so important in obtaining a final count for the reception caterer);

    * gifts received;

    * and thank-you notes sent.

- You may wish to keep alphabetized the names in the main Guest List. If so, set aside approximately the following number of pages for each letter or letter combination (you can use any of the boxes on the left side of the guest list pages as a letter indicator):

A — 1		K-L — 3	
B — 3		M — 3	
C — 2		N-O — 1	
D-E — 2		P-Q — 2	
F — 1		R — 2	
G — 1		S — 4	
H — 2		T — 1	
I-J — 1		U-V — 1	
	W-X-Y-Z — 2		

- Provide your fiancé and his family with a copy of the *Groom's Guest List*. Once they have completed it, you can combine their information into the main Guest List.

- Information in the *Gift Registry* is given as a guide to your suggestion of gift items. Note the places provided for recording the retail price of each item — this may seem time-consuming now, but it will benefit you later when determining the replacement value of your household furnishings for insurance purposes.

Guest List

							thank you:
Name: Victor and Primrose Jensen	**Phone:** 487-1798				**GIFTS:**		
Children: None					shower:		☐
Address: 8620 - 180 ST					shower:		☐
City: EDMONTON	**State:** AB	**Zip:** T5T-0X9	❀		wedding:		☐
Wedding Invitation: ☒	**Reception Invitation:** ☒	**Announcement:** ☐	**RSVP** — yes: ☐ no: ☐	*number invited:* 2	*number attending:* 2		

							thank you:
Name: Dave Rayner	**Phone:** 484·6065				**GIFTS:**		
Children: NONE					shower:		☐
Address:					shower:		☐
City: EDMONTON	**State:** AB	**Zip:**	❀		wedding:		☐
Wedding Invitation: ☐	**Reception Invitation:** ☐	**Announcement:** ☐	**RSVP** — yes: ☐ no: ☐	*number invited:* 1	*number attending:*		

							thank you:
Name: Ruby and Steve	**Phone:**				**GIFTS:**		
Children:					shower:		☐
Address:					shower:		☐
City:	**State:**	**Zip:**	❀		wedding:		☐
Wedding Invitation: ☐	**Reception Invitation:** ☐	**Announcement:** ☐	**RSVP** — yes: ☐ no: ☐	*number invited:* 2	*number attending:*		

							thank you:
Name: Len and Ulla	**Phone:**				**GIFTS:**		
Children:					shower:		☐
Address:					shower:		☐
City: Vancouver	**State:** BC	**Zip:**	❀		wedding:		☐
Wedding Invitation: ☐	**Reception Invitation:** ☐	**Announcement:** ☐	**RSVP** — yes: ☐ no: ☐	*number invited:* 2	*number attending:*		

							thank you:
Name: Lyn and John	**Phone:**				**GIFTS:**		
Children:					shower:		☐
Address:					shower:		☐
City: Vancouver	**State:** B.C.	**Zip:**	❀		wedding:		☐
Wedding Invitation: ☐	**Reception Invitation:** ☐	**Announcement:** ☐	**RSVP** — yes: ☐ no: ☐	*number invited:* 2	*number attending:*		

							thank you:
Name: Antee Laura	**Phone:**				**GIFTS:**		
Children:					shower:		☐
Address:					shower:		☐
City: Vancouver	**State:** BC	**Zip:**	❀		wedding:		☐
Wedding Invitation: ☐	**Reception Invitation:** ☐	**Announcement:** ☐	**RSVP** — yes: ☐ no: ☐	*number invited:* 1	*number attending:*		

							thank you:
Name: Doug and Fazelia	**Phone:**				**GIFTS:**		
Children:					shower:		☐
Address:					shower:		☐
City:	**State:**	**Zip:**	❀		wedding:		☐
Wedding Invitation: ☐	**Reception Invitation:** ☐	**Announcement:** ☐	**RSVP** — yes: ☐ no: ☐	*number invited:* 2	*number attending:*		

							thank you:
Name: Antee Elsie	**Phone:**				**GIFTS:**		
Children:					shower:		☐
Address:					shower:		☐
City:	**State:** England	**Zip:**	❀		wedding:		☐
Wedding Invitation: ☒	**Reception Invitation:** ☒	**Announcement:** ☐	**RSVP** — yes: ☐ no: ☐	*number invited:* 1	*number attending:*		

							thank you:
Name: Uncle Roy	**Phone:**				**GIFTS:**		
Children:					shower:		☐
Address:					shower:		☐
City:	**State:** England	**Zip:**	❀		wedding:		☐
Wedding Invitation: ☒	**Reception Invitation:** ☒	**Announcement:** ☐	**RSVP** — yes: ☐ no: ☐	*number invited:* 1	*number attending:*		

Name: Chris Jensen	Phone:	**GIFTS:**	thank you:
Children:		shower:	❏
Address:		shower:	❏
City: EDMONTON	State: A B	Zip: ❀	wedding:	❏
Wedding Invitation: ☒ Reception Invitation: ☒ Announcement: ❏	RSVP — yes: ❏ no: ❏	number invited: 2 number attending:	

Name: Mom Starratt	Phone:	**GIFTS:**	thank you:
Children:		shower:	❏
Address:		shower:	❏
City: EDMONTON	State:	Zip: ❀	wedding:	❏
Wedding Invitation: ❏ Reception Invitation: ❏ Announcement: ❏	RSVP — yes: ❏ no: ❏	number invited: 2 number attending:	

Name: Dad Paul	Phone:	**GIFTS:**	thank you:
Children:		shower:	❏
Address:		shower:	❏
City: Westlock	State:	Zip: ❀	wedding:	❏
Wedding Invitation: ❏ Reception Invitation: ❏ Announcement: ❏	RSVP — yes: ❏ no: ❏	number invited: 2 number attending:	

Name: Grandma Paul	Phone:	**GIFTS:**	thank you:
Children:		shower:	❏
Address:		shower:	❏
City: Westlock	State:	Zip: ❀	wedding:	❏
Wedding Invitation: ❏ Reception Invitation: ❏ Announcement: ❏	RSVP — yes: ❏ no: ❏	number invited: 2 number attending:	

Name: Lyndy and Connie	Phone:	**GIFTS:**	thank you:
Children:		shower:	❏
Address:		shower:	❏
City: Fort Vermillion	State:	Zip: ❀	wedding:	❏
Wedding Invitation: ❏ Reception Invitation: ❏ Announcement: ❏	RSVP — yes: ❏ no: ❏	number invited: 2 number attending:	

Name: Uncle Amos and Elva	Phone:	**GIFTS:**	thank you:
Children:		shower:	❏
Address:		shower:	❏
City:	State:	Zip: ❀	wedding:	❏
Wedding Invitation: ❏ Reception Invitation: ❏ Announcement: ❏	RSVP — yes: ❏ no: ❏	number invited: 2 number attending:	

Name: Uncle Gerald	Phone:	**GIFTS:**	thank you:
Children: Trina and Trish		shower:	❏
Address:		shower:	❏
City:	State:	Zip: ❀	wedding:	❏
Wedding Invitation: ❏ Reception Invitation: ❏ Announcement: ❏	RSVP — yes: ❏ no: ❏	number invited: 3 number attending:	

Name: David Starrett	Phone:	**GIFTS:**	thank you:
Children:		shower:	❏
Address:		shower:	❏
City:	State:	Zip: ❀	wedding:	❏
Wedding Invitation: ❏ Reception Invitation: ❏ Announcement: ❏	RSVP — yes: ❏ no: ❏	number invited: 2 number attending:	

Name: Fred Paul	Phone:	**GIFTS:**	thank you:
Children:		shower:	❏
Address:		shower:	❏
City:	State:	Zip: ❀	wedding:	❏
Wedding Invitation: ❏ Reception Invitation: ❏ Announcement: ❏	RSVP — yes: ❏ no: ❏	number invited: 2 number attending:	

Name: Gerald and Hiedi	Phone:	**GIFTS:**	thank you:
Children:		shower:	❏
Address:		shower:	❏
City:	State:	Zip: ❀	wedding:	❏
Wedding Invitation: ❏ Reception Invitation: ❏ Announcement: ❏	RSVP — yes: ❏ no: ❏	number invited: 2 number attending:	

Name: Leanne Jody and Julie	Phone:		GIFTS:	thank you:
Children:			shower:	☐
Address:			shower:	☐
City:	State:	Zip:	❀ wedding:	☐
Wedding Invitation: ☐ Reception Invitation: ☐ Announcement: ☐	RSVP — yes: ☐ no: ☐	number invited: 3	number attending: ____	

Name: Charlene Curtis	Phone:		GIFTS:	thank you:
Children:			shower:	☐
Address:			shower:	☐
City:	State:	Zip:	❀ wedding:	☐
Wedding Invitation: ☒ Reception Invitation: ☒ Announcement: ☐	RSVP — yes: ☐ no: ☐	number invited: 2	number attending: ____	

Name: Tina Paul	Phone:		GIFTS:	thank you:
Children:			shower:	☐
Address:			shower:	☐
City:	State:	Zip:	❀ wedding:	☐
Wedding Invitation: ☐ Reception Invitation: ☒ Announcement: ☐	RSVP — yes: ☐ no: ☐	number invited: 2	number attending: ____	

Name: Uncle Allan	Phone:		GIFTS:	thank you:
Children:			shower:	☐
Address:			shower:	☐
City:	State:	Zip:	❀ wedding:	☐
Wedding Invitation: ☐ Reception Invitation: ☐ Announcement: ☐	RSVP — yes: ☐ no: ☐	number invited: 2	number attending: ____	

Name: Antée Laura and Rick	Phone:		GIFTS:	thank you:
Children:			shower:	☐
Address:			shower:	☐
City:	State:	Zip:	❀ wedding:	☐
Wedding Invitation: ☐ Reception Invitation: ☐ Announcement: ☐	RSVP — yes: ☐ no: ☐	number invited: 2	number attending: ____	

Name: Micheal Paul	Phone:		GIFTS:	thank you:
Children:			shower:	☐
Address:			shower:	☐
City:	State:	Zip:	❀ wedding:	☐
Wedding Invitation: ☐ Reception Invitation: ☐ Announcement: ☐	RSVP — yes: ☐ no: ☐	number invited: 1	number attending: ____	

Name: Antie Harriett and Clint	Phone:		GIFTS:	thank you:
Children: 1			shower:	☐
Address:			shower:	☐
City:	State:	Zip:	❀ wedding:	☐
Wedding Invitation: ☐ Reception Invitation: ☐ Announcement: ☐	RSVP — yes: ☐ no: ☐	number invited: 3	number attending: ____	

Name: Conrad	Phone:		GIFTS:	thank you:
Children:			shower:	☐
Address:			shower:	☐
City:	State:	Zip:	❀ wedding:	☐
Wedding Invitation: ☐ Reception Invitation: ☐ Announcement: ☐	RSVP — yes: ☐ no: ☐	number invited: 2	number attending: ____	

Name: Mike Campbell	Phone:		GIFTS:	thank you:
Children:			shower:	☐
Address:			shower:	☐
City:	State:	Zip:	❀ wedding:	☐
Wedding Invitation: ☐ Reception Invitation: ☐ Announcement: ☐	RSVP — yes: ☐ no: ☐	number invited: 2	number attending: ____	

Name: Debbie and Duec	Phone:		GIFTS:	thank you:
Children: 3			shower:	☐
Address:			shower:	☐
City:	State:	Zip:	❀ wedding:	☐
Wedding Invitation: ☒ Reception Invitation: ☒ Announcement: ☐	RSVP — yes: ☐ no: ☐	number invited: 5	number attending: ____	

Name: Dennette	Phone:	**GIFTS:**	thank you:
Children: 3		shower:	❑
Address:		shower:	❑
City:	State:	Zip:	❀ wedding:	❑
Wedding Invitation: ❑ Reception Invitation: ☒ Announcement: ❑ *RSVP* — yes: ❑ no: ❑ *number invited:* **5** *number attending:* ___

Name: Gena and Ryan	Phone:	**GIFTS:**	thank you:
Children: Jesse		shower:	❑
Address:		shower:	❑
City:	State:	Zip:	❀ wedding:	❑
Wedding Invitation: ☒ Reception Invitation: ☒ Announcement: ❑ *RSVP* — yes: ❑ no: ❑ *number invited:* **4** *number attending:* ___

Name: Debbie Dale	Phone:	**GIFTS:**	thank you:
Children:		shower:	❑
Address:		shower:	❑
City:	State:	Zip:	❀ wedding:	❑
Wedding Invitation: ❑ Reception Invitation: ☒ Announcement: ❑ *RSVP* — yes: ❑ no: ❑ *number invited:* **2** *number attending:* ___

Name: Michelle and Dave	Phone:	**GIFTS:**	thank you:
Children: Samantha		shower:	❑
Address:		shower:	❑
City:	State:	Zip:	❀ wedding:	❑
Wedding Invitation: ❑ Reception Invitation: ❑ Announcement: ❑ *RSVP* — yes: ❑ no: ❑ *number invited:* **3** *number attending:* ___

Name: Joan	Phone:	**GIFTS:**	thank you:
Children:		shower:	❑
Address:		shower:	❑
City:	State:	Zip:	❀ wedding:	❑
Wedding Invitation: ❑ Reception Invitation: ❑ Announcement: ❑ *RSVP* — yes: ❑ no: ❑ *number invited:* **1** *number attending:* ___

Name:	Phone:	**GIFTS:**	thank you:
Children:		shower:	❑
Address:		shower:	❑
City:	State:	Zip:	❀ wedding:	❑
Wedding Invitation: ❑ Reception Invitation: ❑ Announcement: ❑ *RSVP* — yes: ❑ no: ❑ *number invited:* ___ *number attending:* ___

Name:	Phone:	**GIFTS:**	thank you:
Children:		shower:	❑
Address:		shower:	❑
City:	State:	Zip:	❀ wedding:	❑
Wedding Invitation: ❑ Reception Invitation: ❑ Announcement: ❑ *RSVP* — yes: ❑ no: ❑ *number invited:* ___ *number attending:* ___

Name:	Phone:	**GIFTS:**	thank you:
Children:		shower:	❑
Address:		shower:	❑
City:	State:	Zip:	❀ wedding:	❑
Wedding Invitation: ❑ Reception Invitation: ❑ Announcement: ❑ *RSVP* — yes: ❑ no: ❑ *number invited:* ___ *number attending:* ___

Name:	Phone:	**GIFTS:**	thank you:
Children:		shower:	❑
Address:		shower:	❑
City:	State:	Zip:	❀ wedding:	❑
Wedding Invitation: ❑ Reception Invitation: ❑ Announcement: ❑ *RSVP* — yes: ❑ no: ❑ *number invited:* ___ *number attending:* ___

Name:	Phone:	**GIFTS:**	thank you:
Children:		shower:	❑
Address:		shower:	❑
City:	State:	Zip:	❀ wedding:	❑
Wedding Invitation: ❑ Reception Invitation: ❑ Announcement: ❑ *RSVP* — yes: ❑ no: ❑ *number invited:* ___ *number attending:* ___

Name:		Phone:	GIFTS:	thank you:
Children:			shower:	❏
Address:			shower:	❏
City:	State:	Zip:	❀ wedding:	❏
Wedding Invitation: ❏	Reception Invitation: ❏	Announcement: ❏	*RSVP* — yes: ❏ no: ❏	*number invited:* ____ *number attending:* ____

Name:		Phone:	GIFTS:	thank you:
Children:			shower:	❏
Address:			shower:	❏
City:	State:	Zip:	❀ wedding:	❏
Wedding Invitation: ❏	Reception Invitation: ❏	Announcement: ❏	*RSVP* — yes: ❏ no: ❏	*number invited:* ____ *number attending:* ____

Name:		Phone:	GIFTS:	thank you:
Children:			shower:	❏
Address:			shower:	❏
City:	State:	Zip:	❀ wedding:	❏
Wedding Invitation: ❏	Reception Invitation: ❏	Announcement: ❏	*RSVP* — yes: ❏ no: ❏	*number invited:* ____ *number attending:* ____

Name:		Phone:	GIFTS:	thank you:
Children:			shower:	❏
Address:			shower:	❏
City:	State:	Zip:	❀ wedding:	❏
Wedding Invitation: ❏	Reception Invitation: ❏	Announcement: ❏	*RSVP* — yes: ❏ no: ❏	*number invited:* ____ *number attending:* ____

Name:		Phone:	GIFTS:	thank you:
Children:			shower:	❏
Address:			shower:	❏
City:	State:	Zip:	❀ wedding:	❏
Wedding Invitation: ❏	Reception Invitation: ❏	Announcement: ❏	*RSVP* — yes: ❏ no: ❏	*number invited:* ____ *number attending:* ____

Name:		Phone:	GIFTS:	thank you:
Children:			shower:	❏
Address:			shower:	❏
City:	State:	Zip:	❀ wedding:	❏
Wedding Invitation: ❏	Reception Invitation: ❏	Announcement: ❏	*RSVP* — yes: ❏ no: ❏	*number invited:* ____ *number attending:* ____

Name:		Phone:	GIFTS:	thank you:
Children:			shower:	❏
Address:			shower:	❏
City:	State:	Zip:	❀ wedding:	❏
Wedding Invitation: ❏	Reception Invitation: ❏	Announcement: ❏	*RSVP* — yes: ❏ no: ❏	*number invited:* ____ *number attending:* ____

Name:		Phone:	GIFTS:	thank you:
Children:			shower:	❏
Address:			shower:	❏
City:	State:	Zip:	❀ wedding:	❏
Wedding Invitation: ❏	Reception Invitation: ❏	Announcement: ❏	*RSVP* — yes: ❏ no: ❏	*number invited:* ____ *number attending:* ____

Name:		Phone:	GIFTS:	thank you:
Children:			shower:	❏
Address:			shower:	❏
City:	State:	Zip:	❀ wedding:	❏
Wedding Invitation: ❏	Reception Invitation: ❏	Announcement: ❏	*RSVP* — yes: ❏ no: ❏	*number invited:* ____ *number attending:* ____

Name:		Phone:	GIFTS:	thank you:
Children:			shower:	❏
Address:			shower:	❏
City:	State:	Zip:	❀ wedding:	❏
Wedding Invitation: ❏	Reception Invitation: ❏	Announcement: ❏	*RSVP* — yes: ❏ no: ❏	*number invited:* ____ *number attending:* ____

Name:		Phone:		GIFTS:	thank you
Children:				shower:	
Address:				shower:	
City:	State:	Zip:	❀	wedding:	
Wedding Invitation: ❏	Reception Invitation: ❏	Announcement: ❏	RSVP — yes: ❏ no: ❏	number invited: ____	number attending: ____

Name:		Phone:		GIFTS:	thank you
Children:				shower:	
Address:				shower:	
City:	State:	Zip:	❀	wedding:	
Wedding Invitation: ❏	Reception Invitation: ❏	Announcement: ❏	RSVP — yes: ❏ no: ❏	number invited: ____	number attending: ____

Name:		Phone:		GIFTS:	thank you
Children:				shower:	
Address:				shower:	
City:	State:	Zip:	❀	wedding:	
Wedding Invitation: ❏	Reception Invitation: ❏	Announcement: ❏	RSVP — yes: ❏ no: ❏	number invited: ____	number attending: ____

Name:		Phone:		GIFTS:	thank you
Children:				shower:	
Address:				shower:	
City:	State:	Zip:	❀	wedding:	
Wedding Invitation: ❏	Reception Invitation: ❏	Announcement: ❏	RSVP — yes: ❏ no: ❏	number invited: ____	number attending: ____

Name:		Phone:		GIFTS:	thank you:
Children:				shower:	
Address:				shower:	
City:	State:	Zip:	❀	wedding:	
Wedding Invitation: ❏	Reception Invitation: ❏	Announcement: ❏	RSVP — yes: ❏ no: ❏	number invited: ____	number attending: ____

Name:		Phone:		GIFTS:	thank you:
Children:				shower:	
Address:				shower:	
City:	State:	Zip:	❀	wedding:	
Wedding Invitation: ❏	Reception Invitation: ❏	Announcement: ❏	RSVP — yes: ❏ no: ❏	number invited: ____	number attending: ____

Name:		Phone:		GIFTS:	thank you:
Children:				shower:	
Address:				shower:	
City:	State:	Zip:	❀	wedding:	
Wedding Invitation: ❏	Reception Invitation: ❏	Announcement: ❏	RSVP — yes: ❏ no: ❏	number invited: ____	number attending: ____

Name:		Phone:		GIFTS:	thank you:
Children:				shower:	
Address:				shower:	
City:	State:	Zip:	❀	wedding:	
Wedding Invitation: ❏	Reception Invitation: ❏	Announcement: ❏	RSVP — yes: ❏ no: ❏	number invited: ____	number attending: ____

Name:		Phone:		GIFTS:	thank you:
Children:				shower:	
Address:				shower:	
City:	State:	Zip:	❀	wedding:	
Wedding Invitation: ❏	Reception Invitation: ❏	Announcement: ❏	RSVP — yes: ❏ no: ❏	number invited: ____	number attending: ____

Name:		Phone:		GIFTS:	thank you:
Children:				shower:	
Address:				shower:	
City:	State:	Zip:	❀	wedding:	
Wedding Invitation: ❏	Reception Invitation: ❏	Announcement: ❏	RSVP — yes: ❏ no: ❏	number invited: ____	number attending: ____

Name:	Phone:	**GIFTS:**	thank you:
Children:		shower:	❑
Address:		shower:	❑
City:	State:	Zip:	❀ wedding:	❑
Wedding Invitation: ❑	Reception Invitation: ❑	Announcement: ❑	*RSVP* — yes: ❑ no: ❑	*number invited:* _____ *number attending:* _____

Name:	Phone:	**GIFTS:**	thank you:
Children:		shower:	❑
Address:		shower:	❑
City:	State:	Zip:	❀ wedding:	❑
Wedding Invitation: ❑	Reception Invitation: ❑	Announcement: ❑	*RSVP* — yes: ❑ no: ❑	*number invited:* _____ *number attending:* _____

Name:	Phone:	**GIFTS:**	thank you:
Children:		shower:	❑
Address:		shower:	❑
City:	State:	Zip:	❀ wedding:	❑
Wedding Invitation: ❑	Reception Invitation: ❑	Announcement: ❑	*RSVP* — yes: ❑ no: ❑	*number invited:* _____ *number attending:* _____

Name:	Phone:	**GIFTS:**	thank you:
Children:		shower:	❑
Address:		shower:	❑
City:	State:	Zip:	❀ wedding:	❑
Wedding Invitation: ❑	Reception Invitation: ❑	Announcement: ❑	*RSVP* — yes: ❑ no: ❑	*number invited:* _____ *number attending:* _____

Name:	Phone:	**GIFTS:**	thank you:
Children:		shower:	❑
Address:		shower:	❑
City:	State:	Zip:	❀ wedding:	❑
Wedding Invitation: ❑	Reception Invitation: ❑	Announcement: ❑	*RSVP* — yes: ❑ no: ❑	*number invited:* _____ *number attending:* _____

Name:	Phone:	**GIFTS:**	thank you:
Children:		shower:	❑
Address:		shower:	❑
City:	State:	Zip:	❀ wedding:	❑
Wedding Invitation: ❑	Reception Invitation: ❑	Announcement: ❑	*RSVP* — yes: ❑ no: ❑	*number invited:* _____ *number attending:* _____

Name:	Phone:	**GIFTS:**	thank you:
Children:		shower:	❑
Address:		shower:	❑
City:	State:	Zip:	❀ wedding:	❑
Wedding Invitation: ❑	Reception Invitation: ❑	Announcement: ❑	*RSVP* — yes: ❑ no: ❑	*number invited:* _____ *number attending:* _____

Name:	Phone:	**GIFTS:**	thank you:
Children:		shower:	❑
Address:		shower:	❑
City:	State:	Zip:	❀ wedding:	❑
Wedding Invitation: ❑	Reception Invitation: ❑	Announcement: ❑	*RSVP* — yes: ❑ no: ❑	*number invited:* _____ *number attending:* _____

Name:	Phone:	**GIFTS:**	thank you:
Children:		shower:	❑
Address:		shower:	❑
City:	State:	Zip:	❀ wedding:	❑
Wedding Invitation: ❑	Reception Invitation: ❑	Announcement: ❑	*RSVP* — yes: ❑ no: ❑	*number invited:* _____ *number attending:* _____

Name:	Phone:	**GIFTS:**	thank you:
Children:		shower:	❑
Address:		shower:	❑
City:	State:	Zip:	❀ wedding:	❑
Wedding Invitation: ❑	Reception Invitation: ❑	Announcement: ❑	*RSVP* — yes: ❑ no: ❑	*number invited:* _____ *number attending:* _____

Name:		Phone:	GIFTS:	thank you
Children:			shower:	
Address:			shower:	
City:	State:	Zip:	❁ wedding:	
Wedding Invitation: ❐	Reception Invitation: ❐	Announcement: ❐	*RSVP* — yes: ❐ no: ❐	*number invited:* ____ *number attending:* ____

Name:		Phone:	GIFTS:	thank you
Children:			shower:	
Address:			shower:	
City:	State:	Zip:	❁ wedding:	
Wedding Invitation: ❐	Reception Invitation: ❐	Announcement: ❐	*RSVP* — yes: ❐ no: ❐	*number invited:* ____ *number attending:* ____

Name:		Phone:	GIFTS:	thank you
Children:			shower:	
Address:			shower:	
City:	State:	Zip:	❁ wedding:	
Wedding Invitation: ❐	Reception Invitation: ❐	Announcement: ❐	*RSVP* — yes: ❐ no: ❐	*number invited:* ____ *number attending:* ____

Name:		Phone:	GIFTS:	thank you
Children:			shower:	
Address:			shower:	
City:	State:	Zip:	❁ wedding:	
Wedding Invitation: ❐	Reception Invitation: ❐	Announcement: ❐	*RSVP* — yes: ❐ no: ❐	*number invited:* ____ *number attending:* ____

Name:		Phone:	GIFTS:	thank you
Children:			shower:	
Address:			shower:	
City:	State:	Zip:	❁ wedding:	
Wedding Invitation: ❐	Reception Invitation: ❐	Announcement: ❐	*RSVP* — yes: ❐ no: ❐	*number invited:* ____ *number attending:* ____

Name:		Phone:	GIFTS:	thank you:
Children:			shower:	
Address:			shower:	
City:	State:	Zip:	❁ wedding:	
Wedding Invitation: ❐	Reception Invitation: ❐	Announcement: ❐	*RSVP* — yes: ❐ no: ❐	*number invited:* ____ *number attending:* ____

Name:		Phone:	GIFTS:	thank you:
Children:			shower:	
Address:			shower:	
City:	State:	Zip:	❁ wedding:	
Wedding Invitation: ❐	Reception Invitation: ❐	Announcement: ❐	*RSVP* — yes: ❐ no: ❐	*number invited:* ____ *number attending:* ____

Name:		Phone:	GIFTS:	thank you:
Children:			shower:	
Address:			shower:	
City:	State:	Zip:	❁ wedding:	
Wedding Invitation: ❐	Reception Invitation: ❐	Announcement: ❐	*RSVP* — yes: ❐ no: ❐	*number invited:* ____ *number attending:* ____

Name:		Phone:	GIFTS:	thank you:
Children:			shower:	
Address:			shower:	
City:	State:	Zip:	❁ wedding:	
Wedding Invitation: ❐	Reception Invitation: ❐	Announcement: ❐	*RSVP* — yes: ❐ no: ❐	*number invited:* ____ *number attending:* ____

Name:		Phone:	GIFTS:	thank you:
Children:			shower:	
Address:			shower:	
City:	State:	Zip:	❁ wedding:	
Wedding Invitation: ❐	Reception Invitation: ❐	Announcement: ❐	*RSVP* — yes: ❐ no: ❐	*number invited:* ____ *number attending:* ____

Name:	Phone:	**GIFTS:** thank you:
Children:		shower: ❏
Address:		shower: ❏
City:	State:	Zip: ✿ wedding: ❏
Wedding Invitation: ❏ Reception Invitation: ❏ Announcement: ❏	*RSVP* — yes: ❏ no: ❏	*number invited:* ____ *number attending:* ____
Name:	Phone:	**GIFTS:** thank you:
Children:		shower: ❏
Address:		shower: ❏
City:	State:	Zip: ✿ wedding: ❏
Wedding Invitation: ❏ Reception Invitation: ❏ Announcement: ❏	*RSVP* — yes: ❏ no: ❏	*number invited:* ____ *number attending:* ____
Name:	Phone:	**GIFTS:** thank you:
Children:		shower: ❏
Address:		shower: ❏
City:	State:	Zip: ✿ wedding: ❏
Wedding Invitation: ❏ Reception Invitation: ❏ Announcement: ❏	*RSVP* — yes: ❏ no: ❏	*number invited:* ____ *number attending:* ____
Name:	Phone:	**GIFTS:** thank you:
Children:		shower: ❏
Address:		shower: ❏
City:	State:	Zip: ✿ wedding: ❏
Wedding Invitation: ❏ Reception Invitation: ❏ Announcement: ❏	*RSVP* — yes: ❏ no: ❏	*number invited:* ____ *number attending:* ____
Name:	Phone:	**GIFTS:** thank you:
Children:		shower: ❏
Address:		shower: ❏
City:	State:	Zip: ✿ wedding: ❏
Wedding Invitation: ❏ Reception Invitation: ❏ Announcement: ❏	*RSVP* — yes: ❏ no: ❏	*number invited:* ____ *number attending:* ____
Name:	Phone:	**GIFTS:** thank you:
Children:		shower: ❏
Address:		shower: ❏
City:	State:	Zip: ✿ wedding: ❏
Wedding Invitation: ❏ Reception Invitation: ❏ Announcement: ❏	*RSVP* — yes: ❏ no: ❏	*number invited:* ____ *number attending:* ____
Name:	Phone:	**GIFTS:** thank you:
Children:		shower: ❏
Address:		shower: ❏
City:	State:	Zip: ✿ wedding: ❏
Wedding Invitation: ❏ Reception Invitation: ❏ Announcement: ❏	*RSVP* — yes: ❏ no: ❏	*number invited:* ____ *number attending:* ____
Name:	Phone:	**GIFTS:** thank you:
Children:		shower: ❏
Address:		shower: ❏
City:	State:	Zip: ✿ wedding: ❏
Wedding Invitation: ❏ Reception Invitation: ❏ Announcement: ❏	*RSVP* — yes: ❏ no: ❏	*number invited:* ____ *number attending:* ____
Name:	Phone:	**GIFTS:** thank you:
Children:		shower: ❏
Address:		shower: ❏
City:	State:	Zip: ✿ wedding: ❏
Wedding Invitation: ❏ Reception Invitation: ❏ Announcement: ❏	*RSVP* — yes: ❏ no: ❏	*number invited:* ____ *number attending:* ____
Name:	Phone:	**GIFTS:** thank you:
Children:		shower: ❏
Address:		shower: ❏
City:	State:	Zip: ✿ wedding: ❏
Wedding Invitation: ❏ Reception Invitation: ❏ Announcement: ❏	*RSVP* — yes: ❏ no: ❏	*number invited:* ____ *number attending:* ____

	Name:	Phone:	GIFTS:	th y
	Children:		shower:	
	Address:		shower:	
	City:	State:	Zip:	❀ wedding:
	Wedding Invitation: ❑	Reception Invitation: ❑	Announcement: ❑	*RSVP* — yes: ❑ no: ❑	*number invited:* ___ *number attending:* ___

	Name:	Phone:	GIFTS:	th y
	Children:		shower:	
	Address:		shower:	
	City:	State:	Zip:	❀ wedding:
	Wedding Invitation: ❑	Reception Invitation: ❑	Announcement: ❑	*RSVP* — yes: ❑ no: ❑	*number invited:* ___ *number attending:* ___

	Name:	Phone:	GIFTS:	tha y
	Children:		shower:	
	Address:		shower:	
	City:	State:	Zip:	❀ wedding:
	Wedding Invitation: ❑	Reception Invitation: ❑	Announcement: ❑	*RSVP* — yes: ❑ no: ❑	*number invited:* ___ *number attending:* ___

	Name:	Phone:	GIFTS:	tha yo
	Children:		shower:	
	Address:		shower:	
	City:	State:	Zip:	❀ wedding:
	Wedding Invitation: ❑	Reception Invitation: ❑	Announcement: ❑	*RSVP* — yes: ❑ no: ❑	*number invited:* ___ *number attending:* ___

	Name:	Phone:	GIFTS:	tha yo
	Children:		shower:	
	Address:		shower:	
	City:	State:	Zip:	❀ wedding:
	Wedding Invitation: ❑	Reception Invitation: ❑	Announcement: ❑	*RSVP* — yes: ❑ no: ❑	*number invited:* ___ *number attending:* ___

	Name:	Phone:	GIFTS:	than yo
	Children:		shower:	
	Address:		shower:	
	City:	State:	Zip:	❀ wedding:
	Wedding Invitation: ❑	Reception Invitation: ❑	Announcement: ❑	*RSVP* — yes: ❑ no: ❑	*number invited:* ___ *number attending:* ___

	Name:	Phone:	GIFTS:	than yo
	Children:		shower:	
	Address:		shower:	
	City:	State:	Zip:	❀ wedding:
	Wedding Invitation: ❑	Reception Invitation: ❑	Announcement: ❑	*RSVP* — yes: ❑ no: ❑	*number invited:* ___ *number attending:* ___

	Name:	Phone:	GIFTS:	than yo
	Children:		shower:	
	Address:		shower:	
	City:	State:	Zip:	❀ wedding:
	Wedding Invitation: ❑	Reception Invitation: ❑	Announcement: ❑	*RSVP* — yes: ❑ no: ❑	*number invited:* ___ *number attending:* ___

	Name:	Phone:	GIFTS:	than yo
	Children:		shower:	
	Address:		shower:	
	City:	State:	Zip:	❀ wedding:
	Wedding Invitation: ❑	Reception Invitation: ❑	Announcement: ❑	*RSVP* — yes: ❑ no: ❑	*number invited:* ___ *number attending:* ___

	Name:	Phone:	GIFTS:	than yo
	Children:		shower:	
	Address:		shower:	
	City:	State:	Zip:	❀ wedding:
	Wedding Invitation: ❑	Reception Invitation: ❑	Announcement: ❑	*RSVP* — yes: ❑ no: ❑	*number invited:* ___ *number attending:* ___

	Name:	Phone:	GIFTS:	than you
	Children:		shower:	
	Address:		shower:	
	City:	State:	Zip:	❀ wedding:
	Wedding Invitation: ❑	Reception Invitation: ❑	Announcement: ❑	*RSVP* — yes: ❑ no: ❑	*number invited:* ___ *number attending:* ___

Name: _____ Phone: _____ **GIFTS:** thank you:
Children: _____ shower: _____ ❑
Address: _____ shower: _____ ❑
City: _____ State: _____ Zip: _____ ✾ wedding: _____ ❑
Wedding Invitation: ❑ Reception Invitation: ❑ Announcement: ❑ *RSVP —* yes: ❑ no: ❑ *number invited:* ____ *number attending:* ____

Name: _____ Phone: _____ **GIFTS:** thank you:
Children: _____ shower: _____ ❑
Address: _____ shower: _____ ❑
City: _____ State: _____ Zip: _____ ✾ wedding: _____ ❑
Wedding Invitation: ❑ Reception Invitation: ❑ Announcement: ❑ *RSVP —* yes: ❑ no: ❑ *number invited:* ____ *number attending:* ____

Name: _____ Phone: _____ **GIFTS:** thank you:
Children: _____ shower: _____ ❑
Address: _____ shower: _____ ❑
City: _____ State: _____ Zip: _____ ✾ wedding: _____ ❑
Wedding Invitation: ❑ Reception Invitation: ❑ Announcement: ❑ *RSVP —* yes: ❑ no: ❑ *number invited:* ____ *number attending:* ____

Name: _____ Phone: _____ **GIFTS:** thank you:
Children: _____ shower: _____ ❑
Address: _____ shower: _____ ❑
City: _____ State: _____ Zip: _____ ✾ wedding: _____ ❑
Wedding Invitation: ❑ Reception Invitation: ❑ Announcement: ❑ *RSVP —* yes: ❑ no: ❑ *number invited:* ____ *number attending:* ____

Name: _____ Phone: _____ **GIFTS:** thank you:
Children: _____ shower: _____ ❑
Address: _____ shower: _____ ❑
City: _____ State: _____ Zip: _____ ✾ wedding: _____ ❑
Wedding Invitation: ❑ Reception Invitation: ❑ Announcement: ❑ *RSVP —* yes: ❑ no: ❑ *number invited:* ____ *number attending:* ____

Name: _____ Phone: _____ **GIFTS:** thank you:
Children: _____ shower: _____ ❑
Address: _____ shower: _____ ❑
City: _____ State: _____ Zip: _____ ✾ wedding: _____ ❑
Wedding Invitation: ❑ Reception Invitation: ❑ Announcement: ❑ *RSVP —* yes: ❑ no: ❑ *number invited:* ____ *number attending:* ____

Name: _____ Phone: _____ **GIFTS:** thank you:
Children: _____ shower: _____ ❑
Address: _____ shower: _____ ❑
City: _____ State: _____ Zip: _____ ✾ wedding: _____ ❑
Wedding Invitation: ❑ Reception Invitation: ❑ Announcement: ❑ *RSVP —* yes: ❑ no: ❑ *number invited:* ____ *number attending:* ____

Name: _____ Phone: _____ **GIFTS:** thank you:
Children: _____ shower: _____ ❑
Address: _____ shower: _____ ❑
City: _____ State: _____ Zip: _____ ✾ wedding: _____ ❑
Wedding Invitation: ❑ Reception Invitation: ❑ Announcement: ❑ *RSVP —* yes: ❑ no: ❑ *number invited:* ____ *number attending:* ____

Name: _____ Phone: _____ **GIFTS:** thank you:
Children: _____ shower: _____ ❑
Address: _____ shower: _____ ❑
City: _____ State: _____ Zip: _____ ✾ wedding: _____ ❑
Wedding Invitation: ❑ Reception Invitation: ❑ Announcement: ❑ *RSVP —* yes: ❑ no: ❑ *number invited:* ____ *number attending:* ____

Name: _____ Phone: _____ **GIFTS:** thank you:
Children: _____ shower: _____ ❑
Address: _____ shower: _____ ❑
City: _____ State: _____ Zip: _____ ✾ wedding: _____ ❑
Wedding Invitation: ❑ Reception Invitation: ❑ Announcement: ❑ *RSVP —* yes: ❑ no: ❑ *number invited:* ____ *number attending:* ____

☐ Name:	Phone:	**GIFTS:** thank you
Children:		shower:
Address:		shower:
City:	State: Zip: ❀	wedding:
Wedding Invitation: ☐ Reception Invitation: ☐ Announcement: ☐	*RSVP* — yes: ☐ no: ☐	*number invited:* _____ *number attending:* _____

☐ Name:	Phone:	**GIFTS:** thank you
Children:		shower:
Address:		shower:
City:	State: Zip: ❀	wedding:
Wedding Invitation: ☐ Reception Invitation: ☐ Announcement: ☐	*RSVP* — yes: ☐ no: ☐	*number invited:* _____ *number attending:* _____

☐ Name:	Phone:	**GIFTS:** thank you
Children:		shower:
Address:		shower:
City:	State: Zip: ❀	wedding:
Wedding Invitation: ☐ Reception Invitation: ☐ Announcement: ☐	*RSVP* — yes: ☐ no: ☐	*number invited:* _____ *number attending:* _____

☐ Name:	Phone:	**GIFTS:** thank you
Children:		shower:
Address:		shower:
City:	State: Zip: ❀	wedding:
Wedding Invitation: ☐ Reception Invitation: ☐ Announcement: ☐	*RSVP* — yes: ☐ no: ☐	*number invited:* _____ *number attending:* _____

☐ Name:	Phone:	**GIFTS:** thank you
Children:		shower:
Address:		shower:
City:	State: Zip: ❀	wedding:
Wedding Invitation: ☐ Reception Invitation: ☐ Announcement: ☐	*RSVP* — yes: ☐ no: ☐	*number invited:* _____ *number attending:* _____

☐ Name:	Phone:	**GIFTS:** thank you
Children:		shower:
Address:		shower:
City:	State: Zip: ❀	wedding:
Wedding Invitation: ☐ Reception Invitation: ☐ Announcement: ☐	*RSVP* — yes: ☐ no: ☐	*number invited:* _____ *number attending:* _____

☐ Name:	Phone:	**GIFTS:** thank you
Children:		shower:
Address:		shower:
City:	State: Zip: ❀	wedding:
Wedding Invitation: ☐ Reception Invitation: ☐ Announcement: ☐	*RSVP* — yes: ☐ no: ☐	*number invited:* _____ *number attending:* _____

☐ Name:	Phone:	**GIFTS:** thank you
Children:		shower:
Address:		shower:
City:	State: Zip: ❀	wedding:
Wedding Invitation: ☐ Reception Invitation: ☐ Announcement: ☐	*RSVP* — yes: ☐ no: ☐	*number invited:* _____ *number attending:* _____

☐ Name:	Phone:	**GIFTS:** thank you
Children:		shower:
Address:		shower:
City:	State: Zip: ❀	wedding:
Wedding Invitation: ☐ Reception Invitation: ☐ Announcement: ☐	*RSVP* — yes: ☐ no: ☐	*number invited:* _____ *number attending:* _____

☐ Name:	Phone:	**GIFTS:** thank you
Children:		shower:
Address:		shower:
City:	State: Zip: ❀	wedding:
Wedding Invitation: ☐ Reception Invitation: ☐ Announcement: ☐	*RSVP* — yes: ☐ no: ☐	*number invited:* _____ *number attending:* _____

Name:		Phone:		GIFTS:	thank you:
Children:				shower:	❑
Address:				shower:	❑
City:	State:	Zip:	❀	wedding:	❑
Wedding Invitation: ❑	Reception Invitation: ❑	Announcement: ❑	RSVP — yes: ❑ no: ❑	number invited: ____	number attending: ____

Name:		Phone:		GIFTS:	thank you:
Children:				shower:	❑
Address:				shower:	❑
City:	State:	Zip:	❀	wedding:	❑
Wedding Invitation: ❑	Reception Invitation: ❑	Announcement: ❑	RSVP — yes: ❑ no: ❑	number invited: ____	number attending: ____

Name:		Phone:		GIFTS:	thank you:
Children:				shower:	❑
Address:				shower:	❑
City:	State:	Zip:	❀	wedding:	❑
Wedding Invitation: ❑	Reception Invitation: ❑	Announcement: ❑	RSVP — yes: ❑ no: ❑	number invited: ____	number attending: ____

Name:		Phone:		GIFTS:	thank you:
Children:				shower:	❑
Address:				shower:	❑
City:	State:	Zip:	❀	wedding:	❑
Wedding Invitation: ❑	Reception Invitation: ❑	Announcement: ❑	RSVP — yes: ❑ no: ❑	number invited: ____	number attending: ____

Name:		Phone:		GIFTS:	thank you:
Children:				shower:	❑
Address:				shower:	❑
City:	State:	Zip:	❀	wedding:	❑
Wedding Invitation: ❑	Reception Invitation: ❑	Announcement: ❑	RSVP — yes: ❑ no: ❑	number invited: ____	number attending: ____

Name:		Phone:		GIFTS:	thank you:
Children:				shower:	❑
Address:				shower:	❑
City:	State:	Zip:	❀	wedding:	❑
Wedding Invitation: ❑	Reception Invitation: ❑	Announcement: ❑	RSVP — yes: ❑ no: ❑	number invited: ____	number attending: ____

Name:		Phone:		GIFTS:	thank you:
Children:				shower:	❑
Address:				shower:	❑
City:	State:	Zip:	❀	wedding:	❑
Wedding Invitation: ❑	Reception Invitation: ❑	Announcement: ❑	RSVP — yes: ❑ no: ❑	number invited: ____	number attending: ____

Name:		Phone:		GIFTS:	thank you:
Children:				shower:	❑
Address:				shower:	❑
City:	State:	Zip:	❀	wedding:	❑
Wedding Invitation: ❑	Reception Invitation: ❑	Announcement: ❑	RSVP — yes: ❑ no: ❑	number invited: ____	number attending: ____

Name:		Phone:		GIFTS:	thank you:
Children:				shower:	❑
Address:				shower:	❑
City:	State:	Zip:	❀	wedding:	❑
Wedding Invitation: ❑	Reception Invitation: ❑	Announcement: ❑	RSVP — yes: ❑ no: ❑	number invited: ____	number attending: ____

Name:		Phone:		GIFTS:	thank you:
Children:				shower:	❑
Address:				shower:	❑
City:	State:	Zip:	❀	wedding:	❑
Wedding Invitation: ❑	Reception Invitation: ❑	Announcement: ❑	RSVP — yes: ❑ no: ❑	number invited: ____	number attending: ____

☐	Name:		Phone:		GIFTS:	thank you:
	Children:				shower:	☐
	Address:				shower:	☐
	City:	State:	Zip:	❀	wedding:	☐
	Wedding Invitation: ☐	Reception Invitation: ☐	Announcement: ☐	RSVP — yes: ☐ no: ☐	number invited: ____	number attending: ____

☐	Name:		Phone:		GIFTS:	thank you:
	Children:				shower:	☐
	Address:				shower:	☐
	City:	State:	Zip:	❀	wedding:	☐
	Wedding Invitation: ☐	Reception Invitation: ☐	Announcement: ☐	RSVP — yes: ☐ no: ☐	number invited: ____	number attending: ____

☐	Name:		Phone:		GIFTS:	thank you
	Children:				shower:	☐
	Address:				shower:	☐
	City:	State:	Zip:	❀	wedding:	☐
	Wedding Invitation: ☐	Reception Invitation: ☐	Announcement: ☐	RSVP — yes: ☐ no: ☐	number invited: ____	number attending: ____

☐	Name:		Phone:		GIFTS:	thank you:
	Children:				shower:	☐
	Address:				shower:	☐
	City:	State:	Zip:	❀	wedding:	☐
	Wedding Invitation: ☐	Reception Invitation: ☐	Announcement: ☐	RSVP — yes: ☐ no: ☐	number invited: ____	number attending: ____

☐	Name:		Phone:		GIFTS:	thank you:
	Children:				shower:	☐
	Address:				shower:	☐
	City:	State:	Zip:	❀	wedding:	☐
	Wedding Invitation: ☐	Reception Invitation: ☐	Announcement: ☐	RSVP — yes: ☐ no: ☐	number invited: ____	number attending: ____

☐	Name:		Phone:		GIFTS:	thank you:
	Children:				shower:	☐
	Address:				shower:	☐
	City:	State:	Zip:	❀	wedding:	☐
	Wedding Invitation: ☐	Reception Invitation: ☐	Announcement: ☐	RSVP — yes: ☐ no: ☐	number invited: ____	number attending: ____

☐	Name:		Phone:		GIFTS:	thank you:
	Children:				shower:	☐
	Address:				shower:	☐
	City:	State:	Zip:	❀	wedding:	☐
	Wedding Invitation: ☐	Reception Invitation: ☐	Announcement: ☐	RSVP — yes: ☐ no: ☐	number invited: ____	number attending: ____

☐	Name:		Phone:		GIFTS:	thank you:
	Children:				shower:	☐
	Address:				shower:	☐
	City:	State:	Zip:	❀	wedding:	☐
	Wedding Invitation: ☐	Reception Invitation: ☐	Announcement: ☐	RSVP — yes: ☐ no: ☐	number invited: ____	number attending: ____

☐	Name:		Phone:		GIFTS:	thank you:
	Children:				shower:	☐
	Address:				shower:	☐
	City:	State:	Zip:	❀	wedding:	☐
	Wedding Invitation: ☐	Reception Invitation: ☐	Announcement: ☐	RSVP — yes: ☐ no: ☐	number invited: ____	number attending: ____

☐	Name:		Phone:		GIFTS:	thank you:
	Children:				shower:	☐
	Address:				shower:	☐
	City:	State:	Zip:	❀	wedding:	☐
	Wedding Invitation: ☐	Reception Invitation: ☐	Announcement: ☐	RSVP — yes: ☐ no: ☐	number invited: ____	number attending: ____

Name:	Phone:	**GIFTS:**	thank you:
Children:		shower:	❏
Address:		shower:	❏
City:	State:	Zip:	❀ wedding:	❏

Wedding Invitation: ❏ Reception Invitation: ❏ Announcement: ❏ *RSVP* — yes: ❏ no: ❏ *number invited:* _____ *number attending:* _____

Name:	Phone:	**GIFTS:**	thank you:
Children:		shower:	❏
Address:		shower:	❏
City:	State:	Zip:	❀ wedding:	❏

Wedding Invitation: ❏ Reception Invitation: ❏ Announcement: ❏ *RSVP* — yes: ❏ no: ❏ *number invited:* _____ *number attending:* _____

Name:	Phone:	**GIFTS:**	thank you:
Children:		shower:	❏
Address:		shower:	❏
City:	State:	Zip:	❀ wedding:	❏

Wedding Invitation: ❏ Reception Invitation: ❏ Announcement: ❏ *RSVP* — yes: ❏ no: ❏ *number invited:* _____ *number attending:* _____

Name:	Phone:	**GIFTS:**	thank you:
Children:		shower:	❏
Address:		shower:	❏
City:	State:	Zip:	❀ wedding:	❏

Wedding Invitation: ❏ Reception Invitation: ❏ Announcement: ❏ *RSVP* — yes: ❏ no: ❏ *number invited:* _____ *number attending:* _____

Name:	Phone:	**GIFTS:**	thank you:
Children:		shower:	❏
Address:		shower:	❏
City:	State:	Zip:	❀ wedding:	❏

Wedding Invitation: ❏ Reception Invitation: ❏ Announcement: ❏ *RSVP* — yes: ❏ no: ❏ *number invited:* _____ *number attending:* _____

Name:	Phone:	**GIFTS:**	thank you:
Children:		shower:	❏
Address:		shower:	❏
City:	State:	Zip:	❀ wedding:	❏

Wedding Invitation: ❏ Reception Invitation: ❏ Announcement: ❏ *RSVP* — yes: ❏ no: ❏ *number invited:* _____ *number attending:* _____

Name:	Phone:	**GIFTS:**	thank you:
Children:		shower:	❏
Address:		shower:	❏
City:	State:	Zip:	❀ wedding:	❏

Wedding Invitation: ❏ Reception Invitation: ❏ Announcement: ❏ *RSVP* — yes: ❏ no: ❏ *number invited:* _____ *number attending:* _____

Name:	Phone:	**GIFTS:**	thank you:
Children:		shower:	❏
Address:		shower:	❏
City:	State:	Zip:	❀ wedding:	❏

Wedding Invitation: ❏ Reception Invitation: ❏ Announcement: ❏ *RSVP* — yes: ❏ no: ❏ *number invited:* _____ *number attending:* _____

Name:	Phone:	**GIFTS:**	thank you:
Children:		shower:	❏
Address:		shower:	❏
City:	State:	Zip:	❀ wedding:	❏

Wedding Invitation: ❏ Reception Invitation: ❏ Announcement: ❏ *RSVP* — yes: ❏ no: ❏ *number invited:* _____ *number attending:* _____

☐ Name:	Phone:	GIFTS:	thank you
Children:		shower:	☐
Address:		shower:	☐
City:	State:	Zip:	❀ wedding:	☐
Wedding Invitation: ☐	Reception Invitation: ☐	Announcement: ☐	*RSVP* — yes: ☐ no: ☐	*number invited:* ____	*number attending:* ____

☐ Name:	Phone:	GIFTS:	thank you
Children:		shower:	☐
Address:		shower:	☐
City:	State:	Zip:	❀ wedding:	☐
Wedding Invitation: ☐	Reception Invitation: ☐	Announcement: ☐	*RSVP* — yes: ☐ no: ☐	*number invited:* ____	*number attending:* ____

☐ Name:	Phone:	GIFTS:	thank you
Children:		shower:	☐
Address:		shower:	☐
City:	State:	Zip:	❀ wedding:	☐
Wedding Invitation: ☐	Reception Invitation: ☐	Announcement: ☐	*RSVP* — yes: ☐ no: ☐	*number invited:* ____	*number attending:* ____

☐ Name:	Phone:	GIFTS:	thank you
Children:		shower:	☐
Address:		shower:	☐
City:	State:	Zip:	❀ wedding:	☐
Wedding Invitation: ☐	Reception Invitation: ☐	Announcement: ☐	*RSVP* — yes: ☐ no: ☐	*number invited:* ____	*number attending:* ____

☐ Name:	Phone:	GIFTS:	thank you
Children:		shower:	☐
Address:		shower:	☐
City:	State:	Zip:	❀ wedding:	☐
Wedding Invitation: ☐	Reception Invitation: ☐	Announcement: ☐	*RSVP* — yes: ☐ no: ☐	*number invited:* ____	*number attending:* ____

☐ Name:	Phone:	GIFTS:	thank you:
Children:		shower:	☐
Address:		shower:	☐
City:	State:	Zip:	❀ wedding:	☐
Wedding Invitation: ☐	Reception Invitation: ☐	Announcement: ☐	*RSVP* — yes: ☐ no: ☐	*number invited:* ____	*number attending:* ____

☐ Name:	Phone:	GIFTS:	thank you:
Children:		shower:	☐
Address:		shower:	☐
City:	State:	Zip:	❀ wedding:	☐
Wedding Invitation: ☐	Reception Invitation: ☐	Announcement: ☐	*RSVP* — yes: ☐ no: ☐	*number invited:* ____	*number attending:* ____

☐ Name:	Phone:	GIFTS:	thank you:
Children:		shower:	☐
Address:		shower:	☐
City:	State:	Zip:	❀ wedding:	☐
Wedding Invitation: ☐	Reception Invitation: ☐	Announcement: ☐	*RSVP* — yes: ☐ no: ☐	*number invited:* ____	*number attending:* ____

☐ Name:	Phone:	GIFTS:	thank you:
Children:		shower:	☐
Address:		shower:	☐
City:	State:	Zip:	❀ wedding:	☐
Wedding Invitation: ☐	Reception Invitation: ☐	Announcement: ☐	*RSVP* — yes: ☐ no: ☐	*number invited:* ____	*number attending:* ____

☐ Name:	Phone:	GIFTS:	thank you:
Children:		shower:	☐
Address:		shower:	☐
City:	State:	Zip:	❀ wedding:	☐
Wedding Invitation: ☐	Reception Invitation: ☐	Announcement: ☐	*RSVP* — yes: ☐ no: ☐	*number invited:* ____	*number attending:* ____

Name:	Phone:	GIFTS:	thank you:
Children:		shower:	❑
Address:		shower:	❑
City:	State: Zip:	✿ wedding:	❑
Wedding Invitation: ❑ Reception Invitation: ❑ Announcement: ❑	*RSVP* — yes: ❑ no: ❑	*number invited:* ____ *number attending:* ____	

Name:	Phone:	GIFTS:	thank you:
Children:		shower:	❑
Address:		shower:	❑
City:	State: Zip:	✿ wedding:	❑
Wedding Invitation: ❑ Reception Invitation: ❑ Announcement: ❑	*RSVP* — yes: ❑ no: ❑	*number invited:* ____ *number attending:* ____	

Name:	Phone:	GIFTS:	thank you:
Children:		shower:	❑
Address:		shower:	❑
City:	State: Zip:	✿ wedding:	❑
Wedding Invitation: ❑ Reception Invitation: ❑ Announcement: ❑	*RSVP* — yes: ❑ no: ❑	*number invited:* ____ *number attending:* ____	

Name:	Phone:	GIFTS:	thank you:
Children:		shower:	❑
Address:		shower:	❑
City:	State: Zip:	✿ wedding:	❑
Wedding Invitation: ❑ Reception Invitation: ❑ Announcement: ❑	*RSVP* — yes: ❑ no: ❑	*number invited:* ____ *number attending:* ____	

Name:	Phone:	GIFTS:	thank you:
Children:		shower:	❑
Address:		shower:	❑
City:	State: Zip:	✿ wedding:	❑
Wedding Invitation: ❑ Reception Invitation: ❑ Announcement: ❑	*RSVP* — yes: ❑ no: ❑	*number invited:* ____ *number attending:* ____	

Name:	Phone:	GIFTS:	thank you:
Children:		shower:	❑
Address:		shower:	❑
City:	State: Zip:	✿ wedding:	❑
Wedding Invitation: ❑ Reception Invitation: ❑ Announcement: ❑	*RSVP* — yes: ❑ no: ❑	*number invited:* ____ *number attending:* ____	

Name:	Phone:	GIFTS:	thank you:
Children:		shower:	❑
Address:		shower:	❑
City:	State: Zip:	✿ wedding:	❑
Wedding Invitation: ❑ Reception Invitation: ❑ Announcement: ❑	*RSVP* — yes: ❑ no: ❑	*number invited:* ____ *number attending:* ____	

Name:	Phone:	GIFTS:	thank you:
Children:		shower:	❑
Address:		shower:	❑
City:	State: Zip:	✿ wedding:	❑
Wedding Invitation: ❑ Reception Invitation: ❑ Announcement: ❑	*RSVP* — yes: ❑ no: ❑	*number invited:* ____ *number attending:* ____	

Name:	Phone:	GIFTS:	thank you:
Children:		shower:	❑
Address:		shower:	❑
City:	State: Zip:	✿ wedding:	❑
Wedding Invitation: ❑ Reception Invitation: ❑ Announcement: ❑	*RSVP* — yes: ❑ no: ❑	*number invited:* ____ *number attending:* ____	

Name:	Phone:	GIFTS:	thank you:
Children:		shower:	❑
Address:		shower:	❑
City:	State: Zip:	✿ wedding:	❑
Wedding Invitation: ❑ Reception Invitation: ❑ Announcement: ❑	*RSVP* — yes: ❑ no: ❑	*number invited:* ____ *number attending:* ____	

☐ Name:	Phone:	**GIFTS:**	thank you:
Children:		shower:	☐
Address:		shower:	☐
City:	State:	Zip:	❀ wedding:	☐
Wedding Invitation: ☐	Reception Invitation: ☐	Announcement: ☐	*RSVP* — yes: ☐ no: ☐	*number invited:* ____ *number attending:* ____

☐ Name:	Phone:	**GIFTS:**	thank you:
Children:		shower:	☐
Address:		shower:	☐
City:	State:	Zip:	❀ wedding:	☐
Wedding Invitation: ☐	Reception Invitation: ☐	Announcement: ☐	*RSVP* — yes: ☐ no: ☐	*number invited:* ____ *number attending:* ____

☐ Name:	Phone:	**GIFTS:**	thank you:
Children:		shower:	☐
Address:		shower:	☐
City:	State:	Zip:	❀ wedding:	☐
Wedding Invitation: ☐	Reception Invitation: ☐	Announcement: ☐	*RSVP* — yes: ☐ no: ☐	*number invited:* ____ *number attending:* ____

☐ Name:	Phone:	**GIFTS:**	thank you:
Children:		shower:	☐
Address:		shower:	☐
City:	State:	Zip:	❀ wedding:	☐
Wedding Invitation: ☐	Reception Invitation: ☐	Announcement: ☐	*RSVP* — yes: ☐ no: ☐	*number invited:* ____ *number attending:* ____

☐ Name:	Phone:	**GIFTS:**	thank you:
Children:		shower:	☐
Address:		shower:	☐
City:	State:	Zip:	❀ wedding:	☐
Wedding Invitation: ☐	Reception Invitation: ☐	Announcement: ☐	*RSVP* — yes: ☐ no: ☐	*number invited:* ____ *number attending:* ____

☐ Name:	Phone:	**GIFTS:**	thank you:
Children:		shower:	☐
Address:		shower:	☐
City:	State:	Zip:	❀ wedding:	☐
Wedding Invitation: ☐	Reception Invitation: ☐	Announcement: ☐	*RSVP* — yes: ☐ no: ☐	*number invited:* ____ *number attending:* ____

☐ Name:	Phone:	**GIFTS:**	thank you:
Children:		shower:	☐
Address:		shower:	☐
City:	State:	Zip:	❀ wedding:	☐
Wedding Invitation: ☐	Reception Invitation: ☐	Announcement: ☐	*RSVP* — yes: ☐ no: ☐	*number invited:* ____ *number attending:* ____

☐ Name:	Phone:	**GIFTS:**	thank you:
Children:		shower:	☐
Address:		shower:	☐
City:	State:	Zip:	❀ wedding:	☐
Wedding Invitation: ☐	Reception Invitation: ☐	Announcement: ☐	*RSVP* — yes: ☐ no: ☐	*number invited:* ____ *number attending:* ____

☐ Name:	Phone:	**GIFTS:**	thank you:
Children:		shower:	☐
Address:		shower:	☐
City:	State:	Zip:	❀ wedding:	☐
Wedding Invitation: ☐	Reception Invitation: ☐	Announcement: ☐	*RSVP* — yes: ☐ no: ☐	*number invited:* ____ *number attending:* ____

☐ Name:	Phone:	**GIFTS:**	thank you:
Children:		shower:	☐
Address:		shower:	☐
City:	State:	Zip:	❀ wedding:	☐
Wedding Invitation: ☐	Reception Invitation: ☐	Announcement: ☐	*RSVP* — yes: ☐ no: ☐	*number invited:* ____ *number attending:* ____

Name:		Phone:	GIFTS:	thank you:
Children:			shower:	☐
Address:			shower:	☐
City:	State:	Zip:	✿ wedding:	☐
Wedding Invitation: ☐	Reception Invitation: ☐	Announcement: ☐	RSVP — yes: ☐ no: ☐	*number invited:* ____ *number attending:* ____

Name:		Phone:	GIFTS:	thank you:
Children:			shower:	☐
Address:			shower:	☐
City:	State:	Zip:	✿ wedding:	☐
Wedding Invitation: ☐	Reception Invitation: ☐	Announcement: ☐	RSVP — yes: ☐ no: ☐	*number invited:* ____ *number attending:* ____

Name:		Phone:	GIFTS:	thank you:
Children:			shower:	☐
Address:			shower:	☐
City:	State:	Zip:	✿ wedding:	☐
Wedding Invitation: ☐	Reception Invitation: ☐	Announcement: ☐	RSVP — yes: ☐ no: ☐	*number invited:* ____ *number attending:* ____

Name:		Phone:	GIFTS:	thank you:
Children:			shower:	☐
Address:			shower:	☐
City:	State:	Zip:	✿ wedding:	☐
Wedding Invitation: ☐	Reception Invitation: ☐	Announcement: ☐	RSVP — yes: ☐ no: ☐	*number invited:* ____ *number attending:* ____

Name:		Phone:	GIFTS:	thank you:
Children:			shower:	☐
Address:			shower:	☐
City:	State:	Zip:	✿ wedding:	☐
Wedding Invitation: ☐	Reception Invitation: ☐	Announcement: ☐	RSVP — yes: ☐ no: ☐	*number invited:* ____ *number attending:* ____

Name:		Phone:	GIFTS:	thank you:
Children:			shower:	☐
Address:			shower:	☐
City:	State:	Zip:	✿ wedding:	☐
Wedding Invitation: ☐	Reception Invitation: ☐	Announcement: ☐	RSVP — yes: ☐ no: ☐	*number invited:* ____ *number attending:* ____

Name:		Phone:	GIFTS:	thank you:
Children:			shower:	☐
Address:			shower:	☐
City:	State:	Zip:	✿ wedding:	☐
Wedding Invitation: ☐	Reception Invitation: ☐	Announcement: ☐	RSVP — yes: ☐ no: ☐	*number invited:* ____ *number attending:* ____

Name:		Phone:	GIFTS:	thank you:
Children:			shower:	☐
Address:			shower:	☐
City:	State:	Zip:	✿ wedding:	☐
Wedding Invitation: ☐	Reception Invitation: ☐	Announcement: ☐	RSVP — yes: ☐ no: ☐	*number invited:* ____ *number attending:* ____

Name:		Phone:	GIFTS:	thank you:
Children:			shower:	☐
Address:			shower:	☐
City:	State:	Zip:	✿ wedding:	☐
Wedding Invitation: ☐	Reception Invitation: ☐	Announcement: ☐	RSVP — yes: ☐ no: ☐	*number invited:* ____ *number attending:* ____

Name:		Phone:	GIFTS:	thank you:
Children:			shower:	☐
Address:			shower:	☐
City:	State:	Zip:	✿ wedding:	☐
Wedding Invitation: ☐	Reception Invitation: ☐	Announcement: ☐	RSVP — yes: ☐ no: ☐	*number invited:* ____ *number attending:* ____

☐ Name: _____ Phone: _____	GIFTS:	thank you:
Children: _____	shower: _____	☐
Address: _____	shower: _____	☐
City: _____ State: ____ Zip: ____ ✿	wedding: _____	☐
Wedding Invitation: ☐ Reception Invitation: ☐ Announcement: ☐ RSVP — yes: ☐ no: ☐	number invited: ____ number attending: ____	

☐ Name: _____ Phone: _____	GIFTS:	thank you:
Children: _____	shower: _____	☐
Address: _____	shower: _____	☐
City: _____ State: ____ Zip: ____ ✿	wedding: _____	☐
Wedding Invitation: ☐ Reception Invitation: ☐ Announcement: ☐ RSVP — yes: ☐ no: ☐	number invited: ____ number attending: ____	

☐ Name: _____ Phone: _____	GIFTS:	thank you:
Children: _____	shower: _____	☐
Address: _____	shower: _____	☐
City: _____ State: ____ Zip: ____ ✿	wedding: _____	☐
Wedding Invitation: ☐ Reception Invitation: ☐ Announcement: ☐ RSVP — yes: ☐ no: ☐	number invited: ____ number attending: ____	

☐ Name: _____ Phone: _____	GIFTS:	thank you:
Children: _____	shower: _____	☐
Address: _____	shower: _____	☐
City: _____ State: ____ Zip: ____ ✿	wedding: _____	☐
Wedding Invitation: ☐ Reception Invitation: ☐ Announcement: ☐ RSVP — yes: ☐ no: ☐	number invited: ____ number attending: ____	

☐ Name: _____ Phone: _____	GIFTS:	thank you:
Children: _____	shower: _____	☐
Address: _____	shower: _____	☐
City: _____ State: ____ Zip: ____ ✿	wedding: _____	☐
Wedding Invitation: ☐ Reception Invitation: ☐ Announcement: ☐ RSVP — yes: ☐ no: ☐	number invited: ____ number attending: ____	

☐ Name: _____ Phone: _____	GIFTS:	thank you:
Children: _____	shower: _____	☐
Address: _____	shower: _____	☐
City: _____ State: ____ Zip: ____ ✿	wedding: _____	☐
Wedding Invitation: ☐ Reception Invitation: ☐ Announcement: ☐ RSVP — yes: ☐ no: ☐	number invited: ____ number attending: ____	

☐ Name: _____ Phone: _____	GIFTS:	thank you:
Children: _____	shower: _____	☐
Address: _____	shower: _____	☐
City: _____ State: ____ Zip: ____ ✿	wedding: _____	☐
Wedding Invitation: ☐ Reception Invitation: ☐ Announcement: ☐ RSVP — yes: ☐ no: ☐	number invited: ____ number attending: ____	

☐ Name: _____ Phone: _____	GIFTS:	thank you:
Children: _____	shower: _____	☐
Address: _____	shower: _____	☐
City: _____ State: ____ Zip: ____ ✿	wedding: _____	☐
Wedding Invitation: ☐ Reception Invitation: ☐ Announcement: ☐ RSVP — yes: ☐ no: ☐	number invited: ____ number attending: ____	

☐ Name: _____ Phone: _____	GIFTS:	thank you:
Children: _____	shower: _____	☐
Address: _____	shower: _____	☐
City: _____ State: ____ Zip: ____ ✿	wedding: _____	☐
Wedding Invitation: ☐ Reception Invitation: ☐ Announcement: ☐ RSVP — yes: ☐ no: ☐	number invited: ____ number attending: ____	

☐ Name: _____ Phone: _____	GIFTS:	thank you:
Children: _____	shower: _____	☐
Address: _____	shower: _____	☐
City: _____ State: ____ Zip: ____ ✿	wedding: _____	☐
Wedding Invitation: ☐ Reception Invitation: ☐ Announcement: ☐ RSVP — yes: ☐ no: ☐	number invited: ____ number attending: ____	

					GIFTS:	thank you:
Name:			Phone:			
Children:					shower:	❑
Address:					shower:	❑
City:		State:	Zip:	❀	wedding:	❑
Wedding Invitation: ❑	Reception Invitation: ❑	Announcement: ❑	RSVP — yes: ❑ no: ❑	number invited: ____	number attending: ____	

					GIFTS:	thank you:
Name:			Phone:			
Children:					shower:	❑
Address:					shower:	❑
City:		State:	Zip:	❀	wedding:	❑
Wedding Invitation: ❑	Reception Invitation: ❑	Announcement: ❑	RSVP — yes: ❑ no: ❑	number invited: ____	number attending: ____	

					GIFTS:	thank you:
Name:			Phone:			
Children:					shower:	❑
Address:					shower:	❑
City:		State:	Zip:	❀	wedding:	❑
Wedding Invitation: ❑	Reception Invitation: ❑	Announcement: ❑	RSVP — yes: ❑ no: ❑	number invited: ____	number attending: ____	

					GIFTS:	thank you:
Name:			Phone:			
Children:					shower:	❑
Address:					shower:	❑
City:		State:	Zip:	❀	wedding:	❑
Wedding Invitation: ❑	Reception Invitation: ❑	Announcement: ❑	RSVP — yes: ❑ no: ❑	number invited: ____	number attending: ____	

					GIFTS:	thank you:
Name:			Phone:			
Children:					shower:	❑
Address:					shower:	❑
City:		State:	Zip:	❀	wedding:	❑
Wedding Invitation: ❑	Reception Invitation: ❑	Announcement: ❑	RSVP — yes: ❑ no: ❑	number invited: ____	number attending: ____	

					GIFTS:	thank you:
Name:			Phone:			
Children:					shower:	❑
Address:					shower:	❑
City:		State:	Zip:	❀	wedding:	❑
Wedding Invitation: ❑	Reception Invitation: ❑	Announcement: ❑	RSVP — yes: ❑ no: ❑	number invited: ____	number attending: ____	

					GIFTS:	thank you:
Name:			Phone:			
Children:					shower:	❑
Address:					shower:	❑
City:		State:	Zip:	❀	wedding:	❑
Wedding Invitation: ❑	Reception Invitation: ❑	Announcement: ❑	RSVP — yes: ❑ no: ❑	number invited: ____	number attending: ____	

					GIFTS:	thank you:
Name:			Phone:			
Children:					shower:	❑
Address:					shower:	❑
City:		State:	Zip:	❀	wedding:	❑
Wedding Invitation: ❑	Reception Invitation: ❑	Announcement: ❑	RSVP — yes: ❑ no: ❑	number invited: ____	number attending: ____	

					GIFTS:	thank you:
Name:			Phone:			
Children:					shower:	❑
Address:					shower:	❑
City:		State:	Zip:	❀	wedding:	❑
Wedding Invitation: ❑	Reception Invitation: ❑	Announcement: ❑	RSVP — yes: ❑ no: ❑	number invited: ____	number attending: ____	

					GIFTS:	thank you:
Name:			Phone:			
Children:					shower:	❑
Address:					shower:	❑
City:		State:	Zip:	❀	wedding:	❑
Wedding Invitation: ❑	Reception Invitation: ❑	Announcement: ❑	RSVP — yes: ❑ no: ❑	number invited: ____	number attending: ____	

	Name:	Phone:	GIFTS:	thank you

Name: _____ Phone: _____ **GIFTS:** thank you
Children: _____ shower: _____
Address: _____ shower: _____
City: _____ State: _____ Zip: _____ ❀ wedding: _____
Wedding Invitation: ❑ Reception Invitation: ❑ Announcement: ❑ *RSVP —* yes: ❑ no: ❑ *number invited:* _____ *number attending:* _____

Name: _____ Phone: _____ **GIFTS:** thank you
Children: _____ shower: _____
Address: _____ shower: _____
City: _____ State: _____ Zip: _____ ❀ wedding: _____
Wedding Invitation: ❑ Reception Invitation: ❑ Announcement: ❑ *RSVP —* yes: ❑ no: ❑ *number invited:* _____ *number attending:* _____

Name: _____ Phone: _____ **GIFTS:** thank you
Children: _____ shower: _____
Address: _____ shower: _____
City: _____ State: _____ Zip: _____ ❀ wedding: _____
Wedding Invitation: ❑ Reception Invitation: ❑ Announcement: ❑ *RSVP —* yes: ❑ no: ❑ *number invited:* _____ *number attending:* _____

Name: _____ Phone: _____ **GIFTS:** thank you
Children: _____ shower: _____
Address: _____ shower: _____
City: _____ State: _____ Zip: _____ ❀ wedding: _____
Wedding Invitation: ❑ Reception Invitation: ❑ Announcement: ❑ *RSVP —* yes: ❑ no: ❑ *number invited:* _____ *number attending:* _____

Name: _____ Phone: _____ **GIFTS:** thank you
Children: _____ shower: _____
Address: _____ shower: _____
City: _____ State: _____ Zip: _____ ❀ wedding: _____
Wedding Invitation: ❑ Reception Invitation: ❑ Announcement: ❑ *RSVP —* yes: ❑ no: ❑ *number invited:* _____ *number attending:* _____

Name: _____ Phone: _____ **GIFTS:** thank you:
Children: _____ shower: _____
Address: _____ shower: _____
City: _____ State: _____ Zip: _____ ❀ wedding: _____
Wedding Invitation: ❑ Reception Invitation: ❑ Announcement: ❑ *RSVP —* yes: ❑ no: ❑ *number invited:* _____ *number attending:* _____

Name: _____ Phone: _____ **GIFTS:** thank you:
Children: _____ shower: _____
Address: _____ shower: _____
City: _____ State: _____ Zip: _____ ❀ wedding: _____
Wedding Invitation: ❑ Reception Invitation: ❑ Announcement: ❑ *RSVP —* yes: ❑ no: ❑ *number invited:* _____ *number attending:* _____

Name: _____ Phone: _____ **GIFTS:** thank you:
Children: _____ shower: _____
Address: _____ shower: _____
City: _____ State: _____ Zip: _____ ❀ wedding: _____
Wedding Invitation: ❑ Reception Invitation: ❑ Announcement: ❑ *RSVP —* yes: ❑ no: ❑ *number invited:* _____ *number attending:* _____

Name: _____ Phone: _____ **GIFTS:** thank you:
Children: _____ shower: _____
Address: _____ shower: _____
City: _____ State: _____ Zip: _____ ❀ wedding: _____
Wedding Invitation: ❑ Reception Invitation: ❑ Announcement: ❑ *RSVP —* yes: ❑ no: ❑ *number invited:* _____ *number attending:* _____

Name: _____ Phone: _____ **GIFTS:** thank you:
Children: _____ shower: _____
Address: _____ shower: _____
City: _____ State: _____ Zip: _____ ❀ wedding: _____
Wedding Invitation: ❑ Reception Invitation: ❑ Announcement: ❑ *RSVP —* yes: ❑ no: ❑ *number invited:* _____ *number attending:* _____

Name:		Phone:		**GIFTS:**	thank you:
Children:				shower:	❑
Address:				shower:	❑
City:	State:	Zip:	❀	wedding:	❑
Wedding Invitation: ❑	Reception Invitation: ❑	Announcement: ❑	*RSVP* — yes: ❑ no: ❑	*number invited:* _____	*number attending:* _____

Name:		Phone:		**GIFTS:**	thank you:
Children:				shower:	❑
Address:				shower:	❑
City:	State:	Zip:	❀	wedding:	❑
Wedding Invitation: ❑	Reception Invitation: ❑	Announcement: ❑	*RSVP* — yes: ❑ no: ❑	*number invited:* _____	*number attending:* _____

Name:		Phone:		**GIFTS:**	thank you:
Children:				shower:	❑
Address:				shower:	❑
City:	State:	Zip:	❀	wedding:	❑
Wedding Invitation: ❑	Reception Invitation: ❑	Announcement: ❑	*RSVP* — yes: ❑ no: ❑	*number invited:* _____	*number attending:* _____

Name:		Phone:		**GIFTS:**	thank you:
Children:				shower:	❑
Address:				shower:	❑
City:	State:	Zip:	❀	wedding:	❑
Wedding Invitation: ❑	Reception Invitation: ❑	Announcement: ❑	*RSVP* — yes: ❑ no: ❑	*number invited:* _____	*number attending:* _____

Name:		Phone:		**GIFTS:**	thank you:
Children:				shower:	❑
Address:				shower:	❑
City:	State:	Zip:	❀	wedding:	❑
Wedding Invitation: ❑	Reception Invitation: ❑	Announcement: ❑	*RSVP* — yes: ❑ no: ❑	*number invited:* _____	*number attending:* _____

Name:		Phone:		**GIFTS:**	thank you:
Children:				shower:	❑
Address:				shower:	❑
City:	State:	Zip:	❀	wedding:	❑
Wedding Invitation: ❑	Reception Invitation: ❑	Announcement: ❑	*RSVP* — yes: ❑ no: ❑	*number invited:* _____	*number attending:* _____

Name:		Phone:		**GIFTS:**	thank you:
Children:				shower:	❑
Address:				shower:	❑
City:	State:	Zip:	❀	wedding:	❑
Wedding Invitation: ❑	Reception Invitation: ❑	Announcement: ❑	*RSVP* — yes: ❑ no: ❑	*number invited:* _____	*number attending:* _____

Name:		Phone:		**GIFTS:**	thank you:
Children:				shower:	❑
Address:				shower:	❑
City:	State:	Zip:	❀	wedding:	❑
Wedding Invitation: ❑	Reception Invitation: ❑	Announcement: ❑	*RSVP* — yes: ❑ no: ❑	*number invited:* _____	*number attending:* _____

Name:		Phone:		**GIFTS:**	thank you:
Children:				shower:	❑
Address:				shower:	❑
City:	State:	Zip:	❀	wedding:	❑
Wedding Invitation: ❑	Reception Invitation: ❑	Announcement: ❑	*RSVP* — yes: ❑ no: ❑	*number invited:* _____	*number attending:* _____

Name:		Phone:		**GIFTS:**	thank you:
Children:				shower:	❑
Address:				shower:	❑
City:	State:	Zip:	❀	wedding:	❑
Wedding Invitation: ❑	Reception Invitation: ❑	Announcement: ❑	*RSVP* — yes: ❑ no: ❑	*number invited:* _____	*number attending:* _____

	Name:	Phone:	GIFTS:	thank you
	Children:		shower:	
	Address:		shower:	
	City:	State:	Zip:	❀ wedding:
	Wedding Invitation: ❏	Reception Invitation: ❏	Announcement: ❏	*RSVP* — yes: ❏ no: ❏	*number invited:* ____ *number attending:* ____

	Name:	Phone:	GIFTS:	thank you
	Children:		shower:	
	Address:		shower:	
	City:	State:	Zip:	❀ wedding:
	Wedding Invitation: ❏	Reception Invitation: ❏	Announcement: ❏	*RSVP* — yes: ❏ no: ❏	*number invited:* ____ *number attending:* ____

	Name:	Phone:	GIFTS:	thank you
	Children:		shower:	
	Address:		shower:	
	City:	State:	Zip:	❀ wedding:
	Wedding Invitation: ❏	Reception Invitation: ❏	Announcement: ❏	*RSVP* — yes: ❏ no: ❏	*number invited:* ____ *number attending:* ____

	Name:	Phone:	GIFTS:	thank you
	Children:		shower:	
	Address:		shower:	
	City:	State:	Zip:	❀ wedding:
	Wedding Invitation: ❏	Reception Invitation: ❏	Announcement: ❏	*RSVP* — yes: ❏ no: ❏	*number invited:* ____ *number attending:* ____

	Name:	Phone:	GIFTS:	thank you
	Children:		shower:	
	Address:		shower:	
	City:	State:	Zip:	❀ wedding:
	Wedding Invitation: ❏	Reception Invitation: ❏	Announcement: ❏	*RSVP* — yes: ❏ no: ❏	*number invited:* ____ *number attending:* ____

	Name:	Phone:	GIFTS:	thank you
	Children:		shower:	
	Address:		shower:	
	City:	State:	Zip:	❀ wedding:
	Wedding Invitation: ❏	Reception Invitation: ❏	Announcement: ❏	*RSVP* — yes: ❏ no: ❏	*number invited:* ____ *number attending:* ____

	Name:	Phone:	GIFTS:	thank you:
	Children:		shower:	
	Address:		shower:	
	City:	State:	Zip:	❀ wedding:
	Wedding Invitation: ❏	Reception Invitation: ❏	Announcement: ❏	*RSVP* — yes: ❏ no: ❏	*number invited:* ____ *number attending:* ____

	Name:	Phone:	GIFTS:	thank you:
	Children:		shower:	
	Address:		shower:	
	City:	State:	Zip:	❀ wedding:
	Wedding Invitation: ❏	Reception Invitation: ❏	Announcement: ❏	*RSVP* — yes: ❏ no: ❏	*number invited:* ____ *number attending:* ____

	Name:	Phone:	GIFTS:	thank you:
	Children:		shower:	
	Address:		shower:	
	City:	State:	Zip:	❀ wedding:
	Wedding Invitation: ❏	Reception Invitation: ❏	Announcement: ❏	*RSVP* — yes: ❏ no: ❏	*number invited:* ____ *number attending:* ____

	Name:	Phone:	GIFTS:	thank you:
	Children:		shower:	
	Address:		shower:	
	City:	State:	Zip:	❀ wedding:
	Wedding Invitation: ❏	Reception Invitation: ❏	Announcement: ❏	*RSVP* — yes: ❏ no: ❏	*number invited:* ____ *number attending:* ____

Name: _____ Phone: _____ **GIFTS:** thank you:
Children: _____ shower: _____ ❑
Address: _____ shower: _____ ❑
City: _____ State: _____ Zip: _____ ❀ wedding: _____ ❑
Wedding Invitation: ❑ Reception Invitation: ❑ Announcement: ❑ *RSVP* — yes: ❑ no: ❑ *number invited:* ____ *number attending:* ____

Name: _____ Phone: _____ **GIFTS:** thank you:
Children: _____ shower: _____ ❑
Address: _____ shower: _____ ❑
City: _____ State: _____ Zip: _____ ❀ wedding: _____ ❑
Wedding Invitation: ❑ Reception Invitation: ❑ Announcement: ❑ *RSVP* — yes: ❑ no: ❑ *number invited:* ____ *number attending:* ____

Name: _____ Phone: _____ **GIFTS:** thank you:
Children: _____ shower: _____ ❑
Address: _____ shower: _____ ❑
City: _____ State: _____ Zip: _____ ❀ wedding: _____ ❑
Wedding Invitation: ❑ Reception Invitation: ❑ Announcement: ❑ *RSVP* — yes: ❑ no: ❑ *number invited:* ____ *number attending:* ____

Name: _____ Phone: _____ **GIFTS:** thank you:
Children: _____ shower: _____ ❑
Address: _____ shower: _____ ❑
City: _____ State: _____ Zip: _____ ❀ wedding: _____ ❑
Wedding Invitation: ❑ Reception Invitation: ❑ Announcement: ❑ *RSVP* — yes: ❑ no: ❑ *number invited:* ____ *number attending:* ____

Name: _____ Phone: _____ **GIFTS:** thank you:
Children: _____ shower: _____ ❑
Address: _____ shower: _____ ❑
City: _____ State: _____ Zip: _____ ❀ wedding: _____ ❑
Wedding Invitation: ❑ Reception Invitation: ❑ Announcement: ❑ *RSVP* — yes: ❑ no: ❑ *number invited:* ____ *number attending:* ____

Name: _____ Phone: _____ **GIFTS:** thank you:
Children: _____ shower: _____ ❑
Address: _____ shower: _____ ❑
City: _____ State: _____ Zip: _____ ❀ wedding: _____ ❑
Wedding Invitation: ❑ Reception Invitation: ❑ Announcement: ❑ *RSVP* — yes: ❑ no: ❑ *number invited:* ____ *number attending:* ____

Name: _____ Phone: _____ **GIFTS:** thank you:
Children: _____ shower: _____ ❑
Address: _____ shower: _____ ❑
City: _____ State: _____ Zip: _____ ❀ wedding: _____ ❑
Wedding Invitation: ❑ Reception Invitation: ❑ Announcement: ❑ *RSVP* — yes: ❑ no: ❑ *number invited:* ____ *number attending:* ____

Name: _____ Phone: _____ **GIFTS:** thank you:
Children: _____ shower: _____ ❑
Address: _____ shower: _____ ❑
City: _____ State: _____ Zip: _____ ❀ wedding: _____ ❑
Wedding Invitation: ❑ Reception Invitation: ❑ Announcement: ❑ *RSVP* — yes: ❑ no: ❑ *number invited:* ____ *number attending:* ____

Name: _____ Phone: _____ **GIFTS:** thank you:
Children: _____ shower: _____ ❑
Address: _____ shower: _____ ❑
City: _____ State: _____ Zip: _____ ❀ wedding: _____ ❑
Wedding Invitation: ❑ Reception Invitation: ❑ Announcement: ❑ *RSVP* — yes: ❑ no: ❑ *number invited:* ____ *number attending:* ____

Name: _____ Phone: _____ **GIFTS:** thank you:
Children: _____ shower: _____ ❑
Address: _____ shower: _____ ❑
City: _____ State: _____ Zip: _____ ❀ wedding: _____ ❑
Wedding Invitation: ❑ Reception Invitation: ❑ Announcement: ❑ *RSVP* — yes: ❑ no: ❑ *number invited:* ____ *number attending:* ____

Name:		Phone:	GIFTS:	th y
Children:			shower:	
Address:			shower:	
City:	State:	Zip:	❀ wedding:	
Wedding Invitation: ❐	Reception Invitation: ❐	Announcement: ❐	RSVP — yes: ❐ no: ❐	number invited: ____ number attending: ____
Name:		Phone:	GIFTS:	th y
Children:			shower:	
Address:			shower:	
City:	State:	Zip:	❀ wedding:	
Wedding Invitation: ❐	Reception Invitation: ❐	Announcement: ❐	RSVP — yes: ❐ no: ❐	number invited: ____ number attending: ____
Name:		Phone:	GIFTS:	tha y
Children:			shower:	
Address:			shower:	
City:	State:	Zip:	❀ wedding:	
Wedding Invitation: ❐	Reception Invitation: ❐	Announcement: ❐	RSVP — yes: ❐ no: ❐	number invited: ____ number attending: ____
Name:		Phone:	GIFTS:	tha yo
Children:			shower:	
Address:			shower:	
City:	State:	Zip:	❀ wedding:	
Wedding Invitation: ❐	Reception Invitation: ❐	Announcement: ❐	RSVP — yes: ❐ no: ❐	number invited: ____ number attending: ____
Name:		Phone:	GIFTS:	tha yo
Children:			shower:	
Address:			shower:	
City:	State:	Zip:	❀ wedding:	
Wedding Invitation: ❐	Reception Invitation: ❐	Announcement: ❐	RSVP — yes: ❐ no: ❐	number invited: ____ number attending: ____
Name:		Phone:	GIFTS:	than yo
Children:			shower:	
Address:			shower:	
City:	State:	Zip:	❀ wedding:	
Wedding Invitation: ❐	Reception Invitation: ❐	Announcement: ❐	RSVP — yes: ❐ no: ❐	number invited: ____ number attending: ____
Name:		Phone:	GIFTS:	thar yo
Children:			shower:	
Address:			shower:	
City:	State:	Zip:	❀ wedding:	
Wedding Invitation: ❐	Reception Invitation: ❐	Announcement: ❐	RSVP — yes: ❐ no: ❐	number invited: ____ number attending: ____
Name:		Phone:	GIFTS:	than yo
Children:			shower:	
Address:			shower:	
City:	State:	Zip:	❀ wedding:	
Wedding Invitation: ❐	Reception Invitation: ❐	Announcement: ❐	RSVP — yes: ❐ no: ❐	number invited: ____ number attending: ____
Name:		Phone:	GIFTS:	than you
Children:			shower:	
Address:			shower:	
City:	State:	Zip:	❀ wedding:	
Wedding Invitation: ❐	Reception Invitation: ❐	Announcement: ❐	RSVP — yes: ❐ no: ❐	number invited: ____ number attending: ____
Name:		Phone:	GIFTS:	than you
Children:			shower:	
Address:			shower:	
City:	State:	Zip:	❀ wedding:	
Wedding Invitation: ❐	Reception Invitation: ❐	Announcement: ❐	RSVP — yes: ❐ no: ❐	number invited: ____ number attending: ____

Name:		Phone:		**GIFTS:**	thank you:
Children:				shower:	❑
Address:				shower:	❑
City:	State:	Zip:	❀	wedding:	❑
Wedding Invitation: ❑	Reception Invitation: ❑	Announcement: ❑	*RSVP* — yes: ❑ no: ❑	*number invited:* _____	*number attending:* _____

Name:		Phone:		**GIFTS:**	thank you:
Children:				shower:	❑
Address:				shower:	❑
City:	State:	Zip:	❀	wedding:	❑
Wedding Invitation: ❑	Reception Invitation: ❑	Announcement: ❑	*RSVP* — yes: ❑ no: ❑	*number invited:* _____	*number attending:* _____

Name:		Phone:		**GIFTS:**	thank you:
Children:				shower:	❑
Address:				shower:	❑
City:	State:	Zip:	❀	wedding:	❑
Wedding Invitation: ❑	Reception Invitation: ❑	Announcement: ❑	*RSVP* — yes: ❑ no: ❑	*number invited:* _____	*number attending:* _____

Name:		Phone:		**GIFTS:**	thank you:
Children:				shower:	❑
Address:				shower:	❑
City:	State:	Zip:	❀	wedding:	❑
Wedding Invitation: ❑	Reception Invitation: ❑	Announcement: ❑	*RSVP* — yes: ❑ no: ❑	*number invited:* _____	*number attending:* _____

Name:		Phone:		**GIFTS:**	thank you:
Children:				shower:	❑
Address:				shower:	❑
City:	State:	Zip:	❀	wedding:	❑
Wedding Invitation: ❑	Reception Invitation: ❑	Announcement: ❑	*RSVP* — yes: ❑ no: ❑	*number invited:* _____	*number attending:* _____

Name:		Phone:		**GIFTS:**	thank you:
Children:				shower:	❑
Address:				shower:	❑
City:	State:	Zip:	❀	wedding:	❑
Wedding Invitation: ❑	Reception Invitation: ❑	Announcement: ❑	*RSVP* — yes: ❑ no: ❑	*number invited:* _____	*number attending:* _____

Name:		Phone:		**GIFTS:**	thank you:
Children:				shower:	❑
Address:				shower:	❑
City:	State:	Zip:	❀	wedding:	❑
Wedding Invitation: ❑	Reception Invitation: ❑	Announcement: ❑	*RSVP* — yes: ❑ no: ❑	*number invited:* _____	*number attending:* _____

Name:		Phone:		**GIFTS:**	thank you:
Children:				shower:	❑
Address:				shower:	❑
City:	State:	Zip:	❀	wedding:	❑
Wedding Invitation: ❑	Reception Invitation: ❑	Announcement: ❑	*RSVP* — yes: ❑ no: ❑	*number invited:* _____	*number attending:* _____

Name:		Phone:		**GIFTS:**	thank you:
Children:				shower:	❑
Address:				shower:	❑
City:	State:	Zip:	❀	wedding:	❑
Wedding Invitation: ❑	Reception Invitation: ❑	Announcement: ❑	*RSVP* — yes: ❑ no: ❑	*number invited:* _____	*number attending:* _____

Name:		Phone:		**GIFTS:**	thank you:
Children:				shower:	❑
Address:				shower:	❑
City:	State:	Zip:	❀	wedding:	❑
Wedding Invitation: ❑	Reception Invitation: ❑	Announcement: ❑	*RSVP* — yes: ❑ no: ❑	*number invited:* _____	*number attending:* _____

☐ Name: _____ Phone: _____	**GIFTS:**	thank you
Children: _____	shower: _____	
Address: _____	shower: _____	
City: _____ State: _____ Zip: _____ ❀	wedding: _____	
Wedding Invitation: ☐ Reception Invitation: ☐ Announcement: ☐ *RSVP* — yes: ☐ no: ☐ *number invited:* ____ *number attending:* ____		

☐ Name: _____ Phone: _____	**GIFTS:**	thank you
Children: _____	shower: _____	
Address: _____	shower: _____	
City: _____ State: _____ Zip: _____ ❀	wedding: _____	
Wedding Invitation: ☐ Reception Invitation: ☐ Announcement: ☐ *RSVP* — yes: ☐ no: ☐ *number invited:* ____ *number attending:* ____		

☐ Name: _____ Phone: _____	**GIFTS:**	thank you
Children: _____	shower: _____	
Address: _____	shower: _____	
City: _____ State: _____ Zip: _____ ❀	wedding: _____	
Wedding Invitation: ☐ Reception Invitation: ☐ Announcement: ☐ *RSVP* — yes: ☐ no: ☐ *number invited:* ____ *number attending:* ____		

☐ Name: _____ Phone: _____	**GIFTS:**	thank you
Children: _____	shower: _____	
Address: _____	shower: _____	
City: _____ State: _____ Zip: _____ ❀	wedding: _____	
Wedding Invitation: ☐ Reception Invitation: ☐ Announcement: ☐ *RSVP* — yes: ☐ no: ☐ *number invited:* ____ *number attending:* ____		

☐ Name: _____ Phone: _____	**GIFTS:**	thank you
Children: _____	shower: _____	
Address: _____	shower: _____	
City: _____ State: _____ Zip: _____ ❀	wedding: _____	
Wedding Invitation: ☐ Reception Invitation: ☐ Announcement: ☐ *RSVP* — yes: ☐ no: ☐ *number invited:* ____ *number attending:* ____		

☐ Name: _____ Phone: _____	**GIFTS:**	thank you
Children: _____	shower: _____	
Address: _____	shower: _____	
City: _____ State: _____ Zip: _____ ❀	wedding: _____	
Wedding Invitation: ☐ Reception Invitation: ☐ Announcement: ☐ *RSVP* — yes: ☐ no: ☐ *number invited:* ____ *number attending:* ____		

☐ Name: _____ Phone: _____	**GIFTS:**	thank you
Children: _____	shower: _____	
Address: _____	shower: _____	
City: _____ State: _____ Zip: _____ ❀	wedding: _____	
Wedding Invitation: ☐ Reception Invitation: ☐ Announcement: ☐ *RSVP* — yes: ☐ no: ☐ *number invited:* ____ *number attending:* ____		

☐ Name: _____ Phone: _____	**GIFTS:**	thank you
Children: _____	shower: _____	
Address: _____	shower: _____	
City: _____ State: _____ Zip: _____ ❀	wedding: _____	
Wedding Invitation: ☐ Reception Invitation: ☐ Announcement: ☐ *RSVP* — yes: ☐ no: ☐ *number invited:* ____ *number attending:* ____		

☐ Name: _____ Phone: _____	**GIFTS:**	thank you
Children: _____	shower: _____	
Address: _____	shower: _____	
City: _____ State: _____ Zip: _____ ❀	wedding: _____	
Wedding Invitation: ☐ Reception Invitation: ☐ Announcement: ☐ *RSVP* — yes: ☐ no: ☐ *number invited:* ____ *number attending:* ____		

☐ Name: _____ Phone: _____	**GIFTS:**	thank you
Children: _____	shower: _____	
Address: _____	shower: _____	
City: _____ State: _____ Zip: _____ ❀	wedding: _____	
Wedding Invitation: ☐ Reception Invitation: ☐ Announcement: ☐ *RSVP* — yes: ☐ no: ☐ *number invited:* ____ *number attending:* ____		

☐ Name: _____ Phone: _____	**GIFTS:**	thank you
Children: _____	shower: _____	
Address: _____	shower: _____	
City: _____ State: _____ Zip: _____ ❀	wedding: _____	
Wedding Invitation: ☐ Reception Invitation: ☐ Announcement: ☐ *RSVP* — yes: ☐ no: ☐ *number invited:* ____ *number attending:* ____		

Name:	Phone:		GIFTS:	thank you:
Children:			shower:	❑
Address:			shower:	❑
City:	State:	Zip:	wedding:	❑
Wedding Invitation: ❑	Reception Invitation: ❑	Announcement: ❑	*RSVP* — yes: ❑ no: ❑	*number invited:* _____ *number attending:* _____

Name:	Phone:		GIFTS:	thank you:
Children:			shower:	❑
Address:			shower:	❑
City:	State:	Zip:	wedding:	❑
Wedding Invitation: ❑	Reception Invitation: ❑	Announcement: ❑	*RSVP* — yes: ❑ no: ❑	*number invited:* _____ *number attending:* _____

Name:	Phone:		GIFTS:	thank you:
Children:			shower:	❑
Address:			shower:	❑
City:	State:	Zip:	wedding:	❑
Wedding Invitation: ❑	Reception Invitation: ❑	Announcement: ❑	*RSVP* — yes: ❑ no: ❑	*number invited:* _____ *number attending:* _____

Name:	Phone:		GIFTS:	thank you:
Children:			shower:	❑
Address:			shower:	❑
City:	State:	Zip:	wedding:	❑
Wedding Invitation: ❑	Reception Invitation: ❑	Announcement: ❑	*RSVP* — yes: ❑ no: ❑	*number invited:* _____ *number attending:* _____

Name:	Phone:		GIFTS:	thank you:
Children:			shower:	❑
Address:			shower:	❑
City:	State:	Zip:	wedding:	❑
Wedding Invitation: ❑	Reception Invitation: ❑	Announcement: ❑	*RSVP* — yes: ❑ no: ❑	*number invited:* _____ *number attending:* _____

Name:	Phone:		GIFTS:	thank you:
Children:			shower:	❑
Address:			shower:	❑
City:	State:	Zip:	wedding:	❑
Wedding Invitation: ❑	Reception Invitation: ❑	Announcement: ❑	*RSVP* — yes: ❑ no: ❑	*number invited:* _____ *number attending:* _____

Name:	Phone:		GIFTS:	thank you:
Children:			shower:	❑
Address:			shower:	❑
City:	State:	Zip:	wedding:	❑
Wedding Invitation: ❑	Reception Invitation: ❑	Announcement: ❑	*RSVP* — yes: ❑ no: ❑	*number invited:* _____ *number attending:* _____

Name:	Phone:		GIFTS:	thank you:
Children:			shower:	❑
Address:			shower:	❑
City:	State:	Zip:	wedding:	❑
Wedding Invitation: ❑	Reception Invitation: ❑	Announcement: ❑	*RSVP* — yes: ❑ no: ❑	*number invited:* _____ *number attending:* _____

Name:	Phone:		GIFTS:	thank you:
Children:			shower:	❑
Address:			shower:	❑
City:	State:	Zip:	wedding:	❑
Wedding Invitation: ❑	Reception Invitation: ❑	Announcement: ❑	*RSVP* — yes: ❑ no: ❑	*number invited:* _____ *number attending:* _____

Name:	Phone:		GIFTS:	thank you:
Children:			shower:	❑
Address:			shower:	❑
City:	State:	Zip:	wedding:	❑
Wedding Invitation: ❑	Reception Invitation: ❑	Announcement: ❑	*RSVP* — yes: ❑ no: ❑	*number invited:* _____ *number attending:* _____

☐ Name:		Phone:	**GIFTS:**	thank you
Children:			shower:	☐
Address:			shower:	☐
City:	State:	Zip:	❀ wedding:	☐
Wedding Invitation: ☐	Reception Invitation: ☐	Announcement: ☐	*RSVP* — yes: ☐ no: ☐	*number invited:* _____ *number attending:* _____
☐ Name:		Phone:	**GIFTS:**	thank you
Children:			shower:	☐
Address:			shower:	☐
City:	State:	Zip:	❀ wedding:	☐
Wedding Invitation: ☐	Reception Invitation: ☐	Announcement: ☐	*RSVP* — yes: ☐ no: ☐	*number invited:* _____ *number attending:* _____
☐ Name:		Phone:	**GIFTS:**	thank you
Children:			shower:	☐
Address:			shower:	☐
City:	State:	Zip:	❀ wedding:	☐
Wedding Invitation: ☐	Reception Invitation: ☐	Announcement: ☐	*RSVP* — yes: ☐ no: ☐	*number invited:* _____ *number attending:* _____
☐ Name:		Phone:	**GIFTS:**	thank you
Children:			shower:	☐
Address:			shower:	☐
City:	State:	Zip:	❀ wedding:	☐
Wedding Invitation: ☐	Reception Invitation: ☐	Announcement: ☐	*RSVP* — yes: ☐ no: ☐	*number invited:* _____ *number attending:* _____
☐ Name:		Phone:	**GIFTS:**	thank you
Children:			shower:	☐
Address:			shower:	☐
City:	State:	Zip:	❀ wedding:	☐
Wedding Invitation: ☐	Reception Invitation: ☐	Announcement: ☐	*RSVP* — yes: ☐ no: ☐	*number invited:* _____ *number attending:* _____
☐ Name:		Phone:	**GIFTS:**	thank you
Children:			shower:	☐
Address:			shower:	☐
City:	State:	Zip:	❀ wedding:	☐
Wedding Invitation: ☐	Reception Invitation: ☐	Announcement: ☐	*RSVP* — yes: ☐ no: ☐	*number invited:* _____ *number attending:* _____
☐ Name:		Phone:	**GIFTS:**	thank you
Children:			shower:	☐
Address:			shower:	☐
City:	State:	Zip:	❀ wedding:	☐
Wedding Invitation: ☐	Reception Invitation: ☐	Announcement: ☐	*RSVP* — yes: ☐ no: ☐	*number invited:* _____ *number attending:* _____
☐ Name:		Phone:	**GIFTS:**	thank you
Children:			shower:	☐
Address:			shower:	☐
City:	State:	Zip:	❀ wedding:	☐
Wedding Invitation: ☐	Reception Invitation: ☐	Announcement: ☐	*RSVP* — yes: ☐ no: ☐	*number invited:* _____ *number attending:* _____
☐ Name:		Phone:	**GIFTS:**	thank you:
Children:			shower:	☐
Address:			shower:	☐
City:	State:	Zip:	❀ wedding:	☐
Wedding Invitation: ☐	Reception Invitation: ☐	Announcement: ☐	*RSVP* — yes: ☐ no: ☐	*number invited:* _____ *number attending:* _____
☐ Name:		Phone:	**GIFTS:**	thank you:
Children:			shower:	☐
Address:			shower:	☐
City:	State:	Zip:	❀ wedding:	☐
Wedding Invitation: ☐	Reception Invitation: ☐	Announcement: ☐	*RSVP* — yes: ☐ no: ☐	*number invited:* _____ *number attending:* _____

Name:		Phone:		**GIFTS:**	thank you:
Children:				shower:	☐
Address:				shower:	☐
City:	State:	Zip:	❀	wedding:	☐
Wedding Invitation: ☐	Reception Invitation: ☐	Announcement: ☐	*RSVP* — yes: ☐ no: ☐	*number invited:* _____	*number attending:* _____

Name:		Phone:		**GIFTS:**	thank you:
Children:				shower:	☐
Address:				shower:	☐
City:	State:	Zip:	❀	wedding:	☐
Wedding Invitation: ☐	Reception Invitation: ☐	Announcement: ☐	*RSVP* — yes: ☐ no: ☐	*number invited:* _____	*number attending:* _____

Name:		Phone:		**GIFTS:**	thank you:
Children:				shower:	☐
Address:				shower:	☐
City:	State:	Zip:	❀	wedding:	☐
Wedding Invitation: ☐	Reception Invitation: ☐	Announcement: ☐	*RSVP* — yes: ☐ no: ☐	*number invited:* _____	*number attending:* _____

Name:		Phone:		**GIFTS:**	thank you:
Children:				shower:	☐
Address:				shower:	☐
City:	State:	Zip:	❀	wedding:	☐
Wedding Invitation: ☐	Reception Invitation: ☐	Announcement: ☐	*RSVP* — yes: ☐ no: ☐	*number invited:* _____	*number attending:* _____

Name:		Phone:		**GIFTS:**	thank you:
Children:				shower:	☐
Address:				shower:	☐
City:	State:	Zip:	❀	wedding:	☐
Wedding Invitation: ☐	Reception Invitation: ☐	Announcement: ☐	*RSVP* — yes: ☐ no: ☐	*number invited:* _____	*number attending:* _____

Name:		Phone:		**GIFTS:**	thank you:
Children:				shower:	☐
Address:				shower:	☐
City:	State:	Zip:	❀	wedding:	☐
Wedding Invitation: ☐	Reception Invitation: ☐	Announcement: ☐	*RSVP* — yes: ☐ no: ☐	*number invited:* _____	*number attending:* _____

Name:		Phone:		**GIFTS:**	thank you:
Children:				shower:	☐
Address:				shower:	☐
City:	State:	Zip:	❀	wedding:	☐
Wedding Invitation: ☐	Reception Invitation: ☐	Announcement: ☐	*RSVP* — yes: ☐ no: ☐	*number invited:* _____	*number attending:* _____

Name:		Phone:		**GIFTS:**	thank you:
Children:				shower:	☐
Address:				shower:	☐
City:	State:	Zip:	❀	wedding:	☐
Wedding Invitation: ☐	Reception Invitation: ☐	Announcement: ☐	*RSVP* — yes: ☐ no: ☐	*number invited:* _____	*number attending:* _____

Name:		Phone:		**GIFTS:**	thank you:
Children:				shower:	☐
Address:				shower:	☐
City:	State:	Zip:	❀	wedding:	☐
Wedding Invitation: ☐	Reception Invitation: ☐	Announcement: ☐	*RSVP* — yes: ☐ no: ☐	*number invited:* _____	*number attending:* _____

Name:		Phone:		**GIFTS:**	thank you:
Children:				shower:	☐
Address:				shower:	☐
City:	State:	Zip:	❀	wedding:	☐
Wedding Invitation: ☐	Reception Invitation: ☐	Announcement: ☐	*RSVP* — yes: ☐ no: ☐	*number invited:* _____	*number attending:* _____

☐ Name: _____	Phone: _____	**GIFTS:** thank you
Children: _____		shower: _____ ☐
Address: _____		shower: _____ ☐
City: _____ State: _____ Zip: _____	✿	wedding: _____ ☐
Wedding Invitation: ☐ Reception Invitation: ☐ Announcement: ☐	*RSVP* — yes: ☐ no: ☐	*number invited:* ____ *number attending:* ____

☐ Name: _____	Phone: _____	**GIFTS:** thank you
Children: _____		shower: _____ ☐
Address: _____		shower: _____ ☐
City: _____ State: _____ Zip: _____	✿	wedding: _____ ☐
Wedding Invitation: ☐ Reception Invitation: ☐ Announcement: ☐	*RSVP* — yes: ☐ no: ☐	*number invited:* ____ *number attending:* ____

☐ Name: _____	Phone: _____	**GIFTS:** thank you
Children: _____		shower: _____ ☐
Address: _____		shower: _____ ☐
City: _____ State: _____ Zip: _____	✿	wedding: _____ ☐
Wedding Invitation: ☐ Reception Invitation: ☐ Announcement: ☐	*RSVP* — yes: ☐ no: ☐	*number invited:* ____ *number attending:* ____

☐ Name: _____	Phone: _____	**GIFTS:** thank you
Children: _____		shower: _____ ☐
Address: _____		shower: _____ ☐
City: _____ State: _____ Zip: _____	✿	wedding: _____ ☐
Wedding Invitation: ☐ Reception Invitation: ☐ Announcement: ☐	*RSVP* — yes: ☐ no: ☐	*number invited:* ____ *number attending:* ____

☐ Name: _____	Phone: _____	**GIFTS:** thank you:
Children: _____		shower: _____ ☐
Address: _____		shower: _____ ☐
City: _____ State: _____ Zip: _____	✿	wedding: _____ ☐
Wedding Invitation: ☐ Reception Invitation: ☐ Announcement: ☐	*RSVP* — yes: ☐ no: ☐	*number invited:* ____ *number attending:* ____

☐ Name: _____	Phone: _____	**GIFTS:** thank you:
Children: _____		shower: _____ ☐
Address: _____		shower: _____ ☐
City: _____ State: _____ Zip: _____	✿	wedding: _____ ☐
Wedding Invitation: ☐ Reception Invitation: ☐ Announcement: ☐	*RSVP* — yes: ☐ no: ☐	*number invited:* ____ *number attending:* ____

☐ Name: _____	Phone: _____	**GIFTS:** thank you:
Children: _____		shower: _____ ☐
Address: _____		shower: _____ ☐
City: _____ State: _____ Zip: _____	✿	wedding: _____ ☐
Wedding Invitation: ☐ Reception Invitation: ☐ Announcement: ☐	*RSVP* — yes: ☐ no: ☐	*number invited:* ____ *number attending:* ____

☐ Name: _____	Phone: _____	**GIFTS:** thank you:
Children: _____		shower: _____ ☐
Address: _____		shower: _____ ☐
City: _____ State: _____ Zip: _____	✿	wedding: _____ ☐
Wedding Invitation: ☐ Reception Invitation: ☐ Announcement: ☐	*RSVP* — yes: ☐ no: ☐	*number invited:* ____ *number attending:* ____

☐ Name: _____	Phone: _____	**GIFTS:** thank you:
Children: _____		shower: _____ ☐
Address: _____		shower: _____ ☐
City: _____ State: _____ Zip: _____	✿	wedding: _____ ☐
Wedding Invitation: ☐ Reception Invitation: ☐ Announcement: ☐	*RSVP* — yes: ☐ no: ☐	*number invited:* ____ *number attending:* ____

☐ Name: _____	Phone: _____	**GIFTS:** thank you:
Children: _____		shower: _____ ☐
Address: _____		shower: _____ ☐
City: _____ State: _____ Zip: _____	✿	wedding: _____ ☐
Wedding Invitation: ☐ Reception Invitation: ☐ Announcement: ☐	*RSVP* — yes: ☐ no: ☐	*number invited:* ____ *number attending:* ____

Groom's Guest List

name:	address:	phone:

name: *address:*   *phone:*

Gift Registry

❁ FINE CHINA

Brand: _____
Pattern: _____

Quantity:	Price:	Item:
_____	_____	5-pc. Setting
_____	_____	Dinner Plate
_____	_____	Salad Plate
_____	_____	Bread/Butter
_____	_____	Cup
_____	_____	Saucer
_____	_____	Soup/Cereal
_____	_____	Fruit Dish
_____	_____	Small Platter
_____	_____	Medium Platter
_____	_____	Large Platter
_____	_____	Covered Vegetable
_____	_____	Oval Vegetable
_____	_____	Round Vegetable
_____	_____	Salt/Pepper
_____	_____	Butter Dish
_____	_____	Gravy Boat
_____	_____	Creamer
_____	_____	Sugar
_____	_____	Teapot
_____	_____	Coffee Pot
_____	_____	_____
_____	_____	_____

❁ FLATWARE—FORMAL

Brand: _____
Pattern: _____

Quantity:	Price:	Item:
_____	_____	4-Pc. Setting
_____	_____	5-Pc.--Soup
_____	_____	5-Pc.--2 Teaspoons
_____	_____	Teaspoon
_____	_____	Salad Fork
_____	_____	Fork
_____	_____	Knife
_____	_____	Place Spoon
_____	_____	Iced Teaspoon
_____	_____	Cocktail Forks
_____	_____	Steak Knives
_____	_____	Butter Spreader
_____	_____	Tablespoon
_____	_____	Pierced Tablespoon
_____	_____	Butter Knife
_____	_____	Sugar Spoon
_____	_____	Meat Fork
_____	_____	Gravy Ladle
_____	_____	Casserole Spoon
_____	_____	Pastry Server
_____	_____	Storage Chest
_____	_____	_____
_____	_____	_____

❁ CRYSTAL ❁

Brand: _____
Pattern: _____
Color: _____

Quantity:	Price:	Item:			
_____	_____	Goblet	_____	_____	Cordial
_____	_____	Wine	_____	_____	Highball
_____	_____	Champagne	_____	_____	Double Old Fashioned
_____	_____	Sherbet	_____	_____	Decanter
			_____	_____	Ice Tea
			_____	_____	_____
			_____	_____	_____
			_____	_____	_____

✿
FLATWARE—CASUAL

Brand: _____
Pattern: _____

Quantity:	Price:	Item:
_____	_____	4-Pc. Setting
_____	_____	5-Pc.--Soup
_____	_____	5-Pc.--2 Teaspoons
_____	_____	Teaspoon
_____	_____	Salad Fork
_____	_____	Fork
_____	_____	Knife
_____	_____	Place Spoon
_____	_____	Iced Teaspoon
_____	_____	Cocktail Forks
_____	_____	Steak Knives
_____	_____	Butter Spreader
_____	_____	Tablespoon
_____	_____	Pierced Tablespoon
_____	_____	Butter Knife
_____	_____	Sugar Spoon
_____	_____	Meat Fork
_____	_____	Gravy Ladle
_____	_____	Casserole Spoon
_____	_____	Pastry Server
_____	_____	Storage Chest

✿
CASUAL DINNERWARE

Brand: _____
Pattern: _____

Quantity:	Price:	Item:
_____	_____	5-Pc. Setting
_____	_____	5-Pc. Server
_____	_____	7-Pc. Hostess
_____	_____	20 Pc. Set
_____	_____	Dinner Plate
_____	_____	Salad Plate
_____	_____	Bread/Butter
_____	_____	Cup
_____	_____	Saucer
_____	_____	Mug
_____	_____	Soup/Cereal
_____	_____	Fruit Dish
_____	_____	Small Platter
_____	_____	Medium Platter
_____	_____	Large Platter
_____	_____	Covered Vegetable
_____	_____	Round Vegetable
_____	_____	Salt/Pepper
_____	_____	Butter Dish
_____	_____	Gravy Boat
_____	_____	Creamer

_____	_____	Sugar
_____	_____	Teapot
_____	_____	Coffee Pot
_____	_____	_____
_____	_____	_____

✿
KITCHEN LINENS

Brand: _____
Pattern: _____

Quantity:	Price:	Item:
_____	_____	Apron
_____	_____	Towels
_____	_____	Mitts
_____	_____	Pot Holders
_____	_____	Toaster Cover
_____	_____	Blender Cover
_____	_____	_____
_____	_____	_____

✿
CASUAL GLASS/BARWARE

Brand: _____
Pattern: _____
Color: _____

Quantity:	Price:	Item:
_____	_____	Goblet
_____	_____	Wine
_____	_____	Champagne
_____	_____	Low Tumbler
_____	_____	High Tumbler
_____	_____	Ice Tea
_____	_____	Juice
_____	_____	Pitcher
_____	_____	24-Pc. Glass Set
_____	_____	Pilsner/Beer Glasses
_____	_____	_____

✿
BAR EQUIPMENT

Brand: _____
Pattern: _____
Color: _____

Quantity:	Price:	Item:
_____	_____	Ice Bucket
_____	_____	Wine Cooler
_____	_____	Wine Rack
_____	_____	Decanter
_____	_____	Punch Bowl Set
_____	_____	Pitcher
_____	_____	Coasters
_____	_____	Cocktail Shaker

❀ COOKWARE

Quantity:	Price:	Item:	Brand:	Pattern:	Color:
___	___	Sauce Pan--1 quart	___	___	___
___	___	Sauce Pan--2 quart	___	___	___
___	___	Sauce Pan--3 quart	___	___	___
___	___	Sauce Pan--4 quart	___	___	___
___	___	Double Boiler	___	___	___
___	___	Small Frying Pan	___	___	___
___	___	Medium Frying Pan	___	___	___
___	___	Large Frying Pan	___	___	___
___	___	Stock Pot	___	___	___
___	___	Dutch Oven	___	___	___
___	___	Lasagna Pan	___	___	___
___	___	Casserole	___	___	___
___	___	Steamer	___	___	___
___	___	Colander	___	___	___
___	___	Tea Kettle	___	___	___
___	___	Microwave Cookware	___	___	___
___	___	Bakeware	___	___	___
___	___	Cookie Sheet	___	___	___
___	___	Quiche Dish	___	___	___
___	___	___	___	___	___
___	___	___	___	___	___
___	___	___	___	___	___
___	___	___	___	___	___

❀ APPLIANCES

Quantity:	Price:	Item:	Brand:	Pattern:	Color:
___	___	Wafflemaker	___	___	___
___	___	Can Opener	___	___	___
___	___	Coffee Maker	___	___	___
___	___	Iron	___	___	___
___	___	Toaster	___	___	___
___	___	Mixer (Hand)	___	___	___
___	___	Blender	___	___	___
___	___	Slow Cooker	___	___	___
___	___	Food Processor	___	___	___
___	___	Popcorn Popper	___	___	___
___	___	Toaster Oven	___	___	___
___	___	Coffee Grinder	___	___	___
___	___	Electric Wok	___	___	___
___	___	Electric Knife	___	___	___
___	___	Electric Juicer	___	___	___
___	___	Ice Cream Maker	___	___	___
___	___	Electric Pasta Machine	___	___	___
___	___	Broil/Rotisserie	___	___	___
___	___	Electric Fondue	___	___	___
___	___	Convection Oven	___	___	___
___	___	Clock	___	___	___
___	___	Vacuum Cleaner	___	___	___
___	___	Espresso Machine	___	___	___
___	___	Microwave Oven	___	___	___
___	___	___	___	___	___
___	___	___	___	___	___

❧ KITCHENWARE

Quantity:	Price:	Item:	Brand:	Pattern:	Color:
		Ironing Board			
		Cutlery			
		Steak Knives			
		Cutting Board			
		Utensil Set			
		Mixing Bowls			
		Canister Set			
		Spice Rack			
		Cook Books			
		Measuring Cups			
		Measuring Spoons			
		Jello Molds			
		Timer			
		Storage Containers			
		Thermometer			

❧ HOLLOWARE/SERVERS

Quantity:	Price:	Item:	Brand:	Pattern:	Color:
		Salt and Pepper			
		Platter			
		Gravy Boat			
		Bread Tray			
		Vegetable Dish			
		Covered Casserole			
		Chafing Dish			
		Salad Bowl			
		Salad Server			
		Butter Dish			
		Relish Dish			
		Chip'n Dip			
		Water Pitcher			
		Serving Tray			
		Sugar and Creamer			
		Coffee/Tea Set			
		Compote			
		Candlesticks (pair)			
		Napkin Rings			

❧ BEDROOM LINENS — Bedroom #1 *(Bed size: _____)*

Quantity:	Price:	Item:	Brand:	Pattern:	Color:
		Flat Sheets			
		Flat Sheets			
		Fitted Sheets			
		Fitted Sheets			
		Pillowcases			
		Pillowcases			
		Pillows			
		Blanket, lightweight			

Quantity:	Price:	Item:	Brand:	Pattern:	Color:
_____	_____	Blanket, woolen	_____	_____	_____
_____	_____	Electric Blanket	_____	_____	_____
_____	_____	Bedspread	_____	_____	_____
_____	_____	Comforter/Quilt	_____	_____	_____
_____	_____	Pillow Shams	_____	_____	_____
_____	_____	Dust Ruffle	_____	_____	_____
_____	_____	Mattress Pad	_____	_____	_____
_____	_____	Pillow Protector	_____	_____	_____
_____	_____	_____	_____	_____	_____
_____	_____	_____	_____	_____	_____
_____	_____	_____	_____	_____	_____

❀ BEDROOM LINENS — Bedroom #2 *(Bed size: _____)*

Quantity:	Price:	Item:	Brand:	Pattern:	Color:
_____	_____	Flat Sheets	_____	_____	_____
_____	_____	Flat Sheets	_____	_____	_____
_____	_____	Fitted Sheets	_____	_____	_____
_____	_____	Fitted Sheets	_____	_____	_____
_____	_____	Pillowcases	_____	_____	_____
_____	_____	Pillowcases	_____	_____	_____
_____	_____	Blanket, lightweight	_____	_____	_____
_____	_____	Blanket, woolen	_____	_____	_____
_____	_____	Electric Blanket	_____	_____	_____
_____	_____	Bedspread	_____	_____	_____
_____	_____	Comforter/Quilt	_____	_____	_____
_____	_____	Pillow Shams	_____	_____	_____
_____	_____	Dust Ruffle	_____	_____	_____
_____	_____	Mattress Pad	_____	_____	_____
_____	_____	Pillow Protector	_____	_____	_____
_____	_____	_____	_____	_____	_____
_____	_____	_____	_____	_____	_____
_____	_____	_____	_____	_____	_____

❀ BATH #1

Quantity:	Price:	Item:	Brand:	Pattern:	Color:
_____	_____	Bath Towels	_____	_____	_____
_____	_____	Bath Towels	_____	_____	_____
_____	_____	Hand Towels	_____	_____	_____
_____	_____	Hand Towels	_____	_____	_____
_____	_____	Washcloths	_____	_____	_____
_____	_____	Washcloths	_____	_____	_____
_____	_____	Fingertip Towels	_____	_____	_____
_____	_____	Fingertip Towels	_____	_____	_____
_____	_____	Bath Sheets	_____	_____	_____
_____	_____	Bath Rug	_____	_____	_____
_____	_____	Contour Rug	_____	_____	_____
_____	_____	Lid Cover	_____	_____	_____
_____	_____	Bath Mat	_____	_____	_____
_____	_____	Shower Curtain	_____	_____	_____
_____	_____	Tissue Holder	_____	_____	_____
_____	_____	Tumbler/Soap Dish	_____	_____	_____
_____	_____	Wastebasket	_____	_____	_____
_____	_____	Hamper	_____	_____	_____
_____	_____	Pool Towels	_____	_____	_____
_____	_____	Tank Set	_____	_____	_____
_____	_____	_____	_____	_____	_____

❀ BATH #2

Quantity:	Price:	Item:	Brand:	Pattern:	Color:
_____	_____	Bath Towels	_____	_____	_____
_____	_____	Bath Towels	_____	_____	_____
_____	_____	Hand Towels	_____	_____	_____
_____	_____	Hand Towels	_____	_____	_____
_____	_____	Washcloths	_____	_____	_____
_____	_____	Washcloths	_____	_____	_____
_____	_____	Fingertip Towels	_____	_____	_____
_____	_____	Fingertip Towels	_____	_____	_____
_____	_____	Bath Sheets	_____	_____	_____
_____	_____	Bath Rug	_____	_____	_____
_____	_____	Contour Rug	_____	_____	_____
_____	_____	Lid Cover	_____	_____	_____
_____	_____	Bath Mat	_____	_____	_____
_____	_____	Shower Curtain	_____	_____	_____
_____	_____	Tissue Holder	_____	_____	_____
_____	_____	Tumbler/Soap Dish	_____	_____	_____
_____	_____	Wastebasket	_____	_____	_____
_____	_____	Tank Set	_____	_____	_____
_____	_____	_____	_____	_____	_____
_____	_____	_____	_____	_____	_____

❀ ELECTRONICS

Quantity:	Price:	Item:	Brand:	Pattern:	Color:
_____	_____	Television	_____	_____	_____
_____	_____	Video System	_____	_____	_____
_____	_____	Radio	_____	_____	_____
_____	_____	Clock/Radio	_____	_____	_____
_____	_____	Stereo System	_____	_____	_____
_____	_____	_____	_____	_____	_____
_____	_____	_____	_____	_____	_____

❀ SPECIALTY ITEMS

Quantity:	Price:	Item:	Brand:	Pattern:	Color:
_____	_____	Luggage	_____	_____	_____
_____	_____	Exercise Equipment	_____	_____	_____
_____	_____	TV Trays	_____	_____	_____
_____	_____	_____	_____	_____	_____
_____	_____	_____	_____	_____	_____
_____	_____	_____	_____	_____	_____

Gift Registry Locations

	#1	#2	#3
Name:	_____	_____	_____
Address:	_____	_____	_____
Contact Persons:	_____	_____	_____
Phone:	_____	_____	_____

BUDGET

BUDGET

- The following percentage estimates are useful in breaking down your total wedding budget into categories.

Stationery	4%	Photographs	9%
Bridal Attire	13%	Bridesmaids' gifts	2%
Music	4%	Rentals	3%
Reception	50%	Transportation	2%
Flowers	10%	Miscellaneous Fees	3%

- To determine a guideline figure for each category in your budget, use this equation:

Your Total Budget × Each Item's Estimated Percentage
(from the list above)

Example:

Assume that your total budget is $5,000, and you want to know a guideline for determining how much to spend for invitations and other stationery. Using the formula above, you multiply $5,000 times .04 (which is 4%, the estimate given above for Stationery):

$$\$5,000 \quad × \quad .04 \quad = \quad \$\underline{200}$$

Therefore, as a guideline for a $5,000 wedding budget, $200 would be an appropriate amount to spend on invitations and other stationery.

- You can change the percentages given above, depending on what you want to emphasize in your wedding.
- After having computed the amounts for each category, you may want to reevaluate your priorities. Make whatever adjustments are necessary to more closely meet your expectations.
- Once you've determined the amounts for each category, enter these amounts in the "Amount Budgeted" column on Worksheet 1 (Bride's Budget).
- For some expenses that are traditionally the groom's responsibility — such as certain flowers and his wedding attire — the cost will be determined by the overall wedding style. Other items in his budget will reflect his own preferences.
- Together you and your fiancé can use Worksheets 1 (Bride's Budget) and 2 (Groom's Budget) to keep a close tab on the budgeted amounts, total costs, deposits made, and the balance due in each category.

We suggest that you set aside a special location for four or five large envelopes to hold the receipts and contracts pertaining to your wedding. The following is an example of how the envelopes may be organized.

Envelope #   *Contains receipts & contracts pertaining to these subjects:*

1. Ceremony site, officiant, wedding coordinator, gift registry, invitations.
2. Wedding attire, special gifts.
3. Reception site, reception caterer, wedding cake, rental equipment, special parties.
4. Music, florist, photographer, video/audio, housing & transportation, newspaper announcement.
5. Honeymoon.

Bride's Budget

(Traditional Expenses)

Budgeted Items	Amount Budgeted	Total Cost	Deposit	Balance Due
Stationery:	360.00	_____		_____
Invitations		_____	_____	_____
Reception Cards		_____	_____	_____
Response Cards		_____	_____	_____
Thank-You Notes		_____	_____	_____
Napkins		_____	_____	_____
Matches		_____	_____	_____
Programs		_____	_____	_____
Announcements		_____	_____	_____
Bridal Attire:	1170.00	_____		
Dress		_____	_____	_____
Headpiece & Veil		_____	_____	_____
Accessories		_____	_____	_____
Groom's Wedding Ring & Gift: _____		_____	_____	_____
Bridal Attendants' Gifts:	180.00	_____	_____	_____
Bride's Medical: _____		_____	_____	_____
Reception:	$4500.00	_____		
Site Fee		_____	_____	_____
Caterer		_____	_____	_____
Food		_____	_____	_____
Beverages		_____	_____	_____
Gratuity & Tax		_____	_____	_____
Cake		_____	_____	_____
Additional Services		_____	_____	_____
Music:	$360	_____		
Ceremony		_____	_____	_____
Reception		_____	_____	_____

(continued)

Budgeted Items	Amount Budgeted	Total Cost	Deposit	Balance Due
Florist:	$900.00	_____		
Ceremony Site Flowers		_____	_____	_____
Bridesmaids' Bouquets		_____	_____	_____
Groom's Boutonniere		_____	_____	_____
Fathers' Boutonnieres		_____	_____	_____
Grandfathers' Boutonnieres		_____	_____	_____
Reception Site Flowers		_____	_____	_____
Special Others		_____	_____	_____
Other		_____	_____	_____
Photographer:	$810.00	_____		
Formal Portraits		_____		
Engagement		_____	_____	
Wedding		_____	_____	
Wedding Package		_____	_____	
Parents' Albums		_____	_____	
Extra Pictures		_____	_____	
Video-taping:	_____	_____	_____	_____
Audio-taping:	_____	_____	_____	_____
Special Parties:	_____	_____		
Bridal Luncheon		_____	_____	_____
Pre-Ceremony Buffet		_____	_____	_____
Rental Equipment:	270.00	_____		
Ceremony		_____	_____	_____
Reception		_____	_____	_____
Transportation:	180.00	_____		
Parking Attendant		_____	_____	_____
Car Rental		_____	_____	_____
Miscellaneous Fees:	270.00	_____		
Ceremony Site Fee		_____	_____	_____
Wedding Coordinator		_____	_____	_____
Maid Service		_____	_____	_____
Guard for Home		_____	_____	_____
Temporary Insurance Policy		_____	_____	_____
Other		_____	_____	_____

Groom's Budget

(Traditional Expenses)

BUDGETED ITEMS	AMOUNT BUDGETED	TOTAL COST	DEPOSIT	BALANCE DUE
Wedding Attire:	_____			
Groom		_____	_____	_____
Mother		_____	_____	_____
Father		_____	_____	_____
Other		_____	_____	_____
		_____	_____	_____
Housing/Transportation:	_____	_____		
Rings:	_____	_____		
Engagement		_____	_____	_____
Wedding		_____	_____	_____
Gift for the Bride:	_____	_____	_____	_____
Attendants' Gifts:	_____	_____	_____	_____
Medical:	_____	_____	_____	_____
Flowers:	_____			
Bride's Bouquet & Corsage		_____	_____	_____
Mothers' Corsages		_____	_____	_____
Grandmothers' Corsages		_____	_____	_____
Ushers' Boutonnieres		_____	_____	_____
Bachelor's Party:	_____	_____	_____	_____
Rehearsal Dinner:	_____	_____	_____	_____
Honeymoon Expenses:	_____	_____	_____	_____

(Include an additional 10% to cover unexpected expenses.)

(continued)

Budgeted Items	Amount Budgeted	Total Cost	Deposit	Balance Due
Marriage License:	_____	_____		
Officiant's fee:	_____	_____	_____	_____
New Home (Buy/Rent):	_____	_____	_____	_____
(related expenses:)		_____	_____	_____
		_____	_____	_____
		_____	_____	_____
Furniture:	_____	_____	_____	_____
(related expenses:)		_____	_____	_____
		_____	_____	_____
		_____	_____	_____
Moving Expenses:	_____	_____	_____	_____
(related expenses)		_____	_____	_____
		_____	_____	_____
Other:	_____	_____	_____	_____
	_____	_____	_____	_____
	_____	_____	_____	_____
	_____	_____	_____	_____
	_____	_____	_____	_____

THE CEREMONY

CEREMONY

- Worksheet 3 (*Style, Date, Time, & Location*) — It is vital that the decisions indicated on this worksheet be made as soon as possible after your engagement.

- Worksheet 4 (*Officiant Selection*) — This form can help you as you choose the person to officiate at your wedding ceremony.

- Worksheet 5 (*Ceremony Site*) — There is much to consider in choosing a ceremony site. This worksheet will help you.

- Worksheet 6 (*Ceremony Order*) — may be used as you plan the ceremony order with your fiancé and officiant.

- Worksheet 7 (*Wording for Vows and Ring Ceremony*) — If you and your fiancé decide to use special vows in your wedding, this worksheet will assist you.

- Worksheet 8 (*Estimate from Wedding Coordinator*) — As you meet with potential coordinators for your wedding, this worksheet will help you decide who to use.

- *Wedding Coordinator's Information List* — Once these pages are completed, a copy should be given to the person who will act as coordinator for your wedding.

- *Rehearsal Information List* — Discuss all items with the officiant and coordinator, and agree on a format applicable to your situation. (A copy of the completed list can be given to the officiant or the person coordinating your wedding.)

- *Position Diagrams* — These diagrams show examples of processionals, positions at the altar, and recessionals for both Christian and Jewish weddings.

Style, Date, Time, & Location

1. **Style of Wedding:** ❑ Formal ☒ Semiformal ❑ Informal
2. **Day of Week:** 1st choice _Saturday_ 2nd choice _____
3. **Time of Day:** (morning, afternoon, evening):
   1st choice _afternoon_ 2nd choice _morning_ 3rd choice _evening_
4. **Desired Wedding Date:** _July 18/98_
   Other possible dates: _____
   _____
5. **Approximate Number of Guests:** _120_
6. **Number of Attendants:** Bride _7_ Groom _7_
7. **Color Scheme:** _purple and white_
   _____
8. **Ceremony Site:**
   ☒ Church _____
   ❑ Synagogue _____
   ❑ Home _____ ❑ Garden _____
   ❑ Hotel _____
   ❑ Other (such as private clubs, parks, rental halls, ships, museums):
   _____
9. **Officiant:** ❑ Clergy _____ ❑ Rabbi _____
   ❑ Judge _____ ❑ Justice _____
10. **Reception Site:**
    ❑ Church _____
    ❑ Hotel _____
    ❑ Club _____
    ❑ Home _____ ❑ Garden _____
    ❑ Other _hall rental_
11. **Special Customs & Traditions to Be Observed:** _____
    _____
    _____
    _____
    _____
    _____
    _____
    _____

Officiant Selection

OPTION #1: Name _____ Phone _____
Address _____
Appointment: Date _____ Time _____
Notes: _____
_____
_____
_____
_____
_____
_____
_____
_____

Fee: _____
Choice: ❏ Yes ❏ No   Date Confirmed _____

OPTION #2: Name _____ Phone _____
Address _____
Appointment: Date _____ Time _____
Notes: _____
_____
_____
_____
_____
_____
_____
_____
_____

Fee: _____
Choice: ❏ Yes ❏ No   Date Confirmed _____

PREMARITAL COUNSELING SCHEDULE:
Dates:_____ Times:_____
Location:_____

Ceremony Site

OPTION #1: Site _____

Address _____

Contact person _____ Phone _____

	Wedding:	*Rehearsal:*
Available dates:	_____	_____
Time preference:	_____	_____
Confirmed:	_____	_____

Questions about facilities and regulations:

1. How many guests can the site accommodate? _____

2. When is the site available for rehearsal? _____

3. What are the church requirements for marriage? _____
   _____

4. What, if any, are the regulations concerning the day or time of day to hold the wedding?
   _____

5. Do special vows need to have approval?   ☐ Yes   ☐ No

6. Is permission required… (a) to marry in case of divorce?   ☐ Yes   ☐ No
   (b) for a marriage of mixed religions?   ☐ Yes   ☐ No

7. What are the restrictions on music? _____

8. What are the restrictions on decorations? _____
   Flowers? _____

9. What accessories does the site provide and what are the fees for using these accessories?
   ☐ Candelabra $_____   ☐ Candles $_____   ☐ Candlelighters $_____   ☐ Arch $_____
   ☐ Kneeling bench $_____   ☐ Flower stands $_____   ☐ Guestbook stand $_____

10. What are the rules regarding photography? _____
    _____

11. Is there a designated room for the photographer to take pictures?   ☐ Yes   ☐ No

12. Is there a sound system for recording the wedding?   ☐ Yes   ☐ No
    Fee for use? $_____   Cost for copies? $_____

13. Are there facilities for the bridal party? ☐ Yes   ☐ No   Restrooms? ☐ Yes   ☐ No
    Designated room for the bride? ☐ Yes   ☐ No

14. What is the fee for the use of the building? $_____ For the custodian? $ _____

15. What are the additional charges for using the site as a reception? $_____
    Notes: _____
    _____
    _____

OPTION #2: Site _____

Address _____

Contact person _____ Phone _____

	Wedding:	*Rehearsal:*
Available dates:	_____	_____
Time preference:	_____	_____
Confirmed:	_____	_____

Questions about facilities and regulations:

1. How many guests can the site accommodate? _____

2. When is the site available for rehearsal? _____

3. What are the church requirements for marriage? _____
   _____

4. What, if any, are the regulations concerning the day or time of day to hold the wedding?
   _____

5. Do special vows need to have approval? ❏ Yes ❏ No

6. Is permission required... (a) to marry in case of divorce? ❏ Yes ❏ No
   (b) for a marriage of mixed religions? ❏ Yes ❏ No

7. What are the restrictions on music? _____

8. What are the restrictions on decorations? _____
   Flowers? _____

9. What accessories does the site provide and what are the fees for using these accessories?
   ❏ Candelabra $_____   ❏ Candles $_____   ❏ Candlelighters $_____   ❏ Arch $_____
   ❏ Kneeling bench $_____   ❏ Flower stands $_____   ❏ Guestbook stand $_____

10. What are the rules regarding photography? _____
    _____

11. Is there a designated room for the photographer to take pictures? ❏ Yes ❏ No

12. Is there a sound system for recording the wedding? ❏ Yes ❏ No
    Fee for use? $_____   Cost for copies? $_____

13. Are there facilities for the bridal party? ❏ Yes ❏ No   Restrooms? ❏ Yes ❏ No
    Designated room for the bride? ❏ Yes ❏ No

14. What is the fee for the use of the building? $_____ For the custodian? $_____

15. What are the additional charges for using the site as a reception? $_____
    Notes: _____
    _____

Choice of Site: _____
Date Confirmed: _____
Notes: _____
_____

Ceremony Order

PRELUDE: _____

_____

_____

PROCESSIONAL: _____

CALL TO WORSHIP: _____

_____

_____

_____

CHARGE: _____

_____

_____

_____

DECLARATION OF CONSENT: _____

_____

_____

_____

EXCHANGE OF VOWS: _____

_____

_____

_____

EXCHANGE OF RINGS: _____

_____

_____

_____

PRONOUNCEMENT OF MARRIAGE: _____

_____

_____

_____

BENEDICTION AND BLESSING: _____

_____

_____

_____

POSTLUDE: _____

_____

Wording for Vows & Ring Ceremony

VOWS OF THE BRIDE TO THE GROOM _____

_____

_____

_____

_____

_____

_____

_____

_____

_____

VOWS OF THE GROOM TO THE BRIDE _____

_____

_____

_____

_____

_____

_____

_____

_____

_____

RING CEREMONY _____

_____

_____

_____

_____

_____

_____

_____

_____

_____

Estimate from Wedding Coordinator

Name _____ Phone _____

Address _____

Appointment: Date _____ Time _____

Fee is based on:

❏ Percentage _____   ❏ Hourly rate _____

❏ Per guest _____   ❏ Flat fee _____

Number of hours needed _____

Services _____

_____

_____

_____

_____

_____

_____

_____

_____

_____

_____

_____

_____

_____

_____

Choice:	Total Cost $ _____
❏ Yes ❏ No	Deposit $ _____
Date Confirmed _____	Balance due $ _____

Planning Schedule:

Date:	*Time:*	*Planning Topic:*
_____	_____	_____
_____	_____	_____
_____	_____	_____
_____	_____	_____
_____	_____	_____

Wedding Coordinator's Information List

1. Bride _____ Phone: *home* _____ *work* _____
   Groom _____ Phone: *home* _____ *work* _____
   Bride's parents _____ Phone: *home* _____ *work* _____
   Groom's parents _____ Phone: *home* _____ *work* _____

2. Wedding Date _____ *Time* _____
   Number of Guests _____
   Rehearsal Date _____ *Time* _____

3. Officiant(s) _____ *Phone* _____
   _____ *Phone* _____

4. Ceremony Site
   Contact Person _____ *Phone* _____
   Custodian _____ *Phone* _____

5. Wedding Color Scheme _____
   Style of Wedding _____

6. Bride's Attendants:
   Maid/Matron of Honor _____ *Phone* _____
   Bridesmaids _____ *Phone* _____
   _____ *Phone* _____
   _____ *Phone* _____
   _____ *Phone* _____
   _____ *Phone* _____
   Flower Girl _____ *Phone* _____
   Bride and Attendants... ❑ dress at home ❑ dress at ceremony site (room # _____)
   Arrival time: Rehearsal _____ Wedding _____

7. Groom's Attendants:
   Best Man _____ *Phone* _____
   Head Usher _____ *Phone* _____
   Ushers _____ *Phone* _____
   _____ *Phone* _____
   _____ *Phone* _____
   _____ *Phone* _____
   Ring Bearer _____ *Phone* _____
   Groom and Attendants... ❑ dress at home ❑ dress at ceremony site (room # _____)
   Arrival time: Rehearsal _____ Wedding _____

8. Musicians:

Organist _____ *Phone* _____

Soloists _____ *Phone* _____

_____ *Phone* _____

Other Musicians _____ *Phone* _____

_____ *Phone* _____

Arrival time: Rehearsal _____ Wedding _____ Set-up room # _____

(See Musicians' Needs Checklist, page 157)

9. Florist _____ *Phone* _____

Arrival time _____

SUPPLIER OF WEDDING ACCESSORIES:

	Ceremony Site:	Florist:	Rental Equipment:
Arch or Canopy	☐	☐	☐
Altar Candelabra	☐	☐	☐
Pew Candelabra	☐	☐	☐
Unity Candelabra	☐	☐	☐
Candles (quantity: _____)	☐	☐	☐
Candlelighters (quantity: _____)	☐	☐	☐
Kneeling Bench	☐	☐	☐
Aisle Runner (length: _____)	☐	☐	☐
Guestbook Stand or Table	☐	☐	☐
Gift Table	☐	☐	☐
Other: _____	☐	☐	☐

(For placement of flowers, wedding accessories, and aisle runner, see the diagrams on page 163)

Persons receiving special corsages: Persons receiving special boutonnieres:

_____ _____

_____ _____

_____ _____

_____ _____

10. Photographer _____ *Phone* _____

Arrival time _____ Room _____ Time when pictures are to be taken _____

11. Video Operator _____ *Phone* _____

Arrival time _____

Audio Operator _____ *Phone* _____

Arrival time _____

(See Video and Audio Planning Worksheets on pages 171-173)

12. Guestbook Attendants _____ *Phone* _____

_____ *Phone* _____

Arrival time _____

Gift Attendant _____ *Phone* _____

Arrival time _____

13. Wedding Day Transportation:

Contact Person _____ *Phone* _____

(continued)

14. If reception is being held at the ceremony site:
    Caterer _____ *Phone* _____
    Arrival time _____
    Bakery _____ *Phone* _____
    Arrival time _____
    Rental Equipment _____ *Phone* _____
    Arrival time _____
15. Reception Hostess _____ *Phone* _____
16. Ceremony Order and Timing: Pre-ceremony ushering begins _____

    CANDLELIGHTING:
    time: *type:*   *Usher:*
    _____   Pew Candles
    _____   Candelabra   _____
    _____   Unity Candelabra   _____
    _____   Other: _____   _____

    SPECIAL SEATING:
    time: *who:*   *which pew:*   *Usher:*

    _____   _____   _____   _____
    _____   _____   _____   _____
    _____   _____   _____   _____
    _____   Mother of the Groom   _____   _____
    _____   Mother of the Bride   _____   _____

    AISLE RIBBONS AND RUNNER:
    time: *aisle to be used:*   *Ushers:*

    _____   _____   _____

    SPECIAL MUSIC:
    time: *who:*

    _____   _____   _____
    _____   _____   _____

    PROCESSIONAL ORDER: (beginning time: _____)

    _____   _____
    _____   _____
    _____   _____
    _____   _____

    RECESSIONAL ORDER:

    _____   _____
    _____   _____

    POSTLUDE: _____
    ORDER OF DISMISSAL OF SPECIAL GUESTS:

    _____   _____
    _____   _____

    REMOVAL OF AISLE RIBBONS: Ushers _____
    DISMISSAL OF REMAINING GUESTS: Ushers _____

Rehearsal Information List

- The Rehearsal should begin with the bridal party taking their positions at the wedding altar. Once all the participants know where to stand, they can be instructed on how to reach that position.

DIAGRAM OF ALTAR POSITIONS:

DIAGRAM OF PROCESSIONAL:

DIAGRAM OF RECESSIONAL:

(continued)

- Type of step used in the processional _____

- Distance between participants during processional _____

- **Special Cues:**
  Mothers' seating _____

  _____

  Entry of bridal party _____

  _____

  Bride's mother rises _____
  Ring bearer and flower girl after reaching altar will…
  ❏ remain with bridal party, or ❏ be seated with parents.
  Father's response _____

  _____

  Other _____

- **Variations in the Service:**
  Special Acknowledgement of Parents? _____
  Kiss or Embrace? _____ By whom? _____
  When? _____
  Mothers' Roses? ❏ Yes ❏ No By whom? _____
  When? _____
  Unity Candle? ❏ Yes ❏ No When? _____
  Lifting of Blusher Veil? ❏ Yes ❏ No By whom? _____
  When? _____

  Other: _____

  _____

- **Ushers' Post-Ceremony Duties:**
  Removal of any flowers to reception site _____

  _____

  Removal of bridal party apparel from ceremony site _____

  _____

Position Diagrams

(Christian Ceremony)

B = Bride   **G** = Groom   **O** = Officiant   **MH** = *Maid (or Matron) of Honor*
BM = Best Man   **Bm** = *Bridesmaids*   **U** = Ushers   **fg** = *Flower Girl*
rb = Ring Bearer   **FB** = Father of the Bride   **HU** = Head Usher

❀ ❀ ❀

IN THE PROCESSIONAL:

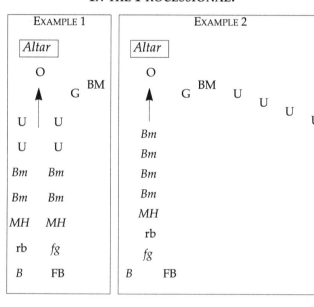

IN THE RECESSIONAL:

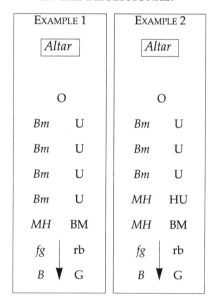

AT THE ALTAR:

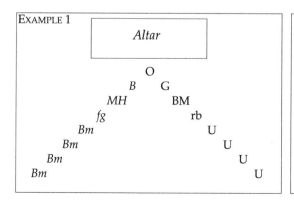

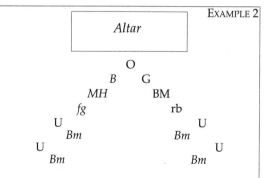

Position Diagrams

(Jewish Ceremony)

B = *Bride*   **G** = Groom
R/C = Rabbi and/or Cantor
MH = *Maid (or Matron) of Honor*   **BM** = Best Man
Bm = *Bridesmaids*   **U** = Ushers
fg/rb = *Flower Girl/Ring Bearer*
FB = Father of the Bride   **MB** = *Mother of the Bride*
FG = Father of the Groom   **MG** = *Mother of the Groom*
BGf = Bride's Grandfather
BGm = *Bride's Grandmother*
GGf = Groom's Grandfather
GGm = *Groom's Grandmother*

❀ ❀ ❀

UNDER THE CHUPPAH:

EXAMPLE 1

FG   R   C   FB
MG   MB
        G   B
    BM   MH

NOTE: When room permits, grandparents may join the Bride, Groom, Honor Attendants, Parents, Rabbi and Cantor under the Chuppah.

EXAMPLE 2

R   C
    G   B
BM   MH

NOTE: *The Bridesmaids, Ushers, Flower Girl and Ring Bearer do not stand under the Chuppah.*

IN THE PROCESSIONAL:

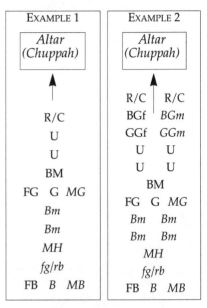

IN THE RECESSIONAL:

ATTIRE & ATTENDANTS

ATTIRE & ATTENDANTS

- *Wedding Gown Search List* — You may use this page to keep track of designs, styles, and costs of gowns that interest you.

- Worksheet 9 *(Bridal Attire)* — Here you can record final decisions on your gown and accessories, and list alteration and delivery schedules.

- Worksheet 10 *(Trousseau Inventory)* — As you plan your wardrobe to fit your lifestyle, this inventory will help you determine what items you might need to purchase.

- *Bride's Honeymoon Packing Checklist* — As you use this checklist, consult your Trousseau Inventory (Worksheet 10).

- *Bride's Wedding Day Checklist* — Use this list to help your wedding day go smoothly.

- Worksheet 11 *(Bridal Attendants' Dresses and Accessories)* — Record here the designs, styles, and cost of attendants' dresses you consider, and list the final choice of dress and accessories.

- *Bridal Attendants List* — Here's a place to record your attendants' names, addresses, and sizes.

- *Bridal Attendants' Guidelines* — Fill out this page and give photocopies to the attendants two weeks before the wedding.

- Worksheet 12 *(Groom's Formal Attire)* — Your fiancé can use this worksheet in selecting formal wear for himself, his attendants, and the fathers.

- *Groom's Honeymoon Packing Checklist*, *Groom's Wedding Day Checklist*, and *Groom's Attendants List* — These can be of help to your fiancé.

- *Groom's Attendants' Guidelines* — When this form is completed, it can be photocopied and given to the groom's attendants two weeks before the wedding.

- Worksheet 13 *(Ushers' Assignments)* — This worksheet may be filled out, photocopied, and given to the head usher at the rehearsal.

Wedding Gown Search List

❀ Description _____
    Manufacturer _____ Model # _____
    Cost _____
    Store _____
    Contact Person _____ *Phone* _____

❀ Description _____
    Manufacturer _____ Model # _____
    Cost _____
    Store _____
    Contact Person _____ *Phone* _____

❀ Description _____
    Manufacturer _____ Model # _____
    Cost _____
    Store _____
    Contact Person _____ *Phone* _____

❀ Description _____
    Manufacturer _____ Model # _____
    Cost _____
    Store _____
    Contact Person _____ *Phone* _____

❀ Description _____
    Manufacturer _____ Model # _____
    Cost _____
    Store _____
    Contact Person _____ *Phone* _____

❀ Description _____
    Manufacturer _____ Model # _____
    Cost _____
    Store _____
    Contact Person _____ *Phone* _____

Bridal Attire

Bridal shop _____

Address _____

Contact person _____ Phone _____

Contract terms _____

Payment schedule _____

	item & description	*cost:*	*deposit:*	*due:*

Wedding gown _____ _____ _____ _____

  Manufacturer: Bridal originals

  Model #: _____

Headpiece _____ _____ _____ _____

  Manufacturer: _____

  Model #: _____

Veil _____ _____ _____ _____

  Manufacturer: _____

  Model #: _____

Accessories:

  Shoes _____ _____ _____ _____

  Hosiery _____ _____ _____ _____

  Slip _____ _____ _____ _____

  Bra _____ _____ _____ _____

  Gloves _____ _____ _____ _____

  Jewelry _____ _____ _____ _____

  Other _____ _____ _____ _____

Alterations:

  Fitting dates/times: _____ / _____ _____ / _____ FINAL: _____ / _____

  Contact person _____ Phone _____

  Address _____ Cost _____

Delivery:

  ❏ church ❏ home ❏ pick-up Date _____ Time _____

Pressing Instructions _____
_____

Date needed for portrait _____

To heirloom gown:

  Name_____

  Address _____ Phone _____

  Contact Person _____ Date _____ Cost _____

Trousseau Inventory

Suits or Dresses	Separates: Blouses, Pants, Skirts, Sweaters	Accessories: Shoes, Jewelry, Scarves, Belts

ITEMS TO BUY:		

Lingerie	Sleepwear	Miscellaneous: special needs for swimming, tennis, golf, etc.

ITEMS TO BUY:		

Bride's Honeymoon Packing Checklist

Honeymoon location _____

Dates _____ Climate _____

CLOTHING NEEDS:

Lingerie/Sleepwear _____
_____
_____

Casual/Sportswear _____
_____
_____
_____
_____

Daytime _____
_____
_____
_____
_____

Evening _____
_____
_____
_____

Accessories _____
_____
_____

COSMETICS, MEDICATIONS:
_____
_____
_____

Bride's Wedding Day Checklist

ITEM:	PACKED & READY:
Wedding Gown _____	☐
Headpiece and Veil _____	☐
Bra, Slip, Panties _____	☐
Hosiery, two pair _____	☐
Shoes _____	☐
Gloves _____	☐
Jewelry _____	☐
Make-up, Nail Polish _____	☐
Comb, Brush, Curling Iron _____	☐
Hairspray and Bobby Pins _____	☐
Mirror _____	☐
Sewing Kit _____	☐
Pressing Iron _____	☐
Other _____	☐
_____	☐
_____	☐

Clothes to change into before leaving reception:

	PACKED & READY:
Going-Away Outfit _____	☐
Bra _____	☐
Slip _____	☐
Hosiery _____	☐
Shoes _____	☐
Accessories _____	☐
_____	☐
_____	☐

Bridal Attendants' Dresses & Accessories

DRESS OPTION #1

Description _____

_____

Manufacturer _____ Style # _____

Store _____

Address _____

Contact person _____ Phone _____

DRESS OPTION #2

Description _____

_____

Manufacturer _____ Style # _____

Store _____

Address _____

Contact person _____ Phone _____

DRESS OPTION #3

Description _____

_____

Manufacturer _____ Style # _____

Store _____

Address _____

Contact person _____ Phone _____

DRESS CHOICE: #____   *Date Ordered* _____ *Delivery Date* _____

Accessories:

Shoes _____ cost _____

Hosiery _____ cost _____

Gloves _____ cost _____

Head Covering _____ cost _____

Jewelry _____ cost _____

Makeup (lipstick, nail polish) _____ cost _____

Other _____ cost _____

Bridal Attendants List

❀ **Maid/Matron of Honor** _Hidi_

Address _____ Phone _488-8921_

City _EDMONTON_ State _ALBERTA_ Zip _T5R-125_

SIZES: _Dress_ _____ _Shoe_ _____ _Hose_ _____ _Glove_ _____ _Head_ _____

Your Gift for Her _____

❀ **Bridesmaid** _Debbie Rossel_

Address _____ Phone _479-7172_

City _EDMONTON_ State _Alberta_ Zip _____

SIZES: _Dress_ _____ _Shoe_ _____ _Hose_ _____ _Glove_ _____ _Head_ _____

Your Gift for Her _____

❀ **Bridesmaid** _Dennette_

Address _____ Phone _____

City _____ State _____ Zip _____

SIZES: _Dress_ _____ _Shoe_ _____ _Hose_ _____ _Glove_ _____ _Head_ _____

Your Gift for Her _____

❀ **Bridesmaid** _Gina_

Address _____ Phone _484-5227_

City _____ State _____ Zip _____

SIZES: _Dress_ _____ _Shoe_ _____ _Hose_ _____ _Glove_ _____ _Head_ _____

Your Gift for Her _____

❀ **Bridesmaid** _Michelle_

Address _____ Phone _____

City _____ State _____ Zip _____

SIZES: _Dress_ _____ _Shoe_ _____ _Hose_ _____ _Glove_ _____ _Head_ _____

Your Gift for Her _____

❀ **Bridesmaid** _____

Address _____ Phone _____

City _____ State _____ Zip _____

SIZES: _Dress_ _____ _Shoe_ _____ _Hose_ _____ _Glove_ _____ _Head_ _____

Your Gift for Her _____

❀ **Bridesmaid / Flower Girl** _Allicia / Katelyn Paul_

Address _____ Phone _____

City _____ State _____ Zip _____

SIZES: _Dress_ _____ _Shoe_ _____ _Hose_ _____ _Glove_ _____ _Head_ _____

Your Gift for Her _____

Bridal Attendants' Guidelines

(For the Week before the Wedding)

- Carefully break in your shoes.
- Have final fittings, if necessary.
- Do you have everything--dress, shoes, hosiery, lingerie, gloves, jewelry, makeup, etc.?
- Gather all essentials ahead of time and place in one area to avoid last-minute frazzled nerves while trying to find something you've forgotten.
- Get plenty of rest.

- BRIDAL LUNCHEON:
  Location _____
  Address _____
  Date _____ Time _____ Phone _____
- REHEARSAL AT CEREMONY SITE:
  Location _____
  Address _____
  Date _____ Time _____ Phone _____
- REHEARSAL DINNER:
  Location _____
  Address _____
  Date _____ Time _____ Phone _____
- ARRIVAL TIME at the wedding site for the ceremony: _____
- WHERE TO DRESS: _____
- PHOTOGRAPHS:
  Location _____
  Address _____
  Date _____ Time _____ Phone _____
- RECEPTION:
  Location _____
  Address _____
  Date _____ Time _____ Phone _____
- TRANSPORTATION:
  To the ceremony site _____
  To the reception site _____
- Other: _____

_____

Groom's Formal Attire

Store _____

Address _____

Contact person _____ Phone _____

Groom's sizes: *Coat* _____   *Sleeve* _____   *Neck* _____

Waist _____   *Trouser Inseam* _____   *Shoe* _____

	GROOM'S ATTIRE:		ATTIRE FOR FATHERS & GROOM'S ATTENDANTS:	
	Option #1	*Option #2*	*Option #1*	*Option #2*
style:				
color:				
coat:				
trousers:				
shirt:				
vest:				
ties:				
ascot:				
cummerbund:				
shoes:				
gloves:				
suspenders:				
studs & cufflinks:				
FINAL CHOICE (✔):	☐	☐	☐	☐
total cost:				
deposit:				
fitting date:				
pickup date:				
return date:				

Groom's Honeymoon Packing Checklist

Honeymoon location _____

Dates _____ Climate _____

CLOTHING NEEDS:

Underwear/Sleepwear _____

_____

_____

Casual/Sportswear _____

_____

_____

_____

_____

Daytime _____

_____

_____

_____

_____

Evening _____

_____

_____

Accessories _____

_____

_____

TOILETRIES, MEDICATIONS:

_____

_____

_____

Groom's Wedding Day Checklist

ITEM:

PACKED
& READY:

Coat _____ ☐

Trousers _____ ☐

Shirt _____ ☐

Vest _____ ☐

Tie _____ ☐

Ascot _____ ☐

Cummerbund _____ ☐

Shoes _____ ☐

Gloves _____ ☐

Suspenders _____ ☐

Studs and Cuff Links _____ ☐

Underwear _____ ☐

Socks _____ ☐

Handkerchief _____ ☐

Toiletries _____ ☐

Other _____ ☐

Clothes to change into before leaving reception:

Jacket _____ ☐

Slacks _____ ☐

Shirt _____ ☐

Tie _____ ☐

Underwear _____ ☐

Socks _____ ☐

Shoes _____ ☐

Accessories _____ ☐

Groom's Attendants List

◆ **Best Man** _Mike_

Address _____ Phone _489 - 4899_

City _____ State _____ Zip _____

SIZES: *Coat* _____ *Sleeve* _____ *Neck* _____ *Waist* _____ *Trouser Inseam* _____ *Shoe* _____

HEIGHT _____ WEIGHT _____   Your Gift to Him _____

◆ **Head Usher** _Conrad_

Address _____ Phone _487 - 6501_

City _____ State _____ Zip _____

SIZES: *Coat* _____ *Sleeve* _____ *Neck* _____ *Waist* _____ *Trouser Inseam* _____ *Shoe* _____

HEIGHT _____ WEIGHT _____   Your Gift to Him _____

◆ **Usher** _Fred_

Address _____ Phone _____

City _____ State _____ Zip _____

SIZES: *Coat* _____ *Sleeve* _____ *Neck* _____ *Waist* _____ *Trouser Inseam* _____ *Shoe* _____

HEIGHT _____ WEIGHT _____   Your Gift to Him _____

◆ **Usher** _Gerald_

Address _____ Phone _488 - 8921_

City _____ State _____ Zip _____

SIZES: *Coat* _____ *Sleeve* _____ *Neck* _____ *Waist* _____ *Trouser Inseam* _____ *Shoe* _____

HEIGHT _____ WEIGHT _____   Your Gift to Him _____

◆ **Usher** _Ryan_

Address _____ Phone _484 - 8227_

City _____ State _____ Zip _____

SIZES: *Coat* _____ *Sleeve* _____ *Neck* _____ *Waist* _____ *Trouser Inseam* _____ *Shoe* _____

HEIGHT _____ WEIGHT _____   Your Gift to Him _____

◆ **Usher**

Address _____ Phone _____

City _____ State _____ Zip _____

SIZES: *Coat* _____ *Sleeve* _____ *Neck* _____ *Waist* _____ *Trouser Inseam* _____ *Shoe* _____

HEIGHT _____ WEIGHT _____   Your Gift to Him _____

◆ **Usher / Ring Bearer** _Alexander / Kyle_

Address _____ Phone _____

City _____ State _____ Zip _____

SIZES: *Coat* _____ *Sleeve* _____ *Neck* _____ *Waist* _____ *Trouser Inseam* _____ *Shoe* _____

HEIGHT _____ WEIGHT _____   Your Gift to Him _____

Groom's Attendants' Guidelines

(For the Week before the Wedding)

- Have final fittings for your wedding attire.
- Do you have everything you need -- coat, trousers, shirt, vest, tie or ascot, cummerbund, shoes, socks, gloves, suspenders, studs, and cuff links?
- Gather all essentials ahead of time and place in one area to avoid last-minute frazzled nerves while trying to find something you've forgotten.
- Get plenty of rest.

- BACHELOR'S PARTY:
  Location _____
  Address _____
  Date _____ Time _____ Phone _____
- REHEARSAL AT CEREMONY SITE:
  Location _____
  Address _____
  Date _____ Time _____ Phone _____
- REHEARSAL DINNER:
  Location _____
  Address _____
  Date _____ Time _____ Phone _____
- ARRIVAL TIME at the wedding site for the ceremony: _____
- WHERE TO DRESS: _____
- PHOTOGRAPHS:
  Location _____
  Address _____
  Date _____ Time _____ Phone _____
- RECEPTION:
  Location _____
  Address _____
  Date _____ Time _____ Phone _____
- TRANSPORTATION:
  To the ceremony site _____
  To the reception site _____
- Other: _____
  _____

Ushers' Assignments

(Indicate ushers responsible for each item.)

1. Inform the groom of the bride's arrival at the ceremony site. _____

2. Candlelighting: _____
   _____

3. Seat and return...
   the groom's grandmother.   Row # _____   _____
   the bride's grandmother.   Row # _____   _____
   the groom's mother.   Row # _____   _____
   the bride's mother.   Row # _____   _____

4. Additional special seating:

Name	*Row #*	
_____	_____	_____
_____	_____	_____
_____	_____	_____
_____	_____	_____
_____	_____	_____
_____	_____	_____
_____	_____	_____

5. Draw and remove aisle ribbons (optional use). _____
   _____

6. Draw aisle runner (may already be in place). _____
   _____

7. Dismiss the remainder of guests. _____

8. Oversee the removal of any flowers to the reception site (especially when the reception is being held elsewhere). _____
   _____

9. Remove any apparel belonging to the bridal party after the ceremony._____
   _____

10. Other assignments: _____
    _____
    _____

THE RECEPTION

RECEPTION

- Worksheet 14 (*Reception Site Estimate*) — Use this form to record information about proposed reception sites and cost estimates.

- Worksheet 15 (*Reception Site Choice*) — Use this to record specific information about the site you have chosen.

- Worksheet 16 (*Caterer Estimate*) — Use this to record information about proposed caterers and their cost estimates.

- Worksheet 17 (*Caterer Choice*)— Use this to record specific information about the caterer you have chosen.

- Worksheet 18 (*Reception Food and Beverages*) — List food and beverage choices here.

- Worksheet 19 (*Cake Estimate*) — Use this form to record information about proposed bakeries and estimates of cost.

- Worksheet 20 (*Design Your Wedding Cake*) — Use this form if the bakery allows you to design your own cake. How much choice you are given depends on the bakery.

- *Reception Seating Chart* — If you're having assigned seating, use these lists to assign tables to the wedding party and guests.

- *Reception Receiving Line* — Use this space to diagram the receiving line. Form the receiving line based on the best traffic flow in the room, with the mother of the bride at the beginning.

- *Reception Room Diagrams* — Use these spaces to indicate the placement of tables in the reception room.

- *Reception Organizer* — These pages may be filled out, photocopied, and given to the person acting as your reception coordinator.

- Worksheet 21 (*Table Layout for the At-Home Reception*) — Use this to plan the placement of tables, food and beverages.

Reception Site Estimate

Option #1	*Option #2*

Option #1

Name ___Sherwood Hall___

Address _____

Contact person _____

Phone _____

Open dates _____

   and times _____

Approximate number of guests __120__

Appointment date and time:

_____

NOTES:

Description of facilities:

   Rental fee __350__

Food and/or Beverage Packages:

   Cost per person _____

Wedding Cake:

   Cost per serving _____

(continued)

Option #2

Name _____

Address _____

Contact person _____

Phone _____

Open dates _____

   and times _____

Approximate number of guests _____

Appointment date and time:

_____

NOTES:

Description of facilities:

   Rental fee _____

Food and/or Beverage Packages:

   Cost per person _____

Wedding Cake:

   Cost per serving _____

(continued)

Services:
- ❏ Cost included
- ❏ Extra cost _____

Seating and table arrangements:

Decorations:

Entertainment:

Equipment:

Miscellaneous:
- Time allowed for reception _____
- Overtime cost _100_____
- Cancellation fee _____

Gratuities included: ❏ Yes ❏ No
Sales tax included in per-person cost:
                                        ❏ Yes ❏ No

Estimated total cost _____

Required deposit $350.00

Services:
- ❏ Cost included
- ❏ Extra cost _____

Seating and table arrangements:

Decorations:

Entertainment:

Equipment:

Miscellaneous:
- Time allowed for reception _____
- Overtime cost _____
- Cancellation fee _____

Gratuities included: ❏ Yes ❏ No
Sales tax included in per-person cost:
                                        ❏ Yes ❏ No

Estimated total cost _____

Required deposit _____

Reception Site Choice

Name _____

Address _____

Contact person _____ Phone _____

Confirmed date _____ Confirmed time period _____

Type of reception _____

Room(s) _____

Date contract signed _____

Deposit of $_____ due on _____; date paid _____

Final head count due on _____

Number of guests (committed) _____

Cost per person _____

Subtotal: Number of guests **X** Cost per person _____

Sales tax _____

Total cost _____

Less deposit _____

BALANCE DUE _____

NOTES:

Caterer Estimate

OPTION #1	OPTION #2

OPTION #1

Name _____

Address _____

Contact person _____

Phone _____

Appointment date and time:

_____

Reception date and time

_____

Number of guests _____

NOTES:

Description of Menu Choices, Food and/or
Beverage Packages:
Cost per person _____

Wedding Cake:
Cost per serving _____

Description of Services:
❏ Cost included
❏ Extra cost _____

Decorations (color of linen, tableware, etc.):

Equipment Needs:

Gratuities included: ❏ Yes   ❏ No
Sales tax included in per-person cost:
                             ❏ Yes   ❏ No
Estimated total cost _____
Required deposit _____
Cancellation fee _____

OPTION #2

Name _____

Address _____

Contact person _____

Phone _____

Appointment date and time:

_____

Reception date and time

_____

Number of guests _____

NOTES:

Description of Menu Choices, Food and/or
Beverage Packages:
Cost per person _____

Wedding Cake:
Cost per serving _____

Description of Services:
❏ Cost included
❏ Extra cost _____

Decorations (color of linen, tableware, etc.):

Equipment Needs:

Gratuities included: ❏ Yes   ❏ No
Sales tax included in per-person cost:
                             ❏ Yes   ❏ No
Estimated total cost _____
Required deposit _____
Cancellation fee _____

Caterer Choice

Name _____

Address _____

Contact person _____ Phone _____

Confirmed date _____ Confirmed time period _____

Type of reception _____

Food and/or Beverage Package _____

_____

_____

Cake _____

_____

_____

Services _____

_____

_____

Date contract signed _____

Deposit of $_____ due on _____; date paid _____

Final head count due on _____

Number of guests (committed) _____

Cost per person _____

Subtotal: Number of guests **X** Cost per person _____

Sales tax _____

Gratuities _____

Total cost _____

Less deposit _____

Balance Due _____

Reception Food & Beverages

Wedding Cake:

Beverages:

Hors d'oeuvres:

Entrées:

Salads & Side Dishes:

Breads:

Cake Estimate

OPTION #1	OPTION #2

OPTION #1

Name _____

Address _____

Contact person _____

Phone _____

Appointment date and time:

_____

Number of guests _____

Cake Description (size, shape, type & number of
   servings, fillings, icing styles & colors, and
   ornaments):
   • *Wedding Cake*

   • *Groom's Cake*

 Cost per serving: Wedding Cake _____
      Groom's Cake _____

Equipment (serving implements, and style &
   number of tables):

Extra Costs:
   Cake tier supports & bases _____
   Cutting and serving fee _____
   Serving implements _____
   Delivery and setup _____
Total Cost _____

OPTION #2

Name _____

Address _____

Contact person _____

Phone _____

Appointment date and time:

_____

Number of guests _____

Cake Description (size, shape, type & number of
   servings, fillings, icing styles & colors, and
   ornaments):
   • *Wedding Cake*

   • *Groom's Cake*

 Cost per serving: Wedding Cake _____
      Groom's Cake _____

Equipment (serving implements, and style &
   number of tables):

Extra Costs:
   Cake tier supports & bases _____
   Cutting and serving fee _____
   Serving implements _____
   Delivery and setup _____
Total Cost _____

Cake choice: #_____   Date confirmed _____

Total cost _____ Deposit paid _____ Balance due _____ by _____

   (Payment increments: $_____ due _____)

Appointment to design and order cake _____

Design Your Wedding Cake

WEDDING CAKE

Size (# of servings, # of layers and sizes):

Shape (round, square, oblong, heart-shaped, flat or graduated in tiers):

Type (white, chocolate, spice, carrot, fruit cake, etc.):

Filling (custard, fruit, icing):

Icing (Style—ornate or plain, Color—white or pastel):

Ornaments (Bride & Groom, swans, bells, doves, hearts, cupids, real flowers):

GROOM'S CAKE

Size:

Shape:

Type:

Icing:

How to serve (individual servings wrapped or boxed, or served along with the wedding cake):

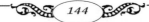

Reception Seating Chart

Bride's Table

Type & size of table _____

Number of chairs _____

    Raised dais: ☐ Yes ☐ No

Order of Seating (diagram or list):

Parents' Table(s)

Type & size of table _____

Number of chairs per table _____

Order of Seating (diagram or list):

Attendants' Table(s)

Type & size of table _____

Number of chairs per table _____

Order of Seating (diagram or list):

Guest Seating

Type & size of table _____

Number of chairs per table _____

Order of Seating (diagram or list):

Table # _____

Table # _____

(continued)

TABLE # _____

TABLE # _____

TABLE # _____

TABLE # _____

TABLE # _____

TABLE # _____

TABLE # _____

TABLE # _____

TABLE # _____

TABLE # _____

Reception Receiving Line

(diagram, showing each participant)

Reception Room Diagrams

Location of receiving line, guestbook, entertainment area, and tables for gifts, cake, and food and beverages

Location of Bride's Table, Attendants' Table(s), Parents' Table(s), and guest tables

Reception Organizer

Reception of: _____

Reception site _____ Room _____

Contact person _____ Phone _____

Date _____ Time _____ Planned length _____

Reception coordinator _____ Phone _____

1. Rooms available for decorating:

    When _____ By whom _____

    _____

    ❀ *For decorations, see the diagram on page 163* ❀

2. Rental equipment to be delivered or picked up:

    When _____ By whom _____

3. Tables and chairs set up:

    When _____ By whom _____

    ❀ *For placement, see the room diagram on page 147* ❀

4. Cake delivered or picked up:

    When _____ By whom _____

    ❀ *For placement, see the room diagram on page 147* ❀

5. Flowers:

    Contact person _____ Phone _____

    Delivered from florist _____

    Flowers delivered from ceremony site

    When _____ By whom _____

6. Musicians:

    Contact person _____ Phone _____

    ❀ *See the Musicians' Needs Checklist on page 157* ❀

(continued)

7. Food and Beverages:

Contact person _____ Phone _____

❀ For placement, see the room diagram on page 147 ❀

8. "Hostesses" (also known as "House Party):

Guest book _____

_____

Gifts _____

_____

Cake cutting and serving _____

_____

Serving beverages _____

_____

Distributing rice _____

9. Cleanup and Storage:

item:	when:	by whom:	deliver to:
Bride's gown	_____	_____	_____
leftover wedding cake	_____	_____	_____
_____	_____	_____	_____
_____	_____	_____	_____
_____	_____	_____	_____
_____	_____	_____	_____
_____	_____	_____	_____
_____	_____	_____	_____
_____	_____	_____	_____
_____	_____	_____	_____
_____	_____	_____	_____
_____	_____	_____	_____
_____	_____	_____	_____
_____	_____	_____	_____
_____	_____	_____	_____
_____	_____	_____	_____
_____	_____	_____	_____
_____	_____	_____	_____

Table Layout for the At-Home Reception

(Diagrams of table locations, and food and beverage placement)

SERVICES

Here are some special tips on just a few of the many worksheets, checklists, and guideline lists included in this section:

- The *Musicians' Guidelines* (there are separate pages for the Ceremony and Reception) may be filled out, photocopied, and given to the musicians who will perform.

- Worksheet 28 (*Floral Planning*) and the *Florist's Guidelines* — may be filled out, photocopied, and given to the florist.

- The *Photographer's Planning List and Guidelines* may be used by you and your photographer to determine what photographs to take. This page can be filled out, photocopied, and given to the photographer.

- Worksheets 31 (*Video Planning & Guidelines*) and 33 (*Audio Planning & Guidelines*) — these may be photocopied and given to those who will operate the recording equipment.

- Provide your out-of-town guests with copies of the *Information List: Guest Housing & Transportation.*

- Photocopies of the *Transportation Guidelines for Drivers* should be given to all the drivers.

- Photocopies of Worksheet 37 (*Equipment Delivery & Pickup*) should go to all those involved in delivering and picking up rental equipment.

- Have fun as you use Worksheet 38 (*Honeymoon Travel & Accommodations*) to plan your special trip.

Stationery Estimate

OPTION #1	OPTION #2

Name _____   Name _____
Contact person _____   Contact person _____
Phone _____   Phone _____
Address _____   Address _____

Invitations—
   Style # _____ Print # _____
   Book _____
   Number needed _____
          Cost _____

Reception Cards—
   Style # _____ Print # _____
   Book _____
   Number needed _____
          Cost _____

Response Cards—
   Style # _____ Print # _____
   Book _____
   Number needed _____
          Cost _____

Thank-You Notes—
   Style # _____ Print # _____
   Book _____
   Number needed _____
          Cost _____

Announcements—
   Style # _____ Print # _____
   Book _____
   Number needed _____
          Cost _____

Napkins—
   Number needed _____
   Style # _____ *Cost* _____

Programs—
   Style # _____ Print # _____
   Book _____
   Number needed _____
          Cost _____
      TOTAL COST _____

Invitations—
   Style # _____ Print # _____
   Book _____
   Number needed _____
          Cost _____

Reception Cards—
   Style # _____ Print # _____
   Book _____
   Number needed _____
          Cost _____

Response Cards—
   Style # _____ Print # _____
   Book _____
   Number needed _____
          Cost _____

Thank-You Notes—
   Style # _____ Print # _____
   Book _____
   Number needed _____
          Cost _____

Announcements—
   Style # _____ Print # _____
   Book _____
   Number needed _____
          Cost _____

Napkins—
   Number needed _____
   Style # _____ *Cost* _____

Programs—
   Style # _____ Print # _____
   Book _____
   Number needed _____
          Cost _____
      TOTAL COST _____

Stationery choice: # _____   Date confirmed _____
Total cost _____ Deposit paid _____ Balance due _____ by _____

Stationery Wording

*(ITEM &
LINE NUMBERS:)*

INVITATION:

1. _____
2. _____
3. _____
4. _____
5. _____
5. _____
7. _____
8. _____
9. _____
10. _____
11. _____
12. _____
13. _____
14. _____
15. _____
16. _____
17. _____
18. _____

RETURN ADDRESS FOR ENVELOPE FLAP:

1. _____
2. _____

RECEPTION CARDS:

1. _____
2. _____
3. _____
4. _____

RESPONSE CARDS:

1. _____
2. _____
3. _____
4. _____

RESPONSE ADDRESS:

1. _____
2. _____
3. _____

THANK-YOU NOTES:

1. _____
2. _____

NAPKINS:

1. _____
2. _____

ANNOUNCEMENTS:

1. _____
2. _____
3. _____
4. _____
5. _____
5. _____
7. _____
8. _____
9. _____
10. _____

Notes:

Music Estimate

Music needed for: *Ceremony only* ❏   *Reception only* ❏   *Both* ❏
Hours needed: *Ceremony* _____   *Reception* _____

Contact/agent _____   Phone _____
Address _____
Rate per hour _____   Overtime rate _____
Rest breaks: How many _____   How often _____
Audition date _____   Time _____   Place _____
Notes:

Choice: Yes ❏   No ❏

Contact/agent _____   Phone _____
Address _____
Rate per hour _____   Overtime rate _____
Rest breaks: How many _____   How often _____
Audition date _____   Time _____   Place _____
Notes:

Choice: Yes ❏   No ❏

Contact/agent _____   Phone _____
Address _____
Rate per hour _____   Overtime rate _____
Rest breaks: How many _____   How often _____
Audition date _____   Time _____   Place _____
Notes:

Choice: Yes ❏   No ❏

Musicians' Needs Checklist

Musicians' needs for: *Ceremony only* ☐   *Reception only* ☐   *Both* ☑

Needs:	*Yes*	*No*	*Number:*
Piano tuned	☐	☐	_____
Folders	☐	☐	_____
Music stands	☐	☐	_____
Seating	☐	☐	_____
Electrical outlets	☐	☐	_____

Sound equipment:

Microphones	☐	☐	_____

placement _____

Amplifiers	☐	☐	_____

placement _____

Sound operator:

name _____

address _____

Organ ☐ ☐ _____

placement _____

Piano ☐ ☐ _____

placement _____

Storage for instruments ☐ ☐ _____

location _____

Dressing area ☐ ☐ _____

location _____

If ceremony or reception is being held outdoors:

Is there a shady spot for musicians? ☐ ☐ _____

Where would they go if it rains? _____

Ceremony Music

Wedding site _____

Contact person _____ Phone _____

Appointment date _____ Time _____ Place_____

Instrumentalists: *phone:*

_____   _____
_____   _____
_____   _____
_____   _____
_____   _____

Soloists: *phone:*

_____   _____
_____   _____
_____   _____

Ceremony Order: *selection:*   *musician:*

Prelude
_____   _____   _____
_____   _____   _____
_____   _____   _____
_____   _____   _____

Processional
_____   _____   _____
_____   _____   _____
_____   _____   _____

Recessional
_____   _____   _____
_____   _____   _____
_____   _____   _____

Postlude
_____   _____   _____
_____   _____   _____
_____   _____   _____
_____   _____   _____

Musicians' Guidelines — Ceremony

Wedding of _____

Ceremony site and address _____

_____

Contact person _____ Phone _____

Wedding date _____ Arrival time _____

What to wear _____

Instrumentalists:	phone:
_____	_____
_____	_____
_____	_____
_____	_____
_____	_____

Soloists:	phone:
_____	_____
_____	_____

Rehearsals:	date:	time:	location:
Special	_____	_____	_____
Special	_____	_____	_____
Wedding	_____	_____	_____

Ceremony Order:	selection:	musician:
Prelude	_____	_____
_____	_____	_____
_____	_____	_____
_____	_____	_____
_____	_____	_____
Processional	_____	_____
_____	_____	_____
_____	_____	_____
Recessional	_____	_____
_____	_____	_____
_____	_____	_____
Postlude	_____	_____
_____	_____	_____
_____	_____	_____

Reception Music

Reception site _____

Contact person _____ Phone _____

Appointment date _____ Time _____ Place_____

General music selection — possible choices:

Live:

Recorded:

Special music — possible choices:

   Fanfares

      Arrival of the bridal couple _____
_____

      Cutting of the cake_____
_____

      Toast to the bridal couple _____
_____

      Throwing of bouquet and garter _____
_____

First Dance _____
_____

Ethnic selections _____
_____
_____
_____
_____

Other: _____
_____
_____
_____

Musicians' Guidelines — Reception

Wedding Reception of _____

Reception site and address _____

_____

Contact person _____ Phone _____

Date _____ Arrival time _____

What to wear _____

Instrumentalists:	*phone:*
_____	_____
_____	_____
_____	_____
_____	_____
_____	_____

Soloists:	*phone:*
_____	_____
_____	_____

program order:	*selection:*	*musician:*
_____	_____	_____
_____	_____	_____
_____	_____	_____
_____	_____	_____
_____	_____	_____
_____	_____	_____
_____	_____	_____
_____	_____	_____
_____	_____	_____
_____	_____	_____
_____	_____	_____
_____	_____	_____
_____	_____	_____
_____	_____	_____
_____	_____	_____
_____	_____	_____
_____	_____	_____
_____	_____	_____

Sound level to be maintained: _____

Florist Estimate

OPTION #1

Name _____

Address _____

Contact person _____

Phone _____

Appointment date and time:

_____

Wedding Package

   Cost _____

   Description: _____

   _____

   _____

   _____

   _____

OPTION #2

Name _____

Address _____

Contact person _____

Phone _____

Appointment date and time:

_____

Wedding Package

   Cost _____

   Description: _____

   _____

   _____

   _____

   _____

INDIVIDUAL CHOICES
(with description)

	COST:	
	Option #1	Option #2
Altar flowers — 1st choice: _____	$_____	$_____
2nd choice: _____	_____	_____
Bride's bouquet — 1st choice _____	_____	_____
2nd choice: _____	_____	_____
Bridesmaids' bouquets — 1st choice _____	_____	_____
2nd choice: _____	_____	_____
Boutonnieres — 1st choice _____	_____	_____
2nd choice: _____	_____	_____
Corsages — 1st choice _____	_____	_____
2nd choice: _____	_____	_____

ACCESSORIES			SERVICES		
	Option #1	Option #2		Option #1	Option #2
Arch/Canopy	$_____	$_____	Delivery	$_____	$_____
Kneeler	_____	_____	Setup	_____	_____
Candelabra	_____	_____	Removal	_____	_____
Candlelighters	_____	_____	Other:		
Candles	_____	_____	_____	_____	_____
Aisle Runner	_____	_____	_____	_____	_____
Other: _____	_____	_____			

Choice: # _____   Date confirmed _____

Total cost _____   Deposit paid _____   Balance due _____ by _____

Floral Diagrams

(For the placement of flowers, plants, and other decorations)

Entry Area
(Including guestbook stand or table, and gift table)

Aisle and Altar

Reception Site

Floral Planning

Florist _____

Address _____

Contact person _____ Phone _____

Date _____ Time _____

Ceremony site & address _____

Contact person _____ Phone _____

Date _____ Time _____

Reception site & address _____

Contact person _____ Phone _____

Date _____ Time _____

❀ CEREMONY FLOWERS ❀

Qty.:   *Description (color, size, type):*   *Cost:*

Bride:

_____   Bouquet _____ _____

_____   Small bouquet for throwing_____ _____

_____   Going-away corsage _____ _____

Bridal Attendants:

_____   Honor Attendant's bouquet _____ _____

      name: _____

_____   Bridesmaid's bouquet _____ _____

      names: _____

      _____

      _____

      _____

      _____

_____   Flower Girl's bouquet _____ _____

      name: _____

_____   Floral headdresses _____ _____

Groom & Attendants

_____   Groom's boutonniere _____ _____

_____   Best Man's boutonniere _____ _____

      name: _____

_____   Groomsmen/Ushers' boutonniere _____ _____

      names: _____

      _____

      _____

      _____

      _____

_____   Ring Bearer's boutonniere _____ _____

      name: _____

Mothers and Grandmothers

_____ Mother of the Bride — corsage _____ _____
   name: _____

_____ Mother of the Groom — corsage _____ _____
   name: _____

_____ Mothers' roses _____ _____

_____ Grandmothers' corsage _____ _____
   names: _____
   _____

_____ Corsage for other female family members (such as stepmothers,
   foster mothers) _____ _____
   names: _____
   _____

Fathers and Grandfathers

_____ Father of the Bride — boutonniere _____ _____
   name: _____

_____ Father of the Groom — boutonniere _____ _____
   name: _____

_____ Boutonnieres for other male family members (such as stepfathers,
   foster fathers) _____ _____
   names: _____
   _____

Altar

_____ Arch/Canopy _____ _____
_____ Kneeling bench _____ _____
   Candelabra:
_____   3 candles, standing _____ _____
_____   3 candles, tabletop unity _____ _____
_____   7 candles, standing _____ _____
_____   15 candles, fan, standing _____ _____
_____   15 candles, spiral, standing _____ _____
_____ Candlelighters _____ _____
_____ White candles _____ _____
_____ Floral sprays _____ _____
_____ Beauty vases _____ _____
_____ Potted flowers _____ _____
_____ Potted plants _____ _____
_____ Potted trees _____ _____
_____ Plant stands _____ _____
_____ Other: _____ _____

Aisle

_____ Pew decorations
_____   Candelabra _____ _____
_____   Floral arrangements _____ _____
_____   Greenery and bows _____ _____
_____ Aisle ribbons _____ _____
_____ Aisle runner (*length:* _____) _____ _____
_____ Other: _____ _____

(continued)

Others for whom you may wish to provide flowers —

_____ Soloist(s) _____ _____
        name:(s) _____

_____ Instrumentalist(s) _____ _____
        name:(s) _____
        _____

_____ Officiant _____ _____
        name: _____

_____ Guestbook attendant(s) _____ _____
        names: _____

_____ Gift attendant(s) _____ _____
        names: _____

_____ Wedding hostess/coordinator(s) _____ _____
        names: _____

_____ Cake servers _____ _____
        names: _____

_____ Hospitality committee _____ _____
        names: _____
        _____

_____ Others: _____ _____
        names: _____

❧ RECEPTION FLOWERS ❧

Qty.:   _Description (color, size, type):_   _Cost:_

Table centerpieces:

_____ Bride's Table _____ _____
_____ Parents' Table _____ _____
_____ Attendants' Table(s) _____ _____
_____ Guest Tables _____ _____
_____ Other: _____ _____

Other decorations:

_____ Table garlands _____ _____
_____ Top of cake _____ _____
_____ Around cake _____ _____
_____ Receiving line area _____ _____
_____ Guestbook stand _____ _____
_____ Table for receiving gifts _____ _____
_____ Ladies' powder room _____ _____
_____ Other: _____ _____

❧ SERVICE COSTS ❧

For the ceremony:	Delivery	$ _____	_For the Reception:_	Delivery	$ _____
	Setup	_____		Setup	_____
	Removal	_____		Removal	_____
Other: _____		_____	Other: _____		_____

Florist's Guidelines

Wedding of _____

Address _____

Phone _____

Ceremony site _____

Address _____

Contact person _____ Phone _____

Date _____ Delivery/Setup time _____

Removal time _____

Reception site _____

Address _____

Contact person _____ Phone _____

Date _____ Delivery/Setup time _____

Removal time _____

NOTES:

Photographer Estimate

OPTION #1	OPTION #2

Photographer _____   Photographer _____

Address _____   Address _____

Contact person _____   Contact person _____

Phone _____   Phone _____

Appointment date and time: Appointment date and time:

_____   _____

DESCRIPTION OF WEDDING PACKAGES   **DESCRIPTION OF WEDDING PACKAGES**
    (including cost and required deposit)   (including cost and required deposit)

_____   _____
_____   _____
_____   _____
_____   _____
_____   _____
_____   _____
_____   _____
_____   _____
_____   _____
_____   _____
_____   _____
_____   _____

INDIVIDUAL PORTRAITS: **INDIVIDUAL PORTRAITS:**

Bridal portrait (part of pkg. ❑   extra ❑)   Bridal portrait (part of pkg. ❑   extra ❑)
    cost _____ deposit _____   cost _____ deposit _____

Engagement photos (part of pkg. ❑   extra ❑) Engagement photos (part of pkg. ❑   extra ❑)
    cost _____ deposit _____   cost _____ deposit _____

Glossies for newspaper (part of pkg. ❑ extra ❑) Glossies for newspaper (part of pkg. ❑ extra ❑)
    cost _____ deposit _____   cost _____ deposit _____

Additional copies   Additional copies
    cost _____ deposit _____   cost _____ deposit _____

Other: _____   Other: _____
    cost _____ deposit _____   cost _____ deposit _____

Photographer choice: # _____   Date confirmed _____

Total cost _____   Deposit paid _____   Balance due _____ by _____

Payment: Credit card ❑   Cash only ❑   Date to view proofs _____

Photographer's Planning List & Guidelines

Bride's name _____ Phone _____

Address _____

Wedding: Date _____ Time _____

  Place _____ Room # _____

Reception: Date _____ Time _____

  Place _____ Room # _____

Engagement pictures:

Time _____ Date _____ Place _____

Formal bridal portrait:

Time _____ Date _____ Place _____

Guidelines/Ceremony site restrictions _____

_____

_____

  What to wear _____

  Other guidelines _____

Suggested formal shots:

BRIDE —	GROOM —	BRIDE & GROOM —
_____ alone	_____ alone	_____ together
with:	*with:*	*with:*
_____ father	_____ father	_____ Best Man
_____ mother	_____ mother	_____ Maid of Honor
_____ parents	_____ parents	_____ Honor Attendants
_____ Maid of Honor	_____ Best Man	_____ Bridesmaids
_____ Bridesmaids	_____ Ushers	_____ Ushers
_____ Flower Girl	_____ Ring Bearer	_____ Flower Girl & Ring Bearer
_____ Grandparents	_____ Grandparents	_____ Grandparents
_____ Family	_____ Family	_____ Both families
_____ _____	_____ _____	_____ Bridal Party
_____ _____	_____ _____	_____ Bride's Parents
_____ _____	_____ _____	_____ Groom's Parents
_____ _____	_____ _____	_____ Officiant
_____ _____	_____ _____	_____ _____
_____ _____	_____ _____	_____ _____

Suggested shots at the reception:

_____ Arrival	_____ Food table	_____ Reception line
_____ Cutting the cake	_____ The toast	_____ Bride throwing bouquet
_____ Cake table	_____ Bridal Table	_____ Bride & Groom feeding each other cake
_____ _____	_____ _____	_____ _____
_____ _____	_____ _____	_____ _____

Video Estimate

<table>
<tr><td>

OPTION #1

Name _____

Address _____

Contact person _____

Phone _____

Appointment date and time:

_____

DESCRIPTION OF SERVICES   *cost:*

   # of hours _____

      (tape length: _____) $ _____

   # of cameras _____   _____

   Planning: ❏ as it unfolds _____

             ❏ tell a story _____

   Editing _____

   Sound:

     ❏ audio capability ❏ dubbing

   Special effects _____ _____

   _____

   Extra cassettes: # _____ _____

   Other: _____ _____

   _____

NOTES:

</td><td>

OPTION #2

Name _____

Address _____

Contact person _____

Phone _____

Appointment date and time:

_____

DESCRIPTION OF SERVICES   *cost:*

   # of hours _____

      (tape length: _____) $ _____

   # of cameras _____   _____

   Planning: ❏ as it unfolds _____

             ❏ tell a story _____

   Editing _____

   Sound:

     ❏ audio capability ❏ dubbing

   Special effects _____ _____

   _____

   Extra cassettes: # _____ _____

   Other: _____ _____

   _____

NOTES:

</td></tr>
</table>

Video choice: # _____   Date confirmed _____

Total cost _____   Deposit paid _____   Balance due _____   by _____

   Date video will be ready _____

Video Planning & Guidelines

Wedding of: _____ Phone _____

Ceremony site & address _____
Contact person _____ Phone _____
Date _____ Time _____

Reception site & address _____
Contact person _____ Phone _____
Date _____ Time _____

What to wear _____

Ceremony site restrictions _____
_____
_____

Planning/Staging:

NOTES:

Audio Estimate

OPTION #1	OPTION #2

OPTION #1

Name _____

Address _____

Contact person _____

Phone _____

Appointment date and time:

_____

Taping is for: ☐ ceremony only
☐ reception only ☐ both

DESCRIPTION OF SERVICES   *cost:*

# of hours _____ $ _____

# of copies _____   _____

Equipment rental:

Taping   _____

Sound   _____

Operator fee   _____

Other: _____   _____

NOTES:

OPTION #2

Name _____

Address _____

Contact person _____

Phone _____

Appointment date and time:

_____

Taping is for: ☐ ceremony only
☐ reception only ☐ both

DESCRIPTION OF SERVICES   *cost:*

# of hours _____ $ _____

# of copies _____   _____

Equipment rental:

Taping   _____

Sound   _____

Operator fee   _____

Other: _____   _____

NOTES:

Equipment:

Taping — privately available from _____

Sound — privately available from _____

Audio choice: # _____   Date confirmed _____

Total cost _____   Deposit paid _____   Balance due _____ by _____

Date tapes will be ready _____

Audio Planning & Guidelines

Wedding of: _____ Phone _____

Ceremony site & address _____
Contact person _____ Phone _____
Date _____ Time _____

Reception site & address _____
Contact person _____ Phone _____
Date _____ Time _____

What to wear _____

Ceremony site restrictions _____
_____
_____

Planning:

NOTES:

Guest Housing & Transportation

Name of Hotel/Host _____
Address _____
     Rates _____ Phone _____
• Guest(s) _____
Arrival date & time _____ Airline flight # _____
Departure date & time _____ Airline flight # _____
Driver to and from airport _____
Driver to and from wedding/reception _____

Name of Hotel/Host _____
Address _____
     Rates _____ Phone _____
• Guest(s) _____
Arrival date & time _____ Airline flight # _____
Departure date & time _____ Airline flight # _____
Driver to and from airport _____
Driver to and from wedding/reception _____

Name of Hotel/Host _____
Address _____
     Rates _____ Phone _____
• Guest(s) _____
Arrival date & time _____ Airline flight # _____
Departure date & time _____ Airline flight # _____
Driver to and from airport _____
Driver to and from wedding/reception _____

Name of Hotel/Host _____
Address _____
     Rates _____ Phone _____
• Guest(s) _____
Arrival date & time _____ Airline flight # _____
Departure date & time _____ Airline flight # _____
Driver to and from airport _____
Driver to and from wedding/reception _____

Name of Hotel/Host _____
Address _____
     Rates _____ Phone _____
• Guest(s) _____
Arrival date & time _____ Airline flight # _____
Departure date & time _____ Airline flight # _____
Driver to and from airport _____
Driver to and from wedding/reception _____

Information List: Guest Housing & Transportation

Guest(s) _____
Staying at _____ Room # _____
Driver to and from airport _____
Driver to and from wedding/reception _____

Guest(s) _____
Staying at _____ Room # _____
Driver to and from airport _____
Driver to and from wedding/reception _____

Guest(s) _____
Staying at _____ Room # _____
Driver to and from airport _____
Driver to and from wedding/reception _____

Guest(s) _____
Staying at _____ Room # _____
Driver to and from airport _____
Driver to and from wedding/reception _____

Guest(s) _____
Staying at _____ Room # _____
Driver to and from airport _____
Driver to and from wedding/reception _____

Guest(s) _____
Staying at _____ Room # _____
Driver to and from airport _____
Driver to and from wedding/reception _____

Guest(s) _____
Staying at _____ Room # _____
Driver to and from airport _____
Driver to and from wedding/reception _____

Guest(s) _____
Staying at _____ Room # _____
Driver to and from airport _____
Driver to and from wedding/reception _____

Guest(s) _____
Staying at _____ Room # _____
Driver to and from airport _____
Driver to and from wedding/reception _____

Transportation Guidelines for Drivers

Guest(s) _____
Arrival date & time _____ Airline flight # _____
Staying at _____ Room # _____
Departure date & time _____ Airline flight # _____
Driver _____

Guest(s) _____
Arrival date & time _____ Airline flight # _____
Staying at _____ Room # _____
Departure date & time _____ Airline flight # _____
Driver _____

Guest(s) _____
Arrival date & time _____ Airline flight # _____
Staying at _____ Room # _____
Departure date & time _____ Airline flight # _____
Driver _____

Guest(s) _____
Arrival date & time _____ Airline flight # _____
Staying at _____ Room # _____
Departure date & time _____ Airline flight # _____
Driver _____

Guest(s) _____
Arrival date & time _____ Airline flight # _____
Staying at _____ Room # _____
Departure date & time _____ Airline flight # _____
Driver _____

Guest(s) _____
Arrival date & time _____ Airline flight # _____
Staying at _____ Room # _____
Departure date & time _____ Airline flight # _____
Driver _____

Guest(s) _____
Arrival date & time _____ Airline flight # _____
Staying at _____ Room # _____
Departure date & time _____ Airline flight # _____
Driver _____

Guest(s) _____
Arrival date & time _____ Airline flight # _____
Staying at _____ Room # _____
Departure date & time _____ Airline flight # _____
Driver _____

Wedding Party Transportation Estimate

OPTION #1

Name _____

Address _____

Contact person _____

Phone _____

Type of vehicle _____

Number needed _____

Per mile cost _____

Hourly rate _____

Overtime _____

Wedding packages:

NOTES:

OPTION #2

Name _____

Address _____

Contact person _____

Phone _____

Type of vehicle _____

Number needed _____

Per mile cost _____

Hourly rate _____

Overtime _____

Wedding packages:

NOTES:

Choice: # _____   Date confirmed _____

Total cost _____   Deposit paid _____   Balance due _____ by _____

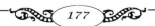

Wedding Party Transportation Guidelines

Wedding of _____   Phone _____
Address _____
_____

Wedding date _____

Ceremony site & address _____
Contact person _____   Phone _____
Date _____   Time _____

Reception site & address _____
Contact person _____   Phone _____
Date _____   Time _____

Type of vehicles _____   Number needed _____

PICK-UP TIMES

    Groom and Best Man _____   *Time* _____
    Address _____   *Phone* _____

    Bridesmaids _____   *Time* _____
    Address _____   *Phone* _____

    Bride's Mother and Honor Attendants _____   *Time* _____
    Address _____   *Phone* _____

    Bride and Her Father _____   *Time* _____
    Address _____   *Phone* _____

    Other: _____   *Time* _____
    Address _____   *Phone* _____

    _____   *Time* _____
    Address _____   *Phone* _____

    _____   *Time* _____
    Address _____   *Phone* _____

Equipment List

Name _____

Address _____

Contact person _____ Phone _____

❁ CEREMONY ACCESSORIES:

_____ _____ Wedding Arch

_____ _____ Wedding Canopy (Chuppah)

_____ _____ Latticework backdrops

Floor Candelabra

_____ _____ 3-light Trinity

_____ _____ 7-light, adjustable

_____ _____ 9-light

_____ _____ 15-light, spiral

_____ _____ 15-light, fan

_____ _____ 17-light, Heart shape

Aisle Candelabra

_____ _____ Clamp type

_____ _____ Free-standing

_____ _____ Candles

_____ _____ Candlelighters

_____ _____ Kneeling bench

_____ _____ Floral baskets

Flower stands

_____ _____ 8"

_____ _____ 12"

_____ _____ 16

_____ _____ 20"

_____ _____ 24"

_____ _____ Aisle stanchions — posts and chains

_____ _____ Aisle runners (differing lengths)

_____ _____ Guest Book stand

❁ CHAIRS: To determine the seating capacity of an area using theater style seating, divide the square footage of the area by 10.

_____ _____ Folding contour seat and back

_____ _____ White wood with padded seat

❁ TABLES: When using the oblong banquet tables, divide the square feet of the area by 8. When using the round banquet tables, divide the square feet of the area by 10.

Oblong tables (30" wide, 29" high)

_____ _____ 6' table seats 6 to 8 people

_____ _____ 8' table seats 8 to 10 people

Round tables

_____ _____ 24" diameter seats 2 people

_____ _____ 36" diameter seats 4 people

_____ _____ 48" diameter seats 6 people

_____ _____ 60" diameter seats 8 people

_____ _____ 72" diameter seats 10 to 12 people

_____ _____ Heart-shaped tables — excellent for cakes

_____ _____ Card tables — 34" square, 28" high

❁ LINENS — usually available in a variety of colors and sizes:

Long cloths

_____ _____ 54" X 54" and 60" X 60" fit card table

_____ _____ 60" X 120" fits 6' and 8' tables

Round cloths

_____ _____ 60" diameter fits 24"-36" round table

_____ _____ 72" diameter drapes 24" round table to the floor; also fits 36"-48" round table

_____ _____ 90" diameter drapes 36" round table to the floor; also fits 48"-60" round table

Qty.	Cost	
_____	_____	100" diameter drapes 48" round table to the floor; also fits 60"-72" round table
_____	_____	120" diameter drapes 60" round table to the floor; also fits 72" round table
		Specialty cloths (lace overlays — same sizing as above)
_____	_____	60" X 60"
_____	_____	60" X 120"
_____	_____	60" diameter
_____	_____	72" diameter
_____	_____	90" diameter
		Napkins
_____	_____	Cocktail size
_____	_____	Dinner size

Table skirting (lace and solid): Rental agencies either charge a flat fee per table or charge by the inch. Lace patterns are usually a bit more expensive. You'll need to know if you want only three or all four sides covered.

To determine the length of skirting needed for 4 sides — multiply the width of the table times 2, then multiply the length of the table times 2, and add the two together.

For 3 sides — multiply the width times 2 and add the length of the table.

For a round table — multiply 3.14 times the diameter of the table.

Rental agencies will send enough skirting for the area to be covered, but it may be in more than one section. Just overlap the ends and continue pinning. Pins are usually included, but it's wise to also have a generous supply of T-pins (wig pins) to firmly secure the skirting to the table.

Qty.	Cost	
		Skirting length
_____	_____	6' table, 4 sides: 204" plus overlap
_____	_____	6' table, 3 sides: 132" plus overlap
_____	_____	8' table, 4 sides: 252" plus overlap

Qty.	Cost	
_____	_____	60" round table: 189" plus overlap
_____	_____	72" round table: 227" plus overlap
_____	_____	90" round table: 283" plus overlap
_____	_____	100" round table: 314" plus overlap
_____	_____	120" round table: 377" plus overlap

❀ FLATWARE: ❑ *Silverplate* ❑ *Stainless*

Qty.	Cost	
_____	_____	Dinner knives
_____	_____	Dinner forks
_____	_____	Salad and dessert forks
_____	_____	Teaspoons
_____	_____	Soup spoons
_____	_____	Butter knives
_____	_____	Shrimp forks
_____	_____	Steak knives
_____	_____	Meat forks
_____	_____	Salad spoon and fork sets
_____	_____	Salad tongs
_____	_____	Serving spoons
_____	_____	Cake knife
_____	_____	Cake server

❀ DINNERWARE:
❑ *China* ❑ *Glass* ❑ *Plastic*

Qty.	Cost	
_____	_____	Dinner plates
_____	_____	Bread and butter plates
_____	_____	Salad plates
_____	_____	Cups
_____	_____	Saucers
_____	_____	Cereal/Soup bowls
_____	_____	Fruit bowls
_____	_____	Creamer and Sugar
_____	_____	Salt and Pepper shakers
_____	_____	Vegetable bowls
_____	_____	Gravy boats
_____	_____	Platters

❀ GLASSWARE: ❑ *Glass* ❑ *Plastic*

Qty.	Cost	
		Stem ware
_____	_____	$4^1/_2$ oz. Champagne
_____	_____	$6^1/_2$ oz. Wine glass

Qty.	Cost	
_____	_____	12 oz. Water goblet
_____	_____	Parfait glass
_____	_____	Sherbet glass
		Glasses
_____	_____	5 oz. Juice glass
_____	_____	Water glass
_____	_____	4 oz. Punch cup
_____		Pitchers

❀ PUNCH FOUNTAINS:

| _____ | _____ | 3 gallon |
| _____ | _____ | 7 gallon |

❀ PUNCH BOWLS (generally 3 gallon capacity)
   ❏ Silver   ❏ Glass   ❏ Plastic

_____	_____	With tray
_____	_____	Without tray
_____	_____	Silver ladle
_____	_____	Plastic ladle

❀ COFFEE MAKERS AND SERVERS:

		Automatic Coffee Makers
_____	_____	35 cup
_____	_____	55 cup
_____	_____	100 cup
		Silver Urns
_____	_____	25 cup
_____	_____	50 cup
_____	_____	Tray
_____	_____	Sugar and Creamer
_____	_____	Silver Coffee and Tea service — complete set of two pots, tray, sugar and creamer
_____	_____	Insulated Coffee Pitchers

❀ MISCELLANEOUS SERVING PIECES:

_____	_____	Silver Bonbon dishes
_____	_____	Silver Revere Bowls — various sizes
_____	_____	Silver Bread dishes
_____	_____	Silver Relish dishes
_____	_____	Silver Sugar Tongs
		Chafing dishes
		❏ Silver ❏ Stainless
_____	_____	2-quart
_____	_____	4-quart
_____	_____	8-quart.

Qty.	Cost	
		Food Pans
		Full pan
_____	_____	4-quart
_____	_____	8-quart
		1/2 pan (divided in half)
_____	_____	4-quart
_____	_____	8-quart
		1/3 pan (divided in thirds)
_____	_____	4-quart
_____	_____	8-quart.

Bowls   ❏ Stainless   ❏ Plastic

_____	_____	12"
_____	_____	14"
_____	_____	16"
_____	_____	18"
_____	_____	20"
_____	_____	24"
_____	_____	Electric Roasters
		Electric Hotplates
_____	_____	Single Burner
_____	_____	Double Burner
		Barbecue
_____	_____	Grills
_____	_____	Equipment
_____	_____	Portable Bar
_____	_____	Bar Stools
_____	_____	Ice Buckets
_____	_____	Ice Tongs
_____	_____	Insulated Coolers
_____	_____	Ice Chests

❀ TRAYS:
   ❏ Silver ❏ Chrome ❏ Stainless ❏ Plastic

_____	_____	10" round
_____	_____	12" round
_____	_____	14" round
_____	_____	16" round
_____	_____	18" round
_____	_____	20" round
_____	_____	22" round
_____	_____	13" X 21" oval
_____	_____	15" X 24" oval
_____	_____	10" X 17" oblong
_____	_____	13" X 19" oblong
_____	_____	14" X 22" oblong
_____	_____	17" X 23" oblong
_____	_____	Waiters' Trays

❀ GARDEN AND PATIO:

_____　_____　Floors — usually 4' X 4' wood sections designed to be set up in any size area, indoors or outdoors on level surfaces. Divide the square footage of the area to be covered by the square footage of one section of wood to determine the number of sections you will need.

_____　_____　Stages, Platform risers — usually in 3' by 6' sections, excellent for head table, bandstands, and walk ways.

Lighting and Electrical
_____　_____　Spotlights
_____　_____　Pole lights
_____　_____　Twinkle lights — strings of small white lights
_____　_____　Tiki Torches
_____　_____　Floating Pool Candles
_____　_____　Hurricane Lights — with glass chimney and candle
_____　_____　Extension cords (25' to 100' in length)

Heating
_____　_____　Indoor Electric Heaters
_____　_____　Outdoor Propane Heaters

Cooling
_____　_____　Table Fans
_____　_____　Floor Fans
_____　_____　Portable Air Conditioners

Canopies and Umbrellas
_____　_____　Canopies — usually available in an assortment of colors and sizes. Keep in mind the site and the size of the area to be covered when ordering.

_____　_____　Sidewalls for canopies — usually rented by the lineal foot, in solid or clear vinyl.

Umbrellas
_____　_____　With stand only

_____　_____　With stand and 48" round table
_____　_____　With stand and 60" round table
_____　_____　With stand and 72" round table
_____　_____　Special linen (necessary for use on umbrella tables)

❀ GUEST ITEMS:
_____　_____　Rollaway Beds
　　　　　　　　❏ 30"　❏ 39"　❏ 48"
_____　_____　Baby Crib
_____　_____　Infant Car Seat
_____　_____　High Chair
_____　_____　Stroller
_____　_____　Play Pen

❀ MISCELLANEOUS
_____　_____　Garment Rack
_____　_____　Garbage Cans
_____　_____　Electric Bug Zapper
_____　_____　Mirror Disc Ball
_____　_____　Movie Projector
_____　_____　Slide Projector
_____　_____　Projector Screen
_____　_____　_____
_____　_____　_____
_____　_____　_____
_____　_____　_____
_____　_____　_____
_____　_____　_____
_____　_____　_____
_____　_____　_____

TOTAL RENTAL COST _____

Deposit _____

Balance Due _____

Date Due _____

Equipment Delivery & Pickup

Name _____

Address _____

Contact person _____ Phone _____

Ceremony Site:

BEFORE:

    Contact person _____ Phone _____

    Date _____ Time _____

    Pickup _____

    Delivery _____

    Setup _____

    Payment _____ When _____

AFTER:

    Date _____ Time _____

    Tear down _____

    Return _____

    Pickup _____

Reception Site:

BEFORE:

    Contact person _____ Phone _____

    Date _____ Time _____

    Pickup _____

    Delivery _____

    Setup _____

    Payment _____ When _____

AFTER:

    Date _____ Time _____

    Tear down _____

    Return _____

    Pickup _____

Honeymoon Travel & Accommodations

Travel Agency _____

Address _____

Agent _____ Phone _____

Total cost _____ Amount due _____

Honeymoon dates: from _____ to _____

WEDDING NIGHT:

Hotel _____

Address _____

Contact person _____ Phone _____

Room accommodations _____

Room # _____ Rate _____ Amount due _____ Reservations: ❏ *Made* ❏ *Confirmed*

Date: Arrival _____ Departure _____

(Notes on wedding night accommodations — Make it at a nearby hotel, if possible. Ask to see the room ahead of time. Is it romantic? Private?)

TRAVEL RESERVATIONS: Airline, Ship, Rental Car

Date:	*Rate:*	*Carrier/Number:*	*Departure/Arrival:*	*Phone:*
_____	_____	_____	_____	_____
_____	_____	_____	_____	_____
_____	_____	_____	_____	_____
_____	_____	_____	_____	_____
_____	_____	_____	_____	_____
_____	_____	_____	_____	_____
_____	_____	_____	_____	_____
_____	_____	_____	_____	_____
_____	_____	_____	_____	_____
_____	_____	_____	_____	_____
_____	_____	_____	_____	_____

With: _____
    Reservations: ❏ *Made* ❏ *Confirmed* Total cost _____ Amount due _____

With: _____
    Reservations: ❏ *Made* ❏ *Confirmed* Total cost _____ Amount due _____

With: _____
    Reservations: ❏ *Made* ❏ *Confirmed* Total cost _____ Amount due _____

HOTEL RESERVATIONS:

Hotel _____

Address _____

Contact person _____ Phone _____

Room accommodations _____

Transportation _____

Room # _____ Rate _____ Amount due _____ Reservations: ❏ *Made* ❏ *Confirmed*

Date: Arrival _____ Departure _____

Hotel _____

Address _____

Contact person _____ Phone _____

Room accommodations _____

Transportation _____

Room # _____ Rate _____ Amount due _____ Reservations: ❏ *Made* ❏ *Confirmed*

Date: Arrival _____ Departure _____

Hotel _____

Address _____

Contact person _____ Phone _____

Room accommodations _____

Transportation _____

Room # _____ Rate _____ Amount due _____ Reservations: ❏ *Made* ❏ *Confirmed*

Date: Arrival _____ Departure _____

Hotel _____

Address _____

Contact person _____ Phone _____

Room accommodations _____

Transportation _____

Room # _____ Rate _____ Amount due _____ Reservations: ❏ *Made* ❏ *Confirmed*

Date: Arrival _____ Departure _____

For Travel Abroad:

Necessary Papers:
   ❏ *Passports*   ❏ *Visas*   ❏ *Marriage License*   ❏ *Travelers Checks*

Inoculations Needed:

_____   _____

_____   _____

_____   _____

_____   _____

_____   _____

SPECIAL PARTIES

SPECIAL PARTIES

- You'll be of great help to the hosts and hostesses who are planning the various special parties if you fill out and photocopy for them the appropriate guest lists in this section. Guest lists are provided here for three Bridal Showers, the Bridal Luncheon, the Pre-Ceremony Buffet, the Bachelor's Party, and the Rehearsal Dinner.

- You can also provide the hosts and hostesses with copies of the estimate and planning worksheets included here.

Bridal Shower Guest List

Hostess _____ Phone _____

Address _____

Date _____ Time _____ Number of guests _____

Yes/No (RSVP)   name & address: phone:

☐ ☐ _____

☐ ☐ _____

☐ ☐ _____

☐ ☐ _____

☐ ☐ _____

☐ ☐ _____

☐ ☐ _____

☐ ☐ _____

☐ ☐ _____

☐ ☐ _____

☐ ☐ _____

☐ ☐ _____

☐ ☐ _____

☐ ☐ _____

☐ ☐ _____

☐ ☐ _____

☐ ☐ _____

☐ ☐ _____

☐ ☐ _____

☐ ☐ _____

☐ ☐ _____

☐ ☐ _____

☐ ☐ _____

☐ ☐ _____

☐ ☐ _____

☐ ☐ _____

☐ ☐ _____

☐ ☐ _____

☐ ☐ _____

☐ ☐ _____

☐ ☐ _____

Bridal Shower Guest List

Hostess _____ Phone _____

Address _____

Date _____ Time _____ Number of guests _____

Yes/No (RSVP)   name & address: phone:

☐ ☐ _____
☐ ☐ _____
☐ ☐ _____
☐ ☐ _____
☐ ☐ _____
☐ ☐ _____
☐ ☐ _____
☐ ☐ _____
☐ ☐ _____
☐ ☐ _____
☐ ☐ _____
☐ ☐ _____
☐ ☐ _____
☐ ☐ _____
☐ ☐ _____
☐ ☐ _____
☐ ☐ _____
☐ ☐ _____
☐ ☐ _____
☐ ☐ _____
☐ ☐ _____
☐ ☐ _____
☐ ☐ _____
☐ ☐ _____
☐ ☐ _____
☐ ☐ _____
☐ ☐ _____
☐ ☐ _____
☐ ☐ _____
☐ ☐ _____

Bridal Shower Guest List

Hostess _____ Phone _____

Address _____

Date _____ Time _____ Number of guests _____

Yes/No (RSVP)   name & address: phone:

☐ ☐ _____

☐ ☐ _____

☐ ☐ _____

☐ ☐ _____

☐ ☐ _____

☐ ☐ _____

☐ ☐ _____

☐ ☐ _____

☐ ☐ _____

☐ ☐ _____

☐ ☐ _____

☐ ☐ _____

☐ ☐ _____

☐ ☐ _____

☐ ☐ _____

☐ ☐ _____

☐ ☐ _____

☐ ☐ _____

☐ ☐ _____

☐ ☐ _____

☐ ☐ _____

☐ ☐ _____

☐ ☐ _____

☐ ☐ _____

☐ ☐ _____

☐ ☐ _____

☐ ☐ _____

☐ ☐ _____

☐ ☐ _____

Bridal Luncheon Guest List

Luncheon site _____

Contact person _____ Phone _____

Address _____

Date _____ Time _____ Number of guests _____

Yes/No (RSVP)   *name & address:*   *phone:*

☐ ☐ _____

☐ ☐ _____

☐ ☐ _____

☐ ☐ _____

☐ ☐ _____

☐ ☐ _____

☐ ☐ _____

☐ ☐ _____

☐ ☐ _____

☐ ☐ _____

☐ ☐ _____

☐ ☐ _____

☐ ☐ _____

☐ ☐ _____

☐ ☐ _____

☐ ☐ _____

☐ ☐ _____

☐ ☐ _____

☐ ☐ _____

☐ ☐ _____

☐ ☐ _____

☐ ☐ _____

☐ ☐ _____

☐ ☐ _____

☐ ☐ _____

☐ ☐ _____

☐ ☐ _____

☐ ☐ _____

☐ ☐ _____

Bridal Luncheon Estimate

OPTION #1

Name _____

Address _____

Contact person _____

Phone _____

Date _____ Time _____

   Number of guests _____

Description of menu choices: cost:

Decorations (color of table linens, centerpieces, candles, etc.):

Suggested seating:

Cost of separate room _____

Estimated total cost _____

Gratuity included: Yes ❑   No ❑

OPTION #2

Name _____

Address _____

Contact person _____

Phone _____

Date _____ Time _____

   Number of guests _____

Description of menu choices: cost:

Decorations (color of table linens, centerpieces, candles, etc.):

Suggested seating:

Cost of separate room _____

Estimated total cost _____

Gratuity included: Yes ❑   No ❑

Choice: #_____   Date confirmed _____

Total cost _____ Deposit paid _____ Balance due _____ by _____

Scheduled date _____ Time _____

Bridal Luncheon Menu

APPETIZER:

SALAD / SOUP:

ENTRÉE:

DESSERT:

BEVERAGE:

Notes:

Pre-Ceremony Buffet Guest List

Buffet site _____ Room # _____

Hostess _____ Phone _____

Address _____

Date _____ Time _____ Number of guests _____

Yes/No (RSVP)   name & address: phone:

☐ ☐ _____
☐ ☐ _____
☐ ☐ _____
☐ ☐ _____
☐ ☐ _____
☐ ☐ _____
☐ ☐ _____
☐ ☐ _____
☐ ☐ _____
☐ ☐ _____
☐ ☐ _____
☐ ☐ _____
☐ ☐ _____
☐ ☐ _____
☐ ☐ _____
☐ ☐ _____
☐ ☐ _____
☐ ☐ _____
☐ ☐ _____
☐ ☐ _____
☐ ☐ _____
☐ ☐ _____
☐ ☐ _____
☐ ☐ _____
☐ ☐ _____
☐ ☐ _____
☐ ☐ _____
☐ ☐ _____

Pre-Ceremony Buffet Planning

Buffet site _____ Room # _____

Hostess _____ Phone _____

Address _____

Date _____ Time _____ Number of guests _____

MENU PLANNING:

DISHWARE, GLASSWARE, FLATWARE, CHAIRS, TABLES, LINENS, etc.

SETUP AND CLEANUP:

Bachelor's Party Guest List

Dinner site _____

Address _____ Room # _____

Contact person _____ Phone _____

Date _____ Time _____ Number of guests _____

Yes/No (RSVP)   name & address: phone:

☐ ☐ _____
☐ ☐ _____
☐ ☐ _____
☐ ☐ _____
☐ ☐ _____
☐ ☐ _____
☐ ☐ _____
☐ ☐ _____
☐ ☐ _____
☐ ☐ _____
☐ ☐ _____
☐ ☐ _____
☐ ☐ _____
☐ ☐ _____
☐ ☐ _____
☐ ☐ _____
☐ ☐ _____
☐ ☐ _____
☐ ☐ _____
☐ ☐ _____
☐ ☐ _____
☐ ☐ _____
☐ ☐ _____
☐ ☐ _____
☐ ☐ _____
☐ ☐ _____
☐ ☐ _____
☐ ☐ _____
☐ ☐ _____

Bachelor's Party Estimate

OPTION #1	*OPTION #2*
Name _____	Name _____
Address _____	Address _____
Contact person _____	Contact person _____
Phone _____	Phone _____
Date _____ Time _____	Date _____ Time _____
Number of guests _____	Number of guests _____

Description of menu choices: cost:

❑ Printed menu (guests can place individual orders)

❑ Special menu:

Description of menu choices: cost:

❑ Printed menu (guests can place individual orders)

❑ Special menu:

Decorations (color of table linens, centerpieces, etc.):

Decorations (color of table linens, centerpieces, etc.):

Suggested seating:

Suggested seating:

Cost of separate room _____

Estimated total cost _____

Gratuity included: Yes ❑   No ❑

Cost of separate room _____

Estimated total cost _____

Gratuity included: Yes ❑   No ❑

Choice: # _____   Date confirmed _____

Total cost _____   Deposit paid _____   Balance due _____   by _____

Scheduled date _____   Time _____

Bachelor's Party Menu

APPETIZER:

SALAD / SOUP:

ENTRÉE:

DESSERT:

BEVERAGE:

Notes:

Rehearsal Dinner Guest List

Dinner site _____

Address _____

Contact person _____ Phone _____

Hosts _____ Phone _____

Date _____ Time _____ Number of guests _____

Yes/No (RSVP)   name & address: phone:

☐ ☐ _____

☐ ☐ _____

☐ ☐ _____

☐ ☐ _____

☐ ☐ _____

☐ ☐ _____

☐ ☐ _____

☐ ☐ _____

☐ ☐ _____

☐ ☐ _____

☐ ☐ _____

☐ ☐ _____

☐ ☐ _____

☐ ☐ _____

☐ ☐ _____

☐ ☐ _____

☐ ☐ _____

☐ ☐ _____

☐ ☐ _____

☐ ☐ _____

☐ ☐ _____

☐ ☐ _____

☐ ☐ _____

☐ ☐ _____

☐ ☐ _____

Rehearsal Dinner Estimate

OPTION #1

Name _____

Address _____

Contact person _____

Phone _____

Date _____ Time _____

  Number of guests _____

Description of menu choices: cost:

Decorations (color of table linens, centerpieces, etc.):

Suggested seating:

Cost of separate room _____

Estimated total cost _____

Gratuity included: Yes ❑   No ❑

OPTION #2

Name _____

Address _____

Contact person _____

Phone _____

Date _____ Time _____

  Number of guests _____

Description of menu choices: cost:

Decorations (color of table linens, centerpieces, etc.):

Suggested seating:

Cost of separate room _____

Estimated total cost _____

Gratuity included: Yes ❑   No ❑

Choice: # _____   Date confirmed _____

Total cost _____   Deposit paid _____   Balance due _____ by _____

Scheduled date _____ Time _____

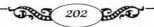

Rehearsal Dinner Menu

APPETIZER:

SALAD / SOUP:

ENTRÉE:

DESSERT:

BEVERAGE:

Notes:

Rehearsal Dinner Program

BEFORE DINNER:

DINNER:

AFTER DINNER:

SPECIAL PRESENTATIONS — *BRIDE & GROOM'S APPRECIATION:*

PERSONAL

Bride's Medical Record

MEDICAL DOCTORS

Specialty _____

Name _____

Address _____

Phone _____

Chart # _____

Specialty _____

Name _____

Address _____

Phone _____

Chart # _____

Specialty _____

Name _____

Address _____

Phone _____

Chart # _____

Specialty _____

Name _____

Address _____

Phone _____

Chart # _____

Specialty _____

Name _____

Address _____

Phone _____

Chart # _____

MEDICAL INSURANCE

Company _____

Policy # _____

DENTAL INSURANCE

Company _____

Policy # _____

PERSONAL HISTORY

Birth weight _____ Length _____

Blood type _____ Rh _____

Present weight _____ height _____

Blood pressure _____ pulse _____

Eyes: Left _____ Right _____

Contacts _____ Glasses _____

Ears: Left _____ Right _____

Have you ever had:

Yes/No

☐ ☐	Allergies	☐ ☐ Kidney trouble
☐ ☐	Anemia	☐ ☐ Measles
☐ ☐	Arthritis	☐ ☐ Menstrual cramps
☐ ☐	Asthma	☐ ☐ Migraine headaches
☐ ☐	Chicken pox	☐ ☐ Mononucleosis
☐ ☐	Concussion	☐ ☐ Mumps
☐ ☐	Diabetes	☐ ☐ Pneumonia
☐ ☐	Eczema	☐ ☐ Polio
☐ ☐	Emotional problems	☐ ☐ Rheumatic fever
☐ ☐	Epilepsy	☐ ☐ Severe sinus trouble
☐ ☐	Frequent fainting	☐ ☐ Chronic sore throats
☐ ☐	Heart murmur	☐ ☐ Tuberculosis
☐ ☐	Hepatitis	☐ ☐ Whooping cough
☐ ☐	Hernia	☐ ☐ Other:
☐ ☐	Hives	_____

Immunizations: date: booster:

DTP (Diphtheria, Tetanus, Pertussis)

_____   _____

TD (Tetanus, Diphtheria, adult type)

_____   _____

Measles   _____   _____

Rubella   _____   _____

Mumps   _____   _____

Polio   _____   _____

Smallpox   _____   _____

Other:

_____   _____

Skin tests:

    Histoplasmosis   _____   _____

    Tuberculosis   _____   _____

    Valley Fever   _____   _____

    Other:

    _____   _____   _____

X-Rays:

date: *hospital:*   *reason:*

_____   _____   _____

_____   _____   _____

_____   _____   _____

_____   _____   _____

Hospitalizations:

date: *hospital:*   *reason:*

_____   _____   _____

_____   _____   _____

_____   _____   _____

_____   _____   _____

Present medical treatment:

_____

_____

_____

_____

_____

Medications you are now taking:

name: *dosage:*   *frequency:*

_____   _____   _____

_____   _____   _____

_____   _____   _____

_____   _____   _____

Allergies:

date: *allergy:*   *reaction:*

_____   _____   _____

_____   _____   _____

_____   _____   _____

_____   _____   _____

Menstrual Period:

Age at first menses _____

Length of monthly cycle _____

Average length of period _____

Type of flow (heavy or light) _____

Other: _____

_____

Other information:

_____

_____

_____

FAMILY HISTORY

Relationship to you:	Serious illnesses experienced (heart disease, hypertension, diabetes, cancer, etc.):	*IF DECEASED:* Age at death:	Cause of death:
Mother			
Father			
Maternal grandmother			
Maternal grandfather			
Paternal grandmother			
Paternal grandfather			
Brothers and sisters:			
Others:			

Groom's Medical Record

Medical Doctors

Specialty _____

Name _____

Address _____

Phone _____

Chart # _____

Specialty _____

Name _____

Address _____

Phone _____

Chart # _____

Specialty _____

Name _____

Address _____

Phone _____

Chart # _____

Specialty _____

Name _____

Address _____

Phone _____

Chart # _____

Specialty _____

Name _____

Address _____

Phone _____

Chart # _____

Medical Insurance

Company _____

Policy # _____

Dental Insurance

Company _____

Policy # _____

Personal History

Birth weight _____ Length _____

Blood type _____ Rh _____

Present weight _____ height _____

Blood pressure _____ pulse _____

Eyes: Left _____ Right _____

Contacts _____ Glasses _____

Ears: Left _____ Right _____

Have you ever had:

Yes/No

❑ ❑	Allergies	❑ ❑ Kidney trouble
❑ ❑	Anemia	❑ ❑ Measles
❑ ❑	Arthritis	❑ ❑ Migraine headaches
❑ ❑	Asthma	❑ ❑ Mononucleosis
❑ ❑	Chicken pox	❑ ❑ Mumps
❑ ❑	Concussion	❑ ❑ Pneumonia
❑ ❑	Diabetes	❑ ❑ Polio
❑ ❑	Eczema	❑ ❑ Rheumatic fever
❑ ❑	Emotional problems	❑ ❑ Severe sinus trouble
❑ ❑	Epilepsy	❑ ❑ Chronic sore throats
❑ ❑	Frequent fainting	❑ ❑ Tuberculosis
❑ ❑	Heart murmur	❑ ❑ Whooping cough
❑ ❑	Hepatitis	❑ ❑ Other:
❑ ❑	Hernia	_____
❑ ❑	Hives	_____

Immunizations: date: booster:

DTP (Diphtheria, Tetanus, Pertussis)

_____ _____

TD (Tetanus, Diphtheria, adult type)

_____ _____

Measles   _____ _____

Rubella   _____ _____

Mumps   _____ _____

Polio   _____ _____

Smallpox   _____ _____

Other:

_____ _____ _____

Skin tests:

Histoplasmosis   _____   _____

Tuberculosis   _____   _____

Valley Fever   _____   _____

Other:

_____   _____

X-Rays:

date:	*hospital:*	*reason:*
_____	_____	_____
_____	_____	_____
_____	_____	_____
_____	_____	_____

Hospitalizations:

date:	*hospital:*	*reason:*
_____	_____	_____
_____	_____	_____
_____	_____	_____

Present medical treatment:

_____

_____

_____

_____

_____

Medications you are now taking:

name:	*dosage:*	*frequency:*
_____	_____	_____
_____	_____	_____
_____	_____	_____
_____	_____	_____

Allergies:

date:	*allergy:*	*reaction:*
_____	_____	_____
_____	_____	_____
_____	_____	_____
_____	_____	_____

Other information:

_____

_____

_____

_____

_____

_____

_____

_____

_____

_____

FAMILY HISTORY

Relationship to you:	Serious illnesses experienced (heart disease, hypertension, diabetes, cancer, etc.):	IF DECEASED: Age at death:	Cause of death:
Mother	_____	____	_____
Father	_____	____	_____
Maternal grandmother	_____	____	_____
Maternal grandfather	_____	____	_____
Paternal grandmother	_____	____	_____
Paternal grandfather	_____	____	_____
Brothers and sisters:			
_____	_____	____	_____
_____	_____	____	_____
_____	_____	____	_____
_____	_____	____	_____
Others:			
_____	_____	____	_____
_____	_____	____	_____

Marriage License Requirements

County Clerk's Office _____

Address _____

Date _____ Time _____ Phone _____

Waiting period required _____

License is valid for _____ days.

Fee _____

Requirements:

❏ Certificate of verification for blood tests

❏ Proof of age or parental consent

❏ Proof of citizenship

❏ Driver's License

❏ Other: _____

Financial/Legal Checklist

Under the appropriate heading, indicate the specific changes to be made:

M = *Marital Status*　　**N** = *Name*　　**A** = *Address*　　**B** = *Beneficiary*

	BRIDE:				GROOM:			
	M	N	A	B	M	N	A	B
Driver's License	❏	❏	❏	❏	❏	❏	❏	❏
Social Security	❏	❏	❏	❏	❏	❏	❏	❏
Professional Records	❏	❏	❏	❏	❏	❏	❏	❏
Employee Records	❏	❏	❏	❏	❏	❏	❏	❏
School Records	❏	❏	❏	❏	❏	❏	❏	❏
Checking Accounts	❏	❏	❏	❏	❏	❏	❏	❏
Saving Accounts	❏	❏	❏	❏	❏	❏	❏	❏
I.R.A. Accounts	❏	❏	❏	❏	❏	❏	❏	❏
Safety Deposit Box	❏	❏	❏	❏	❏	❏	❏	❏
Loans	❏	❏	❏	❏	❏	❏	❏	❏
Stocks and Bonds	❏	❏	❏	❏	❏	❏	❏	❏
Wills	❏	❏	❏	❏	❏	❏	❏	❏
Leases	❏	❏	❏	❏	❏	❏	❏	❏
Property Titles	❏	❏	❏	❏	❏	❏	❏	❏
Insurance	❏	❏	❏	❏	❏	❏	❏	❏
Taxes	❏	❏	❏	❏	❏	❏	❏	❏
Credit Cards	❏	❏	❏	❏	❏	❏	❏	❏
Car Registration	❏	❏	❏	❏	❏	❏	❏	❏
Voter Registration	❏	❏	❏	❏	❏	❏	❏	❏
Passport	❏	❏	❏	❏	❏	❏	❏	❏
Mail Delivery	❏	❏	❏	❏	❏	❏	❏	❏
Business Cards	❏	❏	❏	❏	❏	❏	❏	❏
Magazines/Periodicals	❏	❏	❏	❏	❏	❏	❏	❏
Business Stationery	❏	❏	❏	❏	❏	❏	❏	❏

Your driver's license and/or marriage certificate may be needed to effect these changes.

Newspaper Announcement

Newspaper _____

Address _____

Lifestyle editor _____ Phone _____

To announce: ☐ Wedding ☐ Engagement ☐ Both

Wedding date: _____

Information:	Bride:	Groom:
Names in full	_____	_____
Parents' names	_____	_____
Parents' address	_____	_____
Grandparents'	_____	_____
Schools attended	_____	_____
	_____	_____
Special clubs	_____	_____
	_____	_____
Honoraries	_____	_____
	_____	_____
Military service	_____	_____
Employment	_____	_____

Ceremony site _____

Reception site _____

Names of bridal party members (and their relationship to the bride or groom) _____

_____

_____

Description of bridal gown _____

_____

Description of bridal attendants' dresses _____

_____

Names of: *Officiant* _____ *Soloist(s):* _____

Honeymoon trip _____

Residence after wedding (city and state) _____

Rental Housing Checklist

Name _____

Address _____

Contact person _____ Phone _____

Apartment # _____ Date available _____

Questions to Ask:

1. Is the location convenient to work? ❏ *Yes* ❏ *No*   to school? ❏ *Yes* ❏ *No*
   to church? ❏ *Yes* ❏ *No*   to shopping? ❏ *Yes* ❏ *No*   to entertainment? ❏ *Yes* ❏ *No*

2. Is there a lease? ❏ *Yes* ❏ *No*   If so, for how long? _____
   Can it be broken? ❏ *Yes* ❏ *No*   Sublet? ❏ *Yes* ❏ *No*

3. What are the move-in costs?   First month _____   Last month _____
   Security deposit _____   Cleaning deposit _____   Pet deposit _____

4. How often is the rent raised? _____

5. Can the rent be raised unexpectedly? ❏ *Yes* ❏ *No*

6. Are there laundry facilities? ❏ *Yes* ❏ *No*   Storage facilities? ❏ *Yes* ❏ *No*

7. Is someone readily available for maintenance needs?
   ❏ *Yes* (Name: _____ Phone _____)   ❏ *No*

8. Are there any security provisions? ❏ *Yes* ❏ *No*

9. What is included in the monthly rent?   Water ❏ *Yes* ❏ *No*   Gas ❏ *Yes* ❏ *No*
   Electricity ❏ *Yes* ❏ *No*   Parking ❏ *Yes* (# of spaces: _____) ❏ *No*
   Trash collection ❏ *Yes* ❏ *No*

10. If utility payments are not included in the monthly rent, what are the average monthly
    utility bills?
    Water _____   Gas_____   Electricity_____

What are the heaviest monthly usage payments?

Water _____   Gas_____   Electricity_____

11. Are you allowed to make any improvements — Hang pictures? ❏ *Yes* ❏ *No*
    Wall hangings? ❏ *Yes* ❏ *No*   Shelves? ❏ *Yes* ❏ *No*
    Other: _____? ❏ *Yes* ❏ *No*

12. Are the appliances in good working order? ❏ *Yes* ❏ *No*

13. Are there any leaks in the plumbing? ❏ *Yes* ❏ *No*

14. Is the construction sound? ❏ *Yes* ❏ *No*

15. Can the neighbors be heard through the walls or ceiling? ❏ *Yes* ❏ *No*

16. Is it free of household pests? ❏ *Yes* ❏ *No*

17. Are there any restrictions against children? ❏ *Yes* ❏ *No*

18. Are there any restrictions against pets? ❏ *Yes* ❏ *No*

19. What recreational facilities are offered? _____

    _____

    _____

RENTED: ❏ *Yes* (Move-in date: _____) ❏ *No*

UTILITY SETUP:

Water:	*Turn-on date* _____	*Fee:* _____
Gas:	*Turn-on date* _____	*Fee:* _____
Electricity:	*Turn-on date* _____	*Fee:* _____
Trash collection	*Turn-on date* _____	*Fee:* _____
Phone Service	*Turn-on date* _____	*Fee:* _____
_____	*Turn-on date* _____	*Fee:* _____

Moving Estimate

Your new address _____ Apt. # _____

City _____ State _____ Zip _____

Your new phone _____

TRUCK OR TRAILER RENTAL

Estimate #1

Name _____

Address _____

Contact person _____ Phone _____

Cost: *per hour* _____ *per day* _____ *Deposit* _____

     Payment ❑ *Cash* ❑ *Credit Card* Balance due _____

Pickup: *Date* _____ *Time* _____

     Place _____

Return: *Date* _____ *Time* _____

     Place _____

Confirmed: ❑ *Yes* ❑ *No*

Estimate #2

Name _____

Address _____

Contact person _____ Phone _____

Cost: *per hour* _____ *per day* _____ *Deposit* _____

     Payment ❑ *Cash* ❑ *Credit Card* Balance due _____

Pickup: *Date* _____ *Time* _____

     Place _____

Return: *Date* _____ *Time* _____

     Place _____

Confirmed: ❑ *Yes* ❑ *No*

Estimate #3

Name _____

Address _____

Contact person _____ Phone _____

Cost: *per hour* _____ *per day* _____ *Deposit* _____

     Payment ❑ *Cash* ❑ *Credit Card* Balance due _____

Pickup: *Date* _____ *Time* _____

     Place _____

Return: *Date* _____ *Time* _____

     Place _____

Confirmed: ❑ *Yes* ❑ *No*

PROFESSIONAL MOVERS

Estimate #1

Name _____

Address _____

Contact person _____ Phone _____

Cost, per estimated weight _____ *Deposit* _____

    Payment ❐ *Cash* ❐ *Credit Card* Balance due _____

Insurance coverage _____

Dates: *Packing* _____ *Loading* _____ *Delivery* _____

Confirmed: ❐ *Yes* ❐ *No*

Driver of truck _____ Phone _____

Estimate #2

Name _____

Address _____

Contact person _____ Phone _____

Cost, per estimated weight _____ *Deposit* _____

    Payment ❐ *Cash* ❐ *Credit Card* Balance due _____

Insurance coverage _____

Dates: *Packing* _____ *Loading* _____ *Delivery* _____

Confirmed: ❐ *Yes* ❐ *No*

Driver of truck _____ Phone _____

Estimate #3

Name _____

Address _____

Contact person _____ Phone _____

Cost, per estimated weight _____ *Deposit* _____

    Payment ❐ *Cash* ❐ *Credit Card* Balance due _____

Insurance coverage _____

Dates: *Packing* _____ *Loading* _____ *Delivery* _____

Confirmed: ❐ *Yes* ❐ *No*

Driver of truck _____ Phone _____

Notes:

Home Furnishings Purchase Plan

Style _____

Colors _____

Room: *Item:*   *Cost:*

LIVING

_____   _____

_____   _____

_____   _____

_____   _____

_____   _____

_____   _____

_____   _____

_____   _____

_____   _____

_____   _____

_____   _____

_____   _____

_____   _____

_____   _____

_____   _____

_____   _____

DINING ROOM

_____   _____

_____   _____

_____   _____

_____   _____

_____   _____

BEDROOM

_____   _____

_____   _____

_____   _____

_____   _____

_____   _____

_____   _____

_____   _____

BEDROOM/STUDY _____ _____

_____ _____

_____ _____

_____ _____

_____ _____

KITCHEN _____ _____

_____ _____

_____ _____

_____ _____

_____ _____

_____ _____

_____ _____

BATHROOM _____ _____

_____ _____

_____ _____

_____ _____

BATHROOM _____ _____

_____ _____

_____ _____

_____ _____

_____ _____

OTHER _____ _____

_____ _____

_____ _____

_____ _____

_____ _____

_____ _____

_____ _____

_____ _____

Keep or Toss

Room	Item:	Bride's	Groom's	Keep	Toss
LIVING	_____	☐	☐	☐	☐
	_____	☐	☐	☐	☐
	_____	☐	☐	☐	☐
	_____	☐	☐	☐	☐
	_____	☐	☐	☐	☐
	_____	☐	☐	☐	☐
	_____	☐	☐	☐	☐
	_____	☐	☐	☐	☐
DINING ROOM	_____	☐	☐	☐	☐
	_____	☐	☐	☐	☐
	_____	☐	☐	☐	☐
BEDROOMS	_____	☐	☐	☐	☐
	_____	☐	☐	☐	☐
	_____	☐	☐	☐	☐
	_____	☐	☐	☐	☐
	_____	☐	☐	☐	☐
	_____	☐	☐	☐	☐
	_____	☐	☐	☐	☐
	_____	☐	☐	☐	☐
	_____	☐	☐	☐	☐
	_____	☐	☐	☐	☐
	_____	☐	☐	☐	☐
KITCHEN	_____	☐	☐	☐	☐
	_____	☐	☐	☐	☐
	_____	☐	☐	☐	☐
	_____	☐	☐	☐	☐
	_____	☐	☐	☐	☐
BATHROOM	_____	☐	☐	☐	☐
	_____	☐	☐	☐	☐
	_____	☐	☐	☐	☐
	_____	☐	☐	☐	☐
OTHER	_____	☐	☐	☐	☐
	_____	☐	☐	☐	☐
	_____	☐	☐	☐	☐
	_____	☐	☐	☐	☐
	_____	☐	☐	☐	☐

WEDDING HOW-TO'S

Wedding How-To's

BUDGET

- When forming your budget, decide first how much to spend for the wedding, then how the expenses will be divided.

- Paying for wedding expenses can be handled in a variety of ways. The responsibility can be

  (a) assumed primarily by the bride's parents,
  (b) assumed primarily by the groom's parents,
  (c) shared equally by both sets of parents,
  (d) shared by both families together with the bride and groom, or
  (e) assumed entirely by the bride and groom themselves.

- Final responsibility for wedding costs has been stated by tradition, but there is really no right or wrong way to handle the costs. It's a matter of choice.

- It's appropriate to discuss the budget with both sets of parents, especially when they bear some or all of the financial responsibility. Be sure everyone involved agrees on the budget.

- A spirit of compromise should lessen the possibility of hurt feelings as your families agree together on the budget.

- When setting your budget priorities, compromise on quantity, not quality.

- Your budget should be flexible enough so that unexpected costs will not ruin it.

- The amount of your budget will not necessarily determine the style of your wedding; you can have a formal wedding and reception on a limited budget with careful planning and a smaller guest list.

- You can usually expect to pay from ten to fifty percent as a deposit for services. This deposit often is required in cash.

- Prioritize the following aspects of a wedding according to what you wish to emphasize, and what is most important to you:

  __ Number of guests to be invited
  __ Wedding site (church, synagogue, hotel, club, at home)
  __ Reception location (church hall, hotel, club, at home)
  __ Bridal attire (what you will wear)
  __ Food and beverages (what kind, and how will it be served)
  __ Flowers (what kind and how many)
  __ Photographs (to have a professional photographer or a friend take pictures)
  __ Music (soloists, live music or taped, dancing or not)
  __ Transportation (a limousine, luxury rental car, friend's new car, or family car)

SETTING THE STYLE, DATE, TIME, AND LOCATION

- Before many decisions can be made, you and your fiancé will need to decide if the wedding will be formal or informal, large or small—and when and where it will take place.

- The style of the ceremony should be carried over to the reception.

- When regional or ethnic customs need to be observed, you may flavor your wedding by using one or two songs, by integrating colors in decorations or flowers, or by serving ethnic dishes compatible with other foods chosen for your reception.

- A formal wedding usually has these characteristics:
  — The bride wears a long, white or ivory gown with a chapel train and veil.
  — The bridesmaids wear floor-length gowns.
  — The groom and his attendants wear formal attire.
  — The bride's attendants include a maid or matron of honor, five to ten bridesmaids, and a flower girl.
  — The groom's attendants include a best man, one usher for every fifty guests (or one usher for each bridesmaid), and a ring bearer.

— The ceremony takes place at a church, synagogue, large home, or garden.

— The invitations and announcements are engraved.

- A semiformal wedding usually has these characteristics:
  — The bride wears a long, white or ivory gown with a short train and veil.
  — The bridesmaids wear floor-length gowns or a current style of dress.
  — The groom and his attendants wear tuxedos.
  — The bride's attendants include a maid or matron of honor, and three to seven bridesmaids; a flower girl is optional.
  — The groom's attendants include a best man, and one usher for every 50 guests (or one for each bridesmaid); a ring bearer is optional.
  — The ceremony takes place at a church, synagogue, chapel, home, garden, or hotel.
  — The invitations and announcements are engraved or thermographed.

- An informal wedding usually has these characteristics:
  — The bride wears a white or pastel dress or suit.
  — The bridesmaid wears a dress complementary to the bride's dress.
  — The groom and his attendant wear dark business suits.
  — The bride's attendant is a maid or matron of honor.
  — The groom's attendant is a best man (an usher is selected, if needed to seat guests).
  — The ceremony usually takes place at a chapel, garden, home, or hotel.
  — The invitations are handwritten or verbal.

- The time of your wedding should be compatible with the weather in your area. If your wedding is during the summer or in a warm area of the country, it may be wise to schedule the wedding for early in the morning or in the evening. Likewise, weddings in cold, winter climates would be better scheduled at midday or early afternoon.

- Have a few dates in mind before meeting with your officiant to select a wedding date.

- Verify these dates with possible reception sites before making your final choice.

- Second-time brides are freer today to choose the style of wedding and reception they desire, but in no way should a second wedding be seen as competing with the first.

- If this is a second marriage and you are considering a religious ceremony, you may need to inquire around for a church and a clergy member willing to perform the wedding service.

- Unless military regulations stipulate otherwise, all officers have a choice whether to have a military wedding or civilian wedding.

- Military weddings usually are held in a church or chapel. Military weddings are formal, with military personnel in full-dress uniform, including medals. Civilian members of the wedding party dress in complementary formal attire.

- In a military wedding, the bridal couple usually walks through an arch of swords/sabers in the recessional—as they exit the building. Other aspects of a military wedding are essentially the same as in any other wedding.

- If you have questions regarding military traditions to be followed, or any other aspect of a military wedding, consult with an Officer of Protocol or Commanding Officer.

GUEST LIST

- The size of your guest list will be determined by your budget and by the size of your ceremony and reception sites.

- The list may be divided with one-half of the guests for each family or it can be divided into thirds—one-third for each family and one-third for the bridal couple.

- Generally only sixty-five to eighty-five percent of the invited people attend. The number attending depends on several factors: the time of day, time of year, day of the week, and the social or professional prominence of the bridal couple and their parents.

- State a limit to each family before they begin compiling their lists. It's much easier to add names after the list has been formed, than to have to delete names.

- Set a deadline with your families for giving you the names on their lists.

- Unless it causes a family problem, invite only those you truly want to share your day. This should not be a time for repaying professional or social debts.

- You will need complete names and addresses, including names of any children to be invited.

- Phone numbers will be greatly appreciated if you need to contact any late respondents.

- Knowing the number of guests actually planning to attend is important—it will determine the cost of your reception. The caterer will take your word for the number of guests and charge you accordingly.

- If some have failed to reply by a week before the wedding and you are uncertain of their plans, call them for a response. Your mother, your future mother-in-law, or friends can help you with the calling.

- Everyone invited to the wedding ceremony should also be invited to the reception, but you may invite more people to the reception than to the ceremony.

- Announcement cards can be sent to those who cannot attend, whether they live too far away, or the wedding and reception sites are too small to accommodate them.

GIFT REGISTRY

- You and your fiancé should register your gift preferences at department and specialty stores as soon as your engagement is announced.

- By registering early, you provide a convenient way for your family and friends to select gifts for your showers and wedding.

- If your fiancé and his family are from another city, consider registering there also.

- Once you register, it is your responsibility to keep the registry current by informing the store of gifts received from other sources.

- You can eliminate confusion and save time by having an idea of those things you would like to receive as gifts before meeting with the bridal registrar.

- When your wedding gifts begin arriving,
    - Open each gift immediately and carefully.
    - Record the gift as soon as possible or tape the card to the gift until you do.
    - If the gift arrives marred or broken, immediately call or write the store. If the giver wrapped and mailed the gift without insuring it, thank the person for it but do not mention the damage.

- It's better not to return or exchange anything before the wedding, especially if you display your gifts—some may want to see their gift.

- If you risk offending someone, it's better to keep whatever that person sent—unless you have received an exact duplicate, in which case you may safely exchange one of the gifts.

- If you choose to display your gifts, place the gifts of the same type together—all silver, all china, all linen—on tables covered with floor-length white cloths.

- To save space, you can display only one place setting of your silver, crystal, and china.

- Accompanying cards may or may not be placed with the gifts.

- For gifts of money you may receive, it is considered inappropriate to indicate the amount enclosed. You can either overlap the edges of the checks and gift certificates so only the names are visible, or recognize the gift by writing the name of the sender on a small white card, with the notation: "Gift of money from…" or "Check from…" or "Gift certificate from…"

- Gifts received at the wedding and reception are usually left unopened. You may open the gifts after the reception at the home of the bride's parents, or when you return home from your honeymoon with a small gathering of family and close friends.

- You might consider insuring your gifts with a short-term policy to cover the period of time when the gifts begin arriving until you obtain household insurance after your marriage. As a further precaution, you may want to have someone in your home during the wedding/reception festivities to protect the gifts. Usually, just having someone there is all that's needed to forestall any thievery.

WEDDING COORDINATOR

- Wedding coordinators are available to orchestrate the varied details associated with a successful wedding and reception.

- The cost of a coordinator varies greatly and depends largely on the amount of time spent on your wedding.

- By using the COMPLETE WEDDING PLANNER you can handle the wedding preliminaries yourself, but it is still wise to have a coordinator to help keep your wedding day organized.

- A coordinator can smooth the wedding day's progression, and so help provide the relaxed and enjoyable day you desire.

- A relative or close friend may be able to do the wedding day coordinating for you.

- Many churches have wedding hostesses who know about church facilities and policies.

- During the planning process, have the person designated to coordinate your wedding day use the Wedding and Rehearsal Information Lists on pages 112 to 116, and perhaps the Reception Organizer on page 148.

- Additional tips for the Wedding Coordinator:
  - Acquaint yourself with the ceremony site.
  - Discuss with the bride and groom any wedding policies of the ceremony site.

— Be available to assist the bride and groom by answering questions, offering suggestions, and having names of available resources for services.
— Be as organized as possible, with all wedding day information in one place.
— As you assist the bridal couple in planning their big day, know the following:
  (1) Who will be giving the bride away?
  (2) Will the bridal couple be having a double-ring ceremony? Who will have the rings?
  (3) Will the officiant provide the wording for the vows, or will the bride and groom be writing their own?
  (4) Will communion (the Eucharist) be observed? Who will participate?
  (5) Will the lighting of the Unity Candle be included?
  (6) What other special observance will be a part of the ceremony?
  (7) Who will have the marriage license? When and where will it be signed?
  (8) Will the bridal couple have a receiving line? If so, where? Who will be involved?
  (9) Who will be responsible for any audio and/or video tapes of the ceremony? Of the reception?
  (10) Who will be responsible for cleaning out the bride's dressing room? The groom's dressing room?
  (11) If a preceremony buffet is to be served at the ceremony site, who will be responsible for set-up? Serving? Clean-up?
  (12) Where will the reception be? How soon will it follow the ceremony?
  (13) Who will be responsible for taking the Guest Book to the reception? To whose home afterward?
  (14) Who will be responsible for transporting the gifts from the ceremony site? From the reception site? To whose house?
— Confirm your arrival time for both the rehearsal and ceremony with the custodian of the facility (or other designated person). This time should be early enough to accomplish any necessary advance preparations—unlocking doors, setting up equipment and accessories, and turning on lights, heating or air conditioning, etc.
— Confirm with the bride the arrival times of the bridal party, the bride's and groom's parents, their grandparents, special others, the officiant(s),

musicians, florist, photographer, etc. On the wedding day, be available to greet each one, to answer any questions, and to give any last-minute instructions.

— At the rehearsal, review the wedding day arrival times with the participants—who's to be where and when—and indicate to them the importance of being on time.

— If possible, have all the decisions concerning the ceremony made prior to the rehearsal. If any unexpected changes do occur, they should quickly be addressed to the bride.

— Make certain that each of the ushers receives a list of his responsibilities at the ceremony site ("Responsibilities of the Ushers," p. 231). Also, take time at the rehearsal to demonstrate exactly how they are to usher, and allow them to practice. *Don't assume* they already know what to do.

— As the wedding coordinator you will probably be responsible for collecting any fees or honorariums from the bride and groom. These may be disbursed either at the rehearsal, before the ceremony, or after the reception, as previously indicated by the recipients.

— Determine how many seats (number of pews) need to be reserved for special seating, and who will be sitting where.

— Before the florist leaves the premises on the wedding day, count the bouquets, boutonnieres and corsages to make certain all the needed flowers are there.

— Know when the photographer will be taking pictures.

— When an aisle runner is being used, make certain it has been firmly pinned in place. Pin the runner again once it has been pulled up the aisle.

— If the facility is not equipped with a signaling system, a small flashlight may be used to cue the musicians for the start of the processional and for any other special timing needs.

— Be prepared for possible emergencies with a special bag that includes these items: aspirin, breath mints, clear nail polish, emery boards, facial tissues, hair spray, iron, sanitary pads, scissors, sewing kit, spot remover, static spray, and straight and safety pins.

— Another bag may contain:
  (1) Corsage pins—for flowers, and for pinning the aisle runner in place.
  (2) Flashlight—for signaling musicians.

(3) Hair dryer—for hair needs and candlewax removal.

(4) Masking tape—for marking the positions of the bridal party.

(5) Matches or lighter—for lighting candles or candle-lighters.

(6) Measuring tape—for locating positions of the bridal party.

(7) Scotch tape—for taping gift cards to packages.

(8) Black ink writing pens—for signing the marriage license.

BRIDAL ATTIRE

• It usually takes twelve to sixteen weeks from the time the manufacturer cuts the fabric until the gown is delivered to the store.

• Give the manufacturer a target date which allows ample time for alterations and formal photographs before your wedding day.

• If you need extra fabric to cover a headpiece, for special alterations, or to dress a miniature replica of the bride, it should be ordered at the same time as your gown.

• Generally, once an order has been placed the gown must be purchased, even if your circumstances change.

• Many stores require a fifty-percent deposit when you order your gown.

• It's best to select the headpiece and veil when you select your gown. (If you must buy at another time, try the veil on with the same model of gown or one of similar styling to see how it will look.) Select a headpiece that complements both your gown and your hairstyle.

• Consider ordering your headpiece with a detachable veil. The veil can be removed for the reception, thereby eliminating having your headpiece tugged and pulled by well-wishers.

• When gloves are worn, the underseam of the glove's ring finger is ripped so that the ring may be placed on your finger.

- Wear your engagement ring on the ring finger of your right hand during the ceremony. Then, place it in front of your wedding ring once the ceremony is over.

- Any other jewelry should be simple so as not to detract from the overall effect you desire.

- White satin, lace, or fine leather shoes are usually worn. Heel height is a matter of choice.

- Because of the length of time you'll need to be wearing your shoes, it's important to carefully break them in before the wedding day.

- Your wedding lingerie will be determined by the style of gown you select. The bridal sales-person should be able to advise you in your choice.

- Don't plan your final fitting too early. With all your involvement in pre-wedding activi-ties, you may find yourself gaining or losing weight.

- For the fittings, wear the lingerie and shoes you'll be wearing for your wedding.

- If this is your second marriage, there are many beautiful gowns available from tea length to the more traditional wedding gown style. You may choose white, but a light pastel shade such as iced pink or iced blue is preferred by many.

- It is customary for the bride or her mother to make suggestions to the groom's mother about her outfit—the length of dress, length of sleeves, color, and style.

- The mothers' dresses should be similar in style, and consistent with the style of the wedding (floor-length for formal, floor-length or tea-length for semiformal, street-length dress or suit for informal). Colors should complement both the bride's color and each other.

- Due to the emphasis placed on the bride, many mothers wait too late to order a dress, and often end up with make-do selections. This is both unnecessary and regrettable, because the mothers are in the spotlight too.

- A bride who is in the military may choose to wear either her dress uniform or a traditional wedding gown. Most of these brides choose to wear a gown.

BRIDAL ATTENDANTS

- Bridal attendants are chosen from your close friends and family members, including any sisters of the groom.

- You may elect to have both a maid and matron of honor, but you will have to designate which one will attend you at the altar—to hold your bouquet and the groom's ring, and to help with your veil and train.

- If you decide to have a flower girl, the best ages are between four and nine. If any are younger than this, be prepared for the unex-pected to happen, because a younger child's actions can be very unpredictable. If you decide to have children in your wedding party who are under four years of age, you may want to have them seated with their parents once the officiant has asked, "Who gives this woman?" They can later follow the bride and groom back up the aisle during the recessional.

- Junior bridesmaids are generally between the ages of ten and sixteen.

- Bridesmaids, then, are sixteen years of age and older.

- Special others can be included by having them preside over the Guest Book and gift tables, distributing rice, serving the cake and punch, entertaining the guests, providing housing and transportation, or covering various details for you.

- When a remarriage occurs and there are children involved (yours, the groom's, or both), give them all honored positions in the day's activities.

- If they are willing, you could have the children stand with you at the altar. Teenagers or adult children may serve as your honor attendants. Younger children could serve as flower girls or ring bearers. They could also escort you down the aisle. They can further participate in the ceremony by reading a special poem, Scripture, or prayer.

- When your plans involve children from former marriages, you may need to check with the other parent before involving them in your wedding activities.

- When selecting the bridal attendants' dresses and accessories, consider their financial status and if the dress will be useful to them afterward.

- If possible, have a couple of your attendants try on two or three different styles of dresses. It is nice to ask them for their opinion, but the final choice is yours.

- Order the dresses at the same time to avoid any variations in color and design.

- The flower girl's dress may be the same style as the bridesmaids', or a dress of complementary style and color. It may also be shorter in length for ease of movement.

- In some ceremony locations, your attendants may be required to have their heads covered; otherwise, the choice is yours.

- Their shoes should be of the same style, but the height of the heels may vary according to the girls' heights and their individual need for comfort.

- If the attendants' shoes are being dyed to match, have them done at the same place and time to ensure color conformity.

- Select a complementary shade of hosiery and purchase two pairs for each attendant (an extra pair for emergencies).

- Any jewelry that is worn should be small and dainty, of the same or similar style.

- Any gloves that are worn should be of the same style and length.

- Use fabric swatches to coordinate colors of lipstick and nail polish for the attendants.

- For dresses other than floor length, it's better to have the hems measured down from the knee of each bridesmaid rather than the same distance up from the floor. Just as the head heights of the girls vary, so should their hem lengths. The overall appearance of each girl in her dress is far more important than all dresses being the same distance from the floor.

- If possible, have everyone dress at the ceremony site to avoid wrinkling dresses in transit.

- Bridal attendants should be invited to all parties given for the bride or the bride and groom, including the rehearsal dinner. The only exceptions may be special group or office parties.

- The flower girl is not usually invited to the bridal parties, but her mother is. Her parents may be invited to any parties given for both the bride and groom, and her father to any bachelor parties. Invite the flower girl to the rehearsal dinner. If it's the night before the wedding, her parents may decide to have her forego the dinner so she'll be rested for the wedding day.

- Your gifts to the bridesmaids are usually alike, but the honor attendant's gift may vary from the others in style and design.

- The flower girl may receive a different type of gift than the other attendants.

- Possible gift choices: for the bridesmaids—keepsake boxes, books, compacts, cosmetic bags, crystal, evening bags, engraved pen and pencil sets, jewelry, jewelry cases, perfume, photo albums, picture frames, porcelain, or stationery; and for the flower girl—charm bracelet, china doll, jewelry box, piggy bank, or stuffed animal.

RESPONSIBILITIES OF THE MAID/MATRON OF HONOR:

- Before the wedding, she
  - may help you in such ways as addressing invitations and entertaining out-of-town guests.
  - is responsible for making and keeping any alteration appointments.
  - should wear the lingerie and shoes she will be wearing for the wedding when she goes for fittings, to ensure a more perfect fit.
  - must attend the wedding rehearsal.

— arrives early at a designated place to help you dress.

- During the ceremony, she

  — precedes you and your father in the processional.
  — arranges your train at the altar.
  — holds the bridal bouquet at the required time.
  — may be in charge of the groom's ring in a double-ring ceremony until it is needed.
  — adjusts your veil and again arranges your train for the recessional.
  — usually walks with the best man in the recessional.
  — signs the marriage license.

- At the reception, she

  — stands next to the groom in the receiving line.
  — sits on the groom's left during a sit-down meal.
  — helps you change into you going-away clothes.
  — informs the parents when the bridal couple is ready to leave.

RESPONSIBILITIES OF THE BRIDESMAIDS:

- Before the wedding, they

  — may help you address invitations and assist with any errands.
  — are responsible for individually making and keeping their alteration appointments.
  — should wear the lingerie and shoes they will be wearing for the wedding when they go for fittings, to ensure a more perfect fit.
  — must attend the wedding rehearsal.

- During the ceremony, they

  — either walk alone or in pairs in the processional.
  — are usually escorted by the ushers in the recessional. When there are more bridesmaids than ushers, the extras can walk alone or in pairs.

- At the reception, they

  — stand in the receiving line.
  — sit at either the Bride's Table or a special attendants' table during a sit-down or buffet dinner, alternating positions about the table with the ushers.
  — mingle with the guests, helping the hosts entertain.

RESPONSIBILITIES OF THE FLOWER GIRL:

- Before the wedding, she

  — is responsible for making and keeping her alteration appointments.

— should wear the lingerie and shoes she will be wearing for the wedding when she goes for fittings, to ensure a more perfect fit.
— must attend the wedding rehearsal.
— may attend the rehearsal dinner along with her parents.

- During the ceremony, she

  — walks directly in front of you and your father in the processional.
  — may stand with the bridal party at the altar or be seated with her parents during the ceremony.
  — may follow directly behind the bride and groom in the recessional.

- At the reception, she

  — does not stand in the receiving line.
  — either remains with her parents or sits at a special table for children under adult supervision.

GROOM'S ATTENDANTS

- The best man is usually the groom's most trustworthy and faithful friend or relative.

- The ushers may be the groom's brothers, cousins, or best friends, or brothers and close relatives of the bride.

- The ring bearer, a young boy between the ages of four and nine (using anyone younger than four is not recommended, no matter how cute he is), is usually a relative of the bride or groom or the child of a dear friend.

- When all the groom's attendants live in the same town, they should all visit the same store to be measured and fitted for their formal attire. If someone lives out of town, he should be measured in the shop of his choice. He can then mail his correct measurements to the bride or groom, who will reserve formal wear and accessories for the final fitting.

- In a military wedding, the groom, as a member of the armed forces, chooses attendants from among his military friends. His best man, though, may be civilian.

- The arch of swords (Navy) and sabers (Army) is reserved only for officers. There should be a minimum of four sword/saber bearers, but it is better to have six or eight. The swords or sabers are not worn by the military ushers while seating guests, but are put on just prior to the processional.

- The groom's attendants are invited to attend all parties given for the bridal couple except possibly office or special group parties.

- They are also invited to all bachelor parties.

- You may invite the ring bearer to attend parties for the bride and groom, but because of his age his parents may have him forego attending. But do invite his parents to attend. Also invite his mother to attend any bridal showers, and his father to attend any bachelor parties.

- The ushers' gifts should all be alike.

- The best man's gift may vary from the ushers' in style and design.

- A different kind of gift may be given to the ring bearer, one appropriate for his age.

- Possible gift choices: for the best man and ushers—belt buckles, billfolds, business card cases, collar stay collections, date books, desk accessories, hardbound books, jewelry cases, key rings, money clips, paperweights, pen and pencil sets, pewter mugs, picture frames, record albums/tapes, sports tickets, stationery, or travel clocks; and for the ring bearer—a board game, basketball, model airplane, monogrammed mug, or soccer ball.

RESPONSIBILITIES OF THE BEST MAN:

- Before the wedding, he
  - pays for his own attire—purchased or rented.
  - is responsible for making and keeping appointments for fittings.
  - tries on formal attire before the wedding, preferably before leaving the store in case any sizes need to be exchanged.
  - may confirm the honeymoon travel arrangements for the groom.
  - hosts the bachelor party if other arrangements have not been made.
  - helps the bride's mother with last-minute details.
  - attends the rehearsal and rehearsal dinner.
  - may help the groom finish packing.

  - may provide transportation to the ceremony site for the groom.
  - obtains the marriage license from the groom and holds it until the appropriate time for signing.
  - is in charge of the officiant's fee. May give the envelope to the officiant before the ceremony.
  - may also supervise the ushers, making sure they are thoroughly briefed, dressed, and at the ceremony site at the appropriate time.

- During the ceremony, he
  - is not part of the processional but enters with the groom, standing behind the groom and slightly to the left.
  - may hold the wedding ring until the officiant asks for it.
  - walks with the maid/matron of honor in the recessional.

- After the ceremony, he
  - immediately serves as one of the witnesses in signing the marriage license.
  - helps the bride and groom into their car or other form of transportation if the reception is being held at another location.
  - may drive the bride and groom to the reception.
  - usually drives the maid of honor and other bridesmaids to the reception.

- At the reception, he
  - does not stand in the receiving line unless he is also the father of the groom.
  - sits to the bride's right at a seated reception.
  - proposes the first toast to the new couple for health, happiness, and prosperity.
  - may read aloud any congratulatory telegrams.
  - acts as the master-of-ceremonies, introducing any speakers, the cake-cutting ceremony, the tossing of the bouquet and garter, etc.
  - mingles with guests.
  - helps the groom into his going-away clothes at the end of the reception.
  - checks that all luggage is in the car.
  - leads the couple through the waiting guests to the exit and escorts them to their car.
  - may drive them to the hotel or airport.

- After the reception, he
  - promptly returns both his and the groom's rented formal wear to the appropriate location.
  - may help in entertaining out-of-town guests.

RESPONSIBILITIES OF THE USHERS:

- Before the wedding, they
  - pay for their own wedding attire—purchased or rented.
  - are responsible for making and keeping appointments for fittings.
  - try on formal attire before the wedding, preferably before leaving the store in case any sizes need to be exchanged.
  - attend the rehearsal and rehearsal dinner.

- At the ceremony site, they
  - arrive at the appointed time.
  - assemble to the left of the entrance thirty to forty-five minutes before the ceremony begins.
  - greet arrivals and encourage them to sign the Guest Book, and then be seated.
  - offer their right arms to the women guests. Usher as follows:
    Couple—Take woman's arm, and man follows.
    Family—Take wife's arm; husband and family follow.
    Two girls—Take one on each arm.
    Two women—Escort the elder; the younger woman follows.
    Men—Simply accompany men to their seats unless they need assistance.
    Remain standing by the pew until the person is seated.
  - when the guests do not present a pew card, ask if they are friends of the bride or groom.
  - seat the guests accordingly—the bride's guests on the left, the groom's on the right. (In Jewish weddings, the seating is reversed.) In a military wedding, guests who are officers are seated according to rank.
  - show late-arriving guests to seats on the side with more room.

- During the ceremony, they
  - may participate in the processional (but often enter with the groom).
  - generally escort the bridesmaids in the recessional.

- After the ceremony, they
  - may return to usher out the guests.
  - if asked, should be able to direct guests to restroom and phone facilities, and to the reception site.
  - make certain the ceremony site is cleared of all the wedding party's belongings.

- At the reception, they
  - do not stand in the receiving line.
  - sit at either the Bride's Table or another table designated for the attendants, alternating about the table with the bridesmaids.
  - mingle with guests.

- After the reception, they
  - promptly return any rented formal wear to the appropriate location.

- Throughout the wedding and reception, they are to remain available to assist in whatever capacity asked by the best man or head usher.

RESPONSIBILITIES OF THE HEAD USHER:

(This list is in addition to the previously stated attendant's responsibilities for the position of usher.)

- The head usher is in charge of the other ushers.

- He assures their prompt arrival at the ceremony site for the rehearsal and wedding.

- When the ushers have not been designated by the bride and groom to perform special duties, the head usher appoints them at the rehearsal.

- He informs the ushers of any special seating arrangements.

- He makes certain the groom and the best man have received their boutonnieres.

- He supervises the seating, maintaining a balance of guests on both sides, particularly during the last fifteen minutes prior to the ceremony.

- If one of the ushers is a brother of the bride or groom, he may be designated to escort his own mother. Otherwise, the head usher assumes this honor.

RESPONSIBILITIES OF THE RING BEARER:

- Before the wedding, he
  - pays for his own attire—purchased or rented.
  - is responsible for making and keeping appointments for fittings.
  - tries on formal attire before the wedding, preferably before leaving the store in case any sizes need to be exchanged.

— attends the rehearsal.

— may attend the rehearsal dinner along with his parents.

- During the ceremony, he

  — carries a pillow that may or may not have the official rings attached.

  — either precedes or walks with the flower girl directly in front of you and your father in the processional.

  — may then, if very young, be seated with his parents.

  — if remaining with the bridal party, follows directly behind the bride and groom in the recessional along with the flower girl.

- At the reception, he

  — does not stand in the receiving line.

  — either remains with his parents or sits at a special table for children under adult supervision.

- After the reception, he

  — is responsible for promptly returning any rented formal wear to the appropriate location.

THE CEREMONY

- The ceremony is the most important part of your wedding day.

- It is the position of the officiant (clergy, rabbi, or judge) that determines if the wedding is religious or civil.

- The order of the ceremony is often influenced by the customs and traditions of the area in which you live.

RELIGIOUS CEREMONIES:

- A religious ceremony does not necessarily take place in a church or synagogue. Most officiants will perform a religious ceremony in the location of your choice.

- Use the ceremonial formats appropriate to your faith and to the religious traditions observed at your ceremony site.

CIVIL CEREMONIES:

- Most judges and justices are willing to perform the ceremony at the site of your choice if prior arrangements are made.

- The civil ceremony can be enhanced with music, decorations, and flowers.

THE PRELUDE:

- The organist or other instrumentalist could begin playing thirty minutes before the start of the ceremony.

- The candlelighting can take place anytime before the honor seating occurs.

- The bride's guests sit on the left side and the groom's guests sit on the right side. (In Jewish weddings, the seating is reversed.)

- If more guests have been seated on one side, the ushers should even out the seating during the last fifteen minutes prior to the ceremony.

- If parents are divorced, the father and mother can both sit on the front row if they are agreeable. If the father has remarried, he sits in the third row with his new wife; the mother still sits on the first row.

- The special (honor) seating is usually reserved only for parents and grandparents, but others who have been special to you may be included.

- The honor seating takes place just prior to the start of the ceremony in the order as follows: special guests, the groom's grandparents, the bride's grandparents, the groom's parents, the bride's mother.

- The bride's and groom's mothers may be escorted by specially appointed ushers, by their son or sons (one son on each arm), or by the groom himself.

- After the bride's mother is seated, aisle ribbons, if used, are drawn up the center aisle and across the end pews of the unreserved seating area.

- The two ushers who draw the aisle ribbons then unroll the aisle runner up the aisle from the foot of the wedding altar.

- The aisle ribbons and runner could already be in place before the guests arrive. The guests would then be escorted down the outer aisles to their seats.

THE PROCESSIONAL:

- The organist begins playing the selected music for the processional.

- Today's brides generally ask those participating in the processional to start off on the same foot, to walk with a slow, natural step, and to maintain a distance of eight to ten feet from the attendant who precedes them down the aisle.

- When you are about to enter, the organist increases the volume of the music being played. At this time, the organist could also change to another selection of music.

- Your mother may rise as you enter, a cue for all others to rise and remain standing until seated by the officiant.

- You may be escorted by your father, another close male relative, or a special friend.

- You may wait until the others have reached the altar before making your entrance, or you can double the distance between you and the preceding attendant before starting down the aisle.

- The organist stops playing when you reach the altar.

- For Jewish weddings—refer to the diagrams on page 118. The order of the processional and recessional and the positions under the chuppah are set by local custom.

THE CEREMONY:

- Throughout the ceremony the bride and groom follow the leading of the officiant.

- The custom of giving away the bride is optional. In some services, after escorting the bride to the altar, the father simply takes his seat alongside his wife. In others, the officiant asks, "Who gives this woman…?" The father may respond, "I do," or "Her mother and I do," or "We do."

- You relinquish your father's arm, give your bouquet to your maid of honor, and give your right arm to the groom.

- The wedding rings may be attached to the ring bearer's pillow by tying them with ribbon bows or by securing them with light stitches. It's better, however, for the best man or maid of honor to hold the rings until the appropriate time.

- The groom assists you as you move about the altar area—up and down any steps, kneeling and rising.

- Your maid of honor rearranges your train when necessary.

- After the pronouncement and blessing, the officiant may introduce the newly married couple to the wedding guests as Mr. and Mrs. _____.

- The following list is an example of the ceremony order. (This example is given only as a guide for planning; the officiant or his or her representative has the final word on the order to be observed, including any customs and traditions.)
  — Prelude
  — Solo (special music)
  — Processional
  — Presentation of the Bride
  — Special music
  — Statement about marriage by the officiant
  — Declaration of Consent
  — Exchange of Vows
  — Exchange of Rings
  — Special music
  — Pronouncement and Declaration
  — Benediction and Blessing
  — Kiss
  — Presentation of the Bride and Groom
  — Recessional
  — Postlude

- As a token of your love and appreciation, you and your groom may elect to give your mothers roses at the start or close of the ceremony. The roses can be given in two ways:
  — You and your groom can each give a rose to your respective mothers.

— You can give a rose to your groom's mother, and your groom can give one to your mother.

- You may decide to have a Unity Candle as part of the service.
  — The Unity Candle or Christ Candle is a symbol of the bride and groom—once separate entities, now coming together as one in Christ.
  — The candelabra holds three candles. The outer two may be lit by the ushers during the candlelighting. At the designated time in the ceremony, the bride and groom each take one of the outer candles and together light the middle candle, after which the outer candles are extinguished by the groom.
  — To add a special touch, the mothers, after being escorted in, could individually light the candle representative of their child. Or you can have both sets of parents join in the lighting of the outer candles, symbolizing the union of two families.

- Communion (the Eucharist) could also be observed by the bride and groom only, or by all who wish to partake as part of the wedding ceremony.

- The officiant could invite both sets of parents to come forward to receive the new family member, and to promise to encourage you in your new marriage.

- Both fathers could offer prayers for you and the groom, asking God's blessing upon your marriage.

- The groom could offer a prayer, either following communion or after lighting the Unity Candle.

- The honor attendants may offer special prayers or blessings for the bridal couple.

- Appropriate passages of Scripture could be read by your parents, attendants, or other family members and friends.

- Special letters from both your parents could be read by the best man and maid of honor

- The guests might join in singing one or two verses of an appropriate hymn. Have all members of the bridal party, including the officiant, memorize the song or have them refrain from singing. If the officiant is leading the song, make certain he has a copy of the words.

- If you are planning a Jewish wedding, consult with the rabbi or synagogue of your choice on the ceremony order. The following example is given only as a guide to planning the order of a Jewish ceremony.
  — Processional
  — The Greeting—Traditionally, the rabbi extends a welcome to the bride and groom and their guests.
  — Invocation—The rabbi offers a prayer for God's presence and His blessing on the marriage.
  — First Cup of Wine, with a Betrothal Blessing—The first cup of wine is lifted by the bride and groom to signify their betrothal; they may share this cup with their family and close friends.
  — Vows—These may either precede or follow the Ring Ceremony.
  — Ring Ceremony—Either a single- or double-ring ceremony.
  — Reading of the Ketubah—The Ketubah is the document giving the date and place of the wedding, the names of the bride and groom and their families, and any particulars concerning the marriage. It is much like a marriage contract, though now more only in form than in substance.
  — Second Cup of Wine (or the first cup filled and blessed a second time)—This cup signifies the nuptial ceremony. The rabbi may take a sip before first handing it to the groom, and then to the bride.
  — Special Presentations—Music, poems, prayers, etc., shared by family and friends.
  — The Seven Marriage Blessings—These may be chanted or read by the rabbi both in Hebrew and English. The bridal couple may select special guests to participate in the chanting and reading.
  — The Pronouncement
  — Benediction
  — The Broken Glass—"Mazel tov!"
  — Recessional
  — Yichud—After they leave the chuppah, the bride and groom traditionally spend ten to fifteen minutes alone in a separate room. It's a time to catch their breath, embrace, and share their first meal together, breaking their fast. Afterward they are greeted with a toast, singing and dancing, and a shower of rice.

THE RECESSIONAL:

- At the close of the ceremony, the organist begins playing the music for the recessional.

- The bride takes the groom's right arm as they lead the recessional.

- Other guests remain seated until the mothers and honored guests have been ushered out. Honored guests are ushered out in this order:
  — the bride's mother and father
  — the groom's mother and father
  — the bride's grandparents
  — the groom's grandparents

- After honored guests have been ushered out, the wedding officiant may make an announcement of:
  — Where and when the reception is to be held, and that everyone is invited.
  — Where the receiving line, if any, will be formed.
  — How the guests are to be dismissed.

- Aisle ribbons, if used, are then removed from the unreserved seating areas, and two ushers standing in the main aisle dismiss guests by rows. (Or, the guests may leave corporately.)

- At weddings of less than 250 guests, the bride and groom may return after the parents and grandparents have been ushered out to greet and dismiss their guests individually and by rows. This may be done in lieu of a receiving line.

- Special music, either vocal or instrumental, can also be included during the postlude as the guests are being dismissed, especially at large weddings or when the bride and groom are dismissing the guests themselves.

- For Jewish weddings—refer to page 118.

- As a part of the recessional in a military wedding, the ushers (military officers) draw their swords/sabers and form the arch under which the bridal couple pass. The arch may be formed inside the church at the foot of the altar steps, or outside the church either at the door or on the steps. The arch may also be formed both inside and outside, depending on the church rules and the particular branch of the service.

  When the arch is formed inside, the ushers take their places, facing each other, and on command form the arch. The bride and groom pass through as they walk up the aisle. They are followed by the maid/matron of honor and the best man, then the brides-maids in twos, with the ushers exiting through a side door to form the arch again outside. Or, once the bride and groom have passed through the arch, the ushers may sheath their swords/sabers and escort the bridesmaids up the aisle.

  When the arch is formed outside the church, the bride and groom and their remaining attendants wait in the vestibule until the ushers are in place. The parents and honored guests are escorted from the church in the usual manner and take their positions outside. The rest of the guests are then ushered out to join them. As the bridal couple arrives at the entrance, the head usher gives the command "Draw Swords" or "Draw Sabers." Each usher raises his sword/saber in his right hand with the cutting edge on top. After the bride and groom have passed through the arch, the command is given to "Return Swords" or "Return Sabers." Once this last order is given, the remaining attendants follow the bride and groom outside.

REHEARSAL

- The rehearsal is generally held the day before the wedding.

- In the case of small, intimate weddings, the rehearsal may consist of only a few minutes of instruction prior to the ceremony.

- The rehearsal allows the participants the opportunity to practice specific duties— ushering, lighting of the candles, entrances and exits, special cues, variations in the service, and so on.

- The people required to attend the rehearsal are the officiant or his or her representative, the bride and groom, their parents, all the bridal attendants, and any musicians and soloists.

- Confer with the officiant concerning any last minute changes in the order of the ceremony.

- Make certain the officiant can correctly pronounce the names of the bride and groom.

- It's best to have only one person conduct the rehearsal.

- You and your bridal attendants may use ribbon-bow bouquets from your showers to practice carrying bouquets.

- The musicians should perform enough of each selection so that everyone is acquainted with the music and aware of any necessary cues.

- Bring the following items to the rehearsal.
  - Cellophane tape (two dispensers) for taping cards to gift packages
  - Guest Book and pens
  - Ribbon bouquets
  - Programs

THE RECEPTION

- The type of your reception should be compatible with the ceremony style. There are three general types of receptions:
  - A tea or stand-up buffet, for an early- or late-afternoon wedding, usually consists of hors d'oeuvres, wedding cake, and beverage, and allows approximately eight pieces of finger food in the per-person cost.
  - A sit-down buffet, for a morning, noon or evening wedding, allows guests to serve themselves and then be seated at tables.
  - A sit-down dinner, for a wedding held after 6 P.M., offers a four- or five-course meal that is served to the seated guests.

- The basic requirements for a reception—all that is really needed—are the wedding cake and a beverage for toasting the bridal couple.

- Champagne is traditionally served at formal receptions, but the serving of alcoholic beverages of any kind is a matter of choice.

- The reception is likely to consume the largest portion of your wedding budget.

- You will need to coordinate available dates and times with both the ceremony and reception sites before confirmation can be made.

- The selection of a reception site is largely determined by the size of your guest list.

- It is important to have a room that is neither too large nor too small.
  - Your guests may feel lost in a room too large. To make the room appear smaller, you can partition off an area using potted plants, roping, or moveable room dividers.
  - If a room is too small, it may become cramped and uncomfortable. When weather and location permit, the reception could spill over into a garden or patio to increase the size of the area.

- Allow approximately three hours for your reception. The length will depend upon the style of the reception, the location you have chosen, plus the number of guests to be served.

- Most hotels and caterers, who are involved with more than one reception on any given day, prefer that you select a time for your reception that stays within a single conventional time period: morning, noon, afternoon, or evening. If your reception extends into a second time period—such as from afternoon into evening—you may find difficulty in reserving a room, or an increase in cost for the use of the room and services.

- When you have a choice of using all or some of the services offered with a possible reception site (perhaps in a "package" deal), consider every detail before deciding. "Packages" may include (a) room, food, and service; or (b) room, food, service, cake, and decorations.

- Most hotels require that you use their food and beverage services. Hotels sometimes offer "extras" with their "packages," such as discounted room prices for out-of-town guests, and special wedding night rates for the bride and groom.

- When reserving a reception room months in advance of your wedding, ask for a guaranteed price and get it in writing.

- Make certain that any contract you sign includes only those services you desire, including a cancellation policy whereby you get most of your money back should you cancel, particularly if the room is rebooked by another group.

- Some locations will allow you to reserve a room for a time before signing a contract; however, a deposit is required at signing— usually ten percent of the total estimated cost.

CATERER:

- If you are using a catering service, the time and date of your wedding must be confirmed with them and also with the ceremony and reception sites before you order any invitations.

- When seeking a caterer:
  — ask your family and friends for recommendations;
  — ask any unknown caterers for references, and samples of their food, if possible.

- By informing an experienced caterer of the amount you have budgeted for the event, the facilities to be used, and the number of invited people, he can quickly tell you what can be served, in what amount, and in what style.

- If the caterer is not familiar with the reception site you have selected, have him visit it to determine what is available and what is needed to make it functional for preparing and serving the food.

- Determine who is responsible for renting any needed extras—kitchen and serving equipment, tables, chairs, linens, table settings, etc.

- Most caterers break down the cost into a per-person charge.

- Ask if the quoted price also includes the tax and gratuity.

- You may want to ask who gets the leftover food (since you will have already paid for it).

- Ask how many people the caterer will provide for serving the food.
  — A buffet table requires a server for every main dish.
  — A sit-down dinner requires a server for every ten guests.
  — Beverages require a server for every fifty guests.

- Sometimes, even if you provide the cake, the beverages, and their respective servers, there is a service charge added by the caterer or reception site, especially when they offer the same service. This charge can be extra, or "hidden" in the total per-person charge.

- When you sign a contract, be certain it specifies exactly what is to be served, the number of people serving it, the per-person cost, the payment schedule, and a release clause should you have to cancel.

ORDERING YOUR WEDDING CAKE:

- While seeking estimates for the wedding cake from the banquet manager, caterer, or bakery, taste samples to determine the quality of the cake they offer.

- You'll need an estimate of the number of guests you're expecting when you order your cake.

- Most prices are based on a per-serving cost. A down payment is usually required when ordering.

- The number of needed servings determines both the size and shape of the cake—the number of servings per layer size.

- Do not hesitate to inquire if, with their guidance, you can design your own cake.

- If this is a second marriage, consider having your cake decorated with pastel colored icing and fresh flowers instead of the traditional white with bride-and-groom figurine.

- It's better to have the bakery deliver the cake to the reception site. They can then make any necessary repairs to the icing.

- Do not be afraid to ask friends to cut and serve the cake, even if they have never done it before. It isn't difficult when given proper instruction.

- To preserve the top layer of your cake, wrap it first in plastic wrap, then in two layers of aluminum foil, before sealing with freezer tape.

- If you order more cake than you actually need, you may donate any uncut portions to nursing homes, charitable dining rooms, and others.

CAKE SETUP:

- The wedding cake may be used as a center-piece on the Bride's Table or on the buffet table, or it may be placed on its own table. When deciding on the best location, consider serving accessibility as well as how to best highlight the cake.

- Knowing the design of your cake—round, square, banquet, or heart-shaped—consider what table would best enhance its appearance.

- Cover the table with long cloths. Skirting may be necessary to cover the table to the floor.

- Trim the table and base of the cake with flowers, greenery, garlands, or bows. The bridesmaids' bouquets may also be placed on the table as part of the decorations.

RECEIVING LINE:

- The receiving line is for the bridal couple and their parents to greet guests and receive their congratulations. It should not disband until each guest in the line has been greeted.

- If you choose not to have a receiving line, you may circulate among the guests for the same purpose, greeting each one.

- Though sometimes held at the ceremony site, a receiving line is traditionally formed at the reception.

- You may greet any late arrivals as you mingle with your guests.

- To lessen the amount of time spent receiving guests, include only the bridal couple, parents and honor attendant in the receiving line. Participants traditionally stand in this order: the bride's mother, the groom's mother, the bride, the groom, the maid of

honor, and the bridesmaids (in order, with the girl who led the processional at the end of the line).

- If the fathers are included in the line, the groom's father stands next to the bride's mother and the bride's father stands between the bride and the groom's mother. (If the bride's father participates in the line, the best man assumes the role of reception host until the bride's father is free.)

- Take into consideration your family situation when deciding who will participate in the receiving line and where they will stand, particularly if your parents are divorced.

GUEST BOOK:

- Locate the Guest Book near the entrance or at the end of the receiving line.

- The book can be circulated among the guests to be sure everyone has signed it.

- The person (or persons) who tended the book at the ceremony site could also tend it at the reception (or, others could be designated).

SEATING ARRANGEMENTS:

- Tea or stand-up buffet —
  - You may have a Bride's Table and two or three other tables designated for the bridal party, parents, grandparents, and other family members.
  - It's better to have only half as many chairs as guests, to allow room for people to move about.
  - A few tables should be placed about the room to receive the empty plates, cups and forks.

- Sit-down buffet or dinner —
  - The Bride's Table generally includes the bride's and groom's attendants, other than children, sitting in alternating positions on either side of the bridal couple:

  1 • 2 • 3 • 4 • 5 • **6** • **7** • 8 • 9 • 10 • 11 • 12

  1—Usher   2—*Bridesmaid*   3—Usher   4—*Bridesmaid*
  5—Best Man   **6—BRIDE**   **7—GROOM**   8—*Maid of Honor*
  9—Usher   10—*Bridesmaid*   11—Usher   12—*Bridesmaid*

  - Bridesmaids and ushers may be seated at specially designated tables other than the Bride's Table.

— The Parent's Table can have both sets of parents seated with the officiant and his or her spouse. You could also have separate tables for the bride's and groom's parents. Other honored guests can be seated with the parents with this arrangement:

	1		1—Bride's mother
Groom's father—8	8	2	2—Wedding officiant
Grandparent or friend —7	7	3	3—Grandparent or friend
Officiant's wife —6	6	4	4—Groom's mother
	5		5—Bride's father

— When the bride's parents are divorced, the groom's parents sit with the parent who raised the bride. The other parent sits with his or her family and friends at a separate table.
— If there are children in the wedding party, they may either be seated with their parents or at a special children's table under adult supervision.

CUTTING THE CAKE:

- At a tea or stand-up buffet where the wedding cake is the main part of the menu, you may cut the cake before the receiving line forms.

- At a sit-down buffet you could hold the cake-cutting ceremony once all your guests have gone through the receiving line.

- At a full-course sit-down dinner, the cutting and sharing of the cake by the bridal couple comes just prior to the dessert course.

- Whenever you decide to cut your cake, consider how the timing affects your guests —too long a wait often results in a great deal of leftover cake.

- You and the groom are the first to cut the wedding cake. The groom places his right hand over yours on the knife handle as you together take a slice of cake from the bottom tier. The groom gives you the first bite, and you offer the groom the second.

- After sharing their first piece of cake, you and the groom may serve your respective new in-laws. Afterward, those serving the cake will serve the bridal attendants and remaining guests.

- It is nice to decorate the handle of the cake knife with flowers, bows, or streamers.

- In a military wedding, the bride and groom use his sword/saber to cut the first slice of cake.

ENTERTAINMENT:

- The following are a few of the more common wedding traditions.

  — *Toasting the Bridal Couple*—This usually begins right after the receiving line is completed, and before the food is served at a formal reception. It is traditionally led by the best man. Following a military wedding, the first toast usually welcomes the bride into the service. The arch may again be formed over her head during the toast.

  — *First Dance*—The bride and groom traditionally dance first, followed by these pairings:
    (a) bride and her father, groom and his mother;
    (b) bride and the best man, groom and the maid of honor;
    (c) bride and groom's father, groom and bride's mother;
    (d) everyone joins in.

  It is not necessary for the bridal couple to dance the entire number before the father of the bride cuts in, or everyone is asked to join in.

  When family relationships have been disrupted through divorce, the bride and groom may share their first dance together and then open the floor for everyone else.

  At large formal affairs, dancing may begin at any time, even as early as the first arrival of guests to the reception. When dancing has occurred early, a fanfare may be played to clear the floor and signal the bridal couple's first dance. The first dance may occur immediately following the toasts and reading of any telegrams.

  — *Throwing the Bouquet and Garter*—These popular customs come near the end of the reception just before the bride and groom change into their going-away clothes. The bride first tosses her bouquet over her shoulder to the waiting unmarried women, followed by the groom removing the satin and lace garter from the bride's leg and then tossing it to the waiting single men. Florists will make up a special bouquet for throwing if you want to save your own. (These customs are generally not observed at a second wedding.)

— *Throwing the Rice*—Designate younger sisters, cousins, or friends to distribute the rice or birdseed to guests. (Again, this custom is usually omitted at a second wedding.) Check with the ceremony/reception site on their policy for throwing rice. They may prefer that you use birdseed or confetti, or nothing at all.

- Other forms of entertainment to consider:
  - The best man or emcee could read congratulatory messages received during the day.
  - Slides or a video montage of your individual childhoods and romance could be shown.
  - Solos, poetry, special readings written just for you are some of the ways your loved ones could share in your day.
  - "Your song" could be sung by a group of friends, college pals, co-workers, etc.
  - Speeches could be given by your families or close friends, offering their best wishes and perhaps sharing a few anecdotes from your past. Each should be kept to a minimum of time, no more than one or two minutes.

- Other local and ethnic customs may be observed:
  - *The Dollar Dance.* Guests must pay a dollar each to dance with the bride or groom. They may pin the money to the bride's gown, or put money or checks into a small white satin purse the bride wears on her wrist.
  - *The Grand March.* Near the end of the reception, the emcee announces the Grand March. The bride and groom lead the way, followed by their attendants and guests. As the music is played, the bridal couple leads the crowd around the room and, sometimes, even outside and around the building. At the end, everyone passes by the bridal couple so you can thank each guest for helping you celebrate your wedding day.

AFTER THE RECEPTION:

- After the reception, there is still work to be done—plan for it!

- The amount of work will largely depend on where the reception is held. There will be far less to do when the reception is held at a hotel than in a church, a hall, or at home.

- No matter how much or how little needs to be done, assign people to assist with each cleanup detail. Have plenty of help!

- Appoint someone reliable to oversee the reception—using the Reception Organizer (page 148) to answer questions, coordinate last-minute details, and direct cleanup.

HOME AND/OR GARDEN RECEPTION:

(In addition to much of the preceding information, you must also consider the following when planning a reception at home.)

- Although truly memorable, a home or garden reception is not necessarily less expensive than one held elsewhere, and may entail a great deal more work.

- In preparing for the event, you may find yourselves also involved in special cleaning, painting, and landscaping projects. Therefore, it may be expedient to hire outside professional services to ease the work load.

- If you are not having a caterer, set up a work schedule to plan and prepare the food in advance.

- Particularly with an at-home reception, you will need to study your kitchen and…
  - list any equipment needed to facilitate the preparation and serving of the food and beverages.
  - check to see if you have adequate electrical outlets.
  - check to see if the electrical appliances are in good working condition. Do not be caught at the last minute with a fifty-cup coffee maker that doesn't work.

- Study the general flow of the house and garden as you plan the location of food and beverage tables, the bride's, attendants', and parents' tables, and seating for the guests.

- It may be necessary to remove some of the furniture from your home to allow more room for your guests.

- To avoid any last-minute frustration over where to place a dish on a serving table, prepare a layout of each table showing what dish goes where. Then, prior to the reception, place a slip of paper with the name of the dish at each location.

- At a home or garden reception, you will need additional people assisting you with details:

— A crew to setup the area—tables, chairs, etc.

— Extra people to assist in the kitchen.

— Someone to "pick up" after the family when they leave for the wedding and before they return for the reception. (If the wedding is also being held at home, they could assist in straightening the house just prior to the wedding.)

— Someone to stand at each door or entrance to the house and garden to welcome guests and direct them to the reception area.

— Someone very reliable—perhaps a close personal friend—to supervise the buffet table and keep it well stocked.

— Someone to assist with serving—passing trays of hors d'oeuvres, beverages, etc.

— Others to remove empty plates and cups when guests have finished.

— Someone to keep powder rooms clean and stocked.

— A crew to clean up the entire area. Plan to remove all litter—trash and garbage—after the reception.

- Plan well in advance where to park your guests' cars. It may be necessary to have them park elsewhere, and to provide a shuttle service to your home.

- Parking attendants at your home may be needed. You may also want to consider hiring an off-duty police officer to direct traffic.

- You may need to consider an alternate location in case of undesirable weather (or be prepared with canopies, tents, fans, or heaters). Consider enclosing the following information with your invitations, giving an alternative location:

> *In case of rain the* _____
> *will be held at* _____.

POST-RECEPTION PARTIES

- When all the planning of the past few months has come to fruition, the wedding and reception are over, and the bride and groom have left for their honeymoon…now what? If the festivities occurred early in the day, the bride's parents might consider inviting family members, the groom's parents, and special friends to join them in an informal gathering at home. Continuing the celebration in an intimate home atmo-

sphere, rather than having it come to an abrupt end at the close of the reception, will help the parents to better adjust to the change of pace after the furious activity of the last few months.

- The festivities could extend over the next several days with swimming and boating trips, picnics, and trips to museums, plays, sporting events, etc.

INVITATIONS

- Order invitations only when you have confirmation from your wedding and reception sites.

- Note the time of the reception on the Reception Cards in the event of an extended lag in time between the wedding and reception beyond the normal transit time needed between sites.

- A broad range of prices is available among the different styles of invitations, but the price of comparable invitations varies little from store to store.

- Most stores require a fifty-percent deposit when ordering, with the balance to be paid at delivery.

- It's wise to order about five percent more invitations than needed to cover any mistakes or forgotten people.

- At the time you order the invitations, have the correct form for the names of the persons giving the wedding, the full names of the bride and groom, and the time, date, and location of ceremony.

— If the wedding is given by your mother and father:
> *Mr. and Mrs. James T. Smith*
> *request the honor of your presence*
> *at the marriage of their daughter*
> *Mary Sue*
> *to*
> *Robert John Brown*
> (ETC.)

— If the wedding is given by you and the groom:

Mary Sue Smith
and
Mr. Robert John Brown
request the honor of your presence
at their marriage...
(ETC.)

— If the wedding is given by your mother, and your father is deceased:

Mrs. James T. Smith
requests the honor of your presence
at the marriage of her daughter
Mary Sue
(ETC.)

[If your mother has remarried, use her present husband's name:]

Mr. and Mrs. John C. Howard
request the honor of your presence
at the marriage of her daughter
Mary Sue
(ETC.)

— If the wedding is given by your mother, and your parents are divorced, use your mother's maiden name plus your father's last name:

Mrs. Anne Miller Smith
requests the honor of your presence
at the marriage of her daughter
Mary Sue
(ETC.)

— If the wedding is given by your father, and either your parents are divorced or your mother is deceased:

Mr. James T. Smith
requests the honor of your presence
at the marriage of his daughter
Mary Sue
(ETC.)

[If your father has remarried:]

Mr. and Mrs. James T. Smith
request the honor of your presence
at the marriage of his daughter
Mary Sue

— If the wedding is given by your divorced parents, and each has remarried:

Mr. and Mrs. James T. Smith
and
Mr. and Mrs. Scott M. Jones
request the honor of your presence
at the marriage of their daughter
Mary Sue
(ETC.)

● When deciding what style of wording to use, remember "the honor of your presence" refers to a religious service and "the pleasure of your company" refers to a civil service.

● Consultants at specialty shops are available to help you with any special wording needs.

● The only difference in wording between military and civilian weddings is in the use of service titles. These titles are used in the following manner:

— Army, Marine Corps: rank of Captain or higher
— Navy: rank of Commodore or higher

Their rank precedes their name, and the service designation follows on the next line under their name:

Captain Robert John Brown
United States Army

— For officers whose ranks are below those listed above, list their name on a single line, with the line below showing their rank and service designation:

Robert John Brown
Lieutenant, United States Navy

— For military personnel without rank, list their name on a single line, with the line below showing their service designation:

Robert John Brown
United States Marine Corps

A bride in the military may omit using her own rank and service designation on the invitations unless she plans to be married in her uniform.

● The addressing should be handwritten. Traditionally it is done in black ink, but the same color as the printing may also be used.

● The invitations will come with two sets of envelopes.

● When addressing outer envelopes...

— all formal titles such as Doctor, Captain and The Reverend are written out.
— semiformal titles such as Ms., Mr., and Mrs. are abbreviated.
— Avenue, Street, Road, etc. are written out, as are the city and state.

● The wording on the inner envelope should include the titles and the last names only of the invited adults. If you wish to invite children under the age of eighteen, write their first names on a line below their parents' on the inner envelope. Older children in the family should receive their own invitations. The phrase "and family" instead of the children's names should never be used.

Example:

> Mr. and Mrs. Johnson
> John, Scott, Sarah, and Sue

- Once the invitations are addressed, place all the enclosures in the envelopes in this manner:
  - Place the reception card inside the invitation.
  - Put the response card in its envelope, and place inside invitation.
  - Place map, if used, inside invitation.
  - Place tissue over printing on invitation to prevent smudging.
  - Tuck the invitation, folded side down, into the inner envelope.
  - Place the inner envelope into the outer envelope so the writing on inner envelope faces flap.

- Mail all the invitations at the same time, using first-class stamps.

- A stamp must be provided on the return envelope if response cards are used.

- The following example of response card wording eliminates confusion for your guests and increases the likelihood that they'll return the cards on time.

line 1.	*The favor of a reply*
2.	*is requested before*
3.	*June first.*
4.	M _____
5.	will ____ will not ____ attend.
6.	*Number of Persons:* _____

- When ordering invitations, also order any other stationery accessories you may need.
  - *Reception Cards,* showing the time and place of the event.
  - *Response Cards with Printed Reply-Address Envelopes,* to be enclosed with the invitation so you can plan for the number of guests that will attend the reception.
  - *Informal Thank-You Notes,* having the name of the bride or the bride and groom on the outside, and blank on the inside.

- *Thank-You Notes,* with a pre-printed message to acknowledge when a gift is received.
- *Personalized Napkins and Matches,* for the guests to use or to keep as souvenirs.
- *Announcements,* to be sent to those you would have liked to attend your wedding, but who couldn't.
- *Pew Cards,* rarely used, but appropriate for ultra formal wedding situations, i.e., with celebrities and dignitaries. The cards may be enclosed with the invitation or sent after the acceptance has been received to ensure the correct number of seats.
- *Wedding Programs,* showing the order of the service and listing all participants. These can be folded or rolled like a scroll and tied with ribbon. Not only does a printed program serve as a guide to your wedding ceremony, but it's also a keepsake for your guests.

Programs can be engraved, printed with offset printing, or produced by word processor on a laser-printer, with calligraphy added later.

The program covers may be obtained from printers who offer a variety of paper stocks, from manufacturers of wedding invitations who offer several different styles, or from religious supply houses or bookstores who carry appropriate church bulletin covers. Or they can be of your own creation—including a photograph of the bridal couple, special drawings, etc.

The program could contain the wedding date, time, and location; the names of all the participants, their positions in the wedding, and their relationship to the bride and groom; and the order of the ceremony, with any special readings or observances. Expressions of gratitude from the bridal couple to their families and guests, and any clarifying information regarding the wedding service or reception, could also be included.

If possible, have your programs printed only two weeks or so before the wedding, to include any last-minute changes. Allow enough time, however, for proofreading the copy, making any corrections, and receiving delivery of the finished product.

- Thank-you notes do not have to be long, but they should be personal. To achieve this goal:
  - Mention your spouse's name.
  - Mention the gift.
  - Tell what you liked about the gift.
  - Tell how you will use it.

- It's better to use the blank thank-you notes (Informals) rather than the preprinted ones.

- Thank-you notes which denote the couple as being married—*Mr. and Mrs. Robert Brown,* or *Mary Sue and Robert Brown*—should be reserved for use after the wedding. For notes sent before the wedding, the printing should read as in these examples: *Mary Sue Smith and Robert Brown,* or *Mary Sue and Robert,* or *Mary Sue Smith.*

- If the engagement is broken after the wedding invitations are in the mail and there is sufficient time, you may send a printed announcement of the change of plans, as in this example:

  Mr. and Mrs. _____
  announce that the marriage of their daughter,
  _____, to Mr._____,
  will not take place..

When there isn't enough time, you'll need to phone each invited guest. It isn't necessary to reveal reasons for the break-up. Of course, any gifts must be returned to the sender.

MUSIC

CEREMONY:

- The music should be in keeping with the style of wedding you have chosen—formal, semiformal, or informal. This is achieved through the use of classical, sacred, and contemporary music, combining one or more types of music for a pleasing effect. (See the musical selection ideas on the next page.)

- If you are being married in a church, the church organist can offer many suggestions of appropriate wedding music and acquaint you with any possible restrictions on the type of music that may be used.

- Find out also whether the church requires you to use only their own musicians, before you ask someone else to participate.

- Your choice of instrumentalists and vocalists may be restricted by the ceremony site.

- Be sure you have heard the individuals perform before asking them to be part of your wedding day.

- Be prepared to pay each musician either a fee set by the individual or union scale.

- Give them a payment envelope at the close of the wedding rehearsal.

- If the performers need sheet music, you are responsible for getting it to them as soon as possible.

- They will need time to work any necessary rehearsals into their schedules.

- Have the musicians be responsible for setting their own practice times, dates and locations with each other. You might check later to see if they are prepared.

RECEPTION:

- Use the same procedure in hiring musicians for the reception as you do for the wedding. You might consider using the same musicians for both.

- Especially with groups, be sure you're hiring the musicians you're hearing.

- Use a combination of musical styles to entertain your guests—classical, Broadway tunes, pop, rock, or ethnic.

- To provide continuous music, you may use a combination of "live" and taped music.

- You may decide to have only recorded music. A professional radio "disc jockey" is usually an experienced emcee and is able to entertain your guests with a variety of music styles.

- Be sure to set a limit on the level of sound for any amplified instruments. The sound level should not hinder conversation.

- Payment to the musicians should be made immediately before they leave the reception area.

- You might consider inviting your guests to have a special part in your day by sharing their talents during the reception.

MUSICAL SELECTION IDEAS:

KEY to Selection Use: [1] Prelude [2] Processional [3] Vocal Solo [4] Instrumental Solo [5] Recessional

Bach —
Adagio Cantabile [1]
Andante from *Brandenburg Concerto No. 2* [2]
Arioso in A [1]
Jesu, Joy of Man's Desiring [1, 3]
Sheep May Safely Graze [1]

Bach, Gounod —
Ave Maria [4]

Beethoven —
Joyful, Joyful, We Adore Thee [3, 5]
Ode to Joy: Theme from Ninth
Symphony [2, 3]

Berlioz —
Trio for Two Flutes and Harp from
L'Enfance du Christ [1]

Bradbury —
Savior, Like a Shepherd Lead Us [4]

Brown —
This Is the Day (or, A Wedding Song) [3]

Campra —
Riguadon [2]

Clarke —
Trumpet Voluntary: Prince of Denmark's
March [2]

Copeland —
Bridal Prayer [3]

Cutting, Anonymous —
Greensleeves [4]

Diggle —
Wedding Prelude {1]

Fettke —
When You Created Love [3]

Gounod —
Entreat Me Not to Leave Thee [3, 4]

Grieg —
I Love Thee [3]

Handel —
Largo [2]
Allegro Maestoso from
Water Music Suite [2, 5]

Harris —
In This Very Room [3]

Hustad —
O Love That Wilt Not Let Me Go [3]

Johnson, D. —
Keep Us One [3]

Johnson, P. —
Make Us One (from *Here Comes the Son*) [3]

Lamb, Rosasco —
Household of Faith [3]

Liles, Borop —
Only God Would Love You More [3]

Limpic —
Time for Joy [3]

Liszt —
Liebestraum [1]

Malotte —
The Lord's Prayer [3, 4]

Marcello —
Psalm 19 [5]

Mendelssohn —
On Wings of Song [1]
Wedding March from
Midsummer Night's Dream [5]

Mouret —
Rondeau [1]

Pachabel —
Canon [1]

Patillo —
Flesh of My Flesh [3]

Peterson —
Jesus, Guest at Cana's Wedding [3]

Purcell —
Trumpet Tune and Air [2, 5]

Purifoy —
Here We Are Now [3]

Schumann —
Thou Art Like a Flower [3, 4]

Scott, Coomes, North —
Our Love [3]

Sheppard —
Me and My House [3]

Strader —
Together [3]

Traditional —
The Wedding Song (There Is Love) [3]

Wagner —
Bridal Chorus from *Lohrengrin* [2]

Widor —
Toccata from Symphony No. 5 [5]

Williams —
A Wedding Prayer [3]

FLOWERS

- Does the florist offer a wedding package? What is included? Can you make any substitutions?

- When you visit the florist of your choice, have the following information: your wedding style, your wedding gown color and style, your bridal attendants' colored fabric swatches, the colors of the mothers' and grandmothers' dresses and what type of corsage they prefer (pinned to the shoulder, waist, or purse, or carried or worn on the wrist), pictures or diagrams of the ceremony and reception sites and their color schemes, any restrictions concerning the floral decorations or use of candles, an approximate number and types of arrangements you will need, and the length of the aisle you'll be using.

- A skilled florist can stay within your floral budget by selecting flowers that are in season, by controlling the sizes of bouquets and corsages, by interspersing more greenery with the flowers, and by utilizing many of the flowers from the ceremony at the reception site.

- You might also consider renting potted plants, flowers, and trees for decorations.

- The bridal bouquet may be very colorful or done entirely with white flowers and greenery, using a combination of flowers in a variety of sizes. The style of the bouquet should complement the style of the gown:
  - Formal gowns: cascade, crescent, or over-arm bouquets.
  - Informal gowns: nosegay and oval-shaped bouquets or a few flowers wrapped with ribbon.
  The style of the bouquet should also complement the bride's height—smaller bouquets using more delicate flowers for petite brides, longer and larger bouquets with larger flowers for taller brides.

- Flowers to consider for your wedding are asters, camellias, daisies, freesia, gardenias, irises, lilies, lilies of the valley, orchids, roses, stephanotis, tulips, violets, and others.

- If you decide to have a "going away" corsage, it can be made as part of your bridal bouquet. The florists term this a "break-away bouquet."

- To identify the honor attendant, her bouquet can be a different color or larger than the other attendants.

- The flower girl can carry petals or flowers in a basket or a miniature bouquet.

- The groom's boutonniere is usually taken from the flowers in the bride's bouquet and is different from all the other boutonnieres.

- Extra corsages and boutonnieres could be provided for the soloists, instrumentalists, the officiant—if he isn't wearing a robe—the Guest Book and gift attendants, the wedding hostess, the cake server and hospitality committee, and any other special people. Flowers are not necessary for those who charge a fee.

- Have the florist pin the individual names to the corsages, bouquets, and boutonnieres for easy dispersal at the ceremony site. To aid your wedding coordinator, have a family member or close friend available to identify those people other than the bridal party who are to receive flowers at your wedding.

- Keep the flowers refrigerated until the last possible moment.

- If you're not using spring-loaded candles, freeze the candles ahead of time to prevent or lessen their dripping. Then, pre-light them to ensure easy lighting during the ceremony.

- Don't use spring-loaded candles in the Unity candelabra.

- If the aisle runner is to extend up the altar steps, be certain it's firmly secured to prevent slippage.

- The decorations for a military wedding may include the American flag and the colors of the bride's and/or groom's military units. Consult with the ceremony site for permission to use these.

- Boutonnieres are not worn with military uniforms.

- It's best at large weddings to have a Guest Book that can have its pages easily removed. By placing the pages on opposites ends of the table, you create two areas for signing. A floral table spray placed in the middle of the table could be used for decoration.

- If, however, you are having only one place for your guests to register, then a small arrangement—perhaps two or three flowers, baby's breath, greenery and a bow—could be used for the Guest Book stand.

- Stanchions placed outdoors and decorated with bows and greenery could be used to direct those guests unfamiliar with either the ceremony or reception sites.

- If your reception is a stand-up affair, only a few arrangements and garlands for the serving, punch, and cake tables will be needed.

- If, however, the reception is a sit-down dinner, you will need to plan centerpieces for each table in addition to any other decoration you might desire.

- The bridal attendants' bouquets can be used as decorations by placing them around the cake or on the Bride's Table.

- To fully utilize your flowers, designate someone to transfer them from the ceremony site to the reception.

- The floral baskets from your ceremony could be positioned at either end of the receiving line, beside the cake table, or even behind the Bride's Table.

- Any floral pew arrangements could also be used as decorations at the reception. Have the florist fix them for easy transferral.

- It's nice to order flowers to be sent to your parents' homes one or two days after the wedding as a special thank-you gift.

- Another nice gesture is to send flowers to your bridal shower and party hostesses. Tell the florist the kind, date, time and place of each event.

PHOTOGRAPHY

- To ensure good quality pictures, it's best to employ a professional photographer.

- When you're selecting a photographer, study his portfolio; ask if the same person who shot the pictures you're examining will be the one to shoot your wedding; and ask about any "package" plans he offers.

- The cost of the different "packages" is controlled by adjusting the quality and sizes of prints, the size of the album, and any extra services. These vary from one photographer to another, so be sure you understand exactly what is being offered.

- When you have decided on a photographer, discuss any restrictions to be observed during the ceremony—concerning such details as flash bulbs and the photographer's being at the altar or otherwise visible to guests.

- More and more couples are having their formal pictures taken—including the bridal portrait—at the ceremony site *before* the service. It is a tradition, but one based on superstition, that prevents the bride and groom from seeing each other on their wedding day before the ceremony.

- By having your portrait taken on your wedding day —
  — You avoid having to transport your gown to a studio and back, running the risk of soiling it.
  — You will have your own wedding bouquet in the picture.
  — You will be photographed at your best—a glowing bride.

- To accomplish this, you, your groom, your attendants, and families will need to be at the ceremony site approximately three hours before the wedding—allowing thirty to forty-five minutes to dress, up to two hours for photographs, and thirty to forty-five minutes to prepare for the arrival of the wedding guests.

- By taking all the formal pictures before the wedding, the groom will not have that special moment of first seeing you as you come down the aisle. Therefore, arrange a time for the two of you to be alone immediately before having your pictures taken. This could also be a special time spent with both sets of parents or with your maid of honor and best man. Be creative with this time—the sharing of special music, poetry, Scripture, or prayer.

- If you really want to wait until the ceremony for the groom to see you, then schedule only the taking of the separate formals and individual family pictures just prior to the ceremony time. But out of consideration for your guests, set a time limit for finishing the formal pictures after the ceremony.

- You may want to designate a close friend or family member to assist the photographer at the reception by identifying other special people to be photographed.

- Be aware that viewing your proofs can be an emotion-packed time. Undoubtedly you will need to eliminate some great pictures to maintain your budget.

VIDEO-TAPING AND AUDIO-TAPING

VIDEO:

- Again, view the product before buying it. Check sample tape for quality of coverage, movement, color, clarity, and sound.

- The least expensive type of videotaping uses only one camera in a more or less stationary position. The shots are taken as the action unfolds, in a straightforward manner. There's no post-production work on the tape —no editing, sound dubbing, or special effects.

- Find out about any restrictions concerning videotaping at the ceremony site.

- Ask the videographer to attend the rehearsal to determine exactly where to position the camera(s) for the best possible results while taking into consideration the location of the

bridal couple, their attendants, and the officiant during the ceremony, as well as the location of flowers, greenery, candelabra, etc.

- The rehearsal time also gives the videographer an understanding of your particular wedding ceremony so he can plan ahead for any special shots.

- Suggest to camera operators that they be as unobtrusive as possible during the ceremony.

AUDIO:

- If the ceremony site is not equipped with an audio-taping system, use a hidden cassette recorder to record the service. Adequate results can be obtained with a quality recorder.

HOUSING AND TRANSPORTATION

OUT-OF-TOWN GUESTS:

- Accommodations for out-of-town guests can be arranged at a friend's home or at a hotel.

- Hotel and travel expenses for out-of-town guests are *not* the bride or groom's responsibility.

- It is nice to provide entertainment for your out-of-town guests. This is a time to ask your friends for help. They could host a party before the wedding, an informal supper, a pool-side party, a post-reception party, or a tour of the area.

- Send the following to out-of-town guests one to two weeks before their planned arrival:
  — a copy of the information sheet on page 175— listing where everyone is staying;
  — a list of sight-seeing activities and maps of the area;
  — agendas of all activities and maps to reach their locations;
  — a list of needed clothes and leisure equipment.

- If out-of-town guests are not driving their own cars, and if they have not reserved rental cars for their use on arrival, then you could arrange their transportation or make them aware of what is available.

WEDDING PARTY TRANSPORTATION:

- Many different modes of transportation can be used for the bride, groom, parents, and attendants: from antique cars or horse-drawn carriages to limousines, privately owned cars, or whatever your imagination comes up with—antique trolley cars, bicycles, helicopters, or hot-air balloons.

- If possible, four or more vehicles should be reserved to provide transportation to the ceremony for the following: (a) the groom and best man, (b) the bridesmaids, (c) the bride's mother and honor attendant, and (d) the bride and her father.

- Transportation to the reception requires vehicles for the following: (a) the bride and groom, (b) the best man and honor attendant, (c) the bridesmaids and ushers, (d) the ring bearer and flower girl and their parents, and (e) the parents of both the bride and groom.

RENTAL EQUIPMENT

- The charge is usually based on a daily rate or a single-use price per item.
- A required security deposit generally serves to guarantee item availability.
- The deposit is refunded if items are returned in a satisfactory condition. A replacement cost is usually charged for any losses.
- Payment is generally required upon delivery or when you pick up any rented items.
- Delivery, setup and pickup fees may also be charged.

HONEYMOON

- The groom will need to arrange for a nearby hotel for your wedding night.

- If you will be traveling out of town, consult with a travel agent, who can offer valuable tips on vacation sites—available activities and weather probabilities, and take advantage of the best rates for hotel and travel accommodations.

- If you are flying, take a carry-on bag which contains all the essentials for a day.

- If you are driving a long distance, lock all luggage in the truck as a deterrent to a robbery.

- Carry a copy of your marriage certificate with you when traveling abroad, particularly if your passport is in your former name.

- Remember, do not over-schedule. Your honeymoon is a time to get to know each other.

- It's a nice gesture for you and your groom to telephone both your parents as soon as you arrive at your travel destination. It will let them know you have arrived safely and will also offer another opportunity to thank them for the wedding.

SPECIAL PARTIES

BRIDAL SHOWERS:

- Traditionally, bridal showers are given by friends rather than relatives; although relatives can help.

- Today, showers often are given not only for the bride but also for the bride and groom together.

- Since you may be given more than one bridal shower, you might suggest a different guest list for each party.

- When some guests, including family members and bridal attendants, are invited to attend more than one shower, you may suggest they bring a gift to only one.

- At the showers, have someone record the gifts and who gave them, thus helping you avoid mistakes when you send thank-you notes.

- Make "bouquets" from the ribbons and bows for you and your bridal attendants to practice with at the wedding rehearsal.

BRIDAL LUNCHEON:

- The bride usually hosts a luncheon for her attendants, her mother, and the groom's mother. It can be held a week or two before the wedding.

- If time commitments prohibit a luncheon, it's appropriate to schedule it in the evening, perhaps the same time as the Bachelor's Party.

- You can hold the luncheon at home, in a restaurant, or at a club, or even have a picnic in the park—wherever your imagination leads.

- The degree of formality is strictly your choice.

REHEARSAL DINNER:

- The Rehearsal Dinner provides a special time for the bride and groom to express their appreciation to everyone.

- Traditionally the groom's parents host the Rehearsal Dinner. The bride's family, a close relative, or a special friend may host the dinner if the groom's parents are unable to do so.

- It is usually a sit-down dinner held immediately following the rehearsal. It may be held at home, or in a restaurant, resort, or club.

- If the hosts are from out of town, you may facilitate their search for a dinner site by offering suggestions on available places to hold the dinner. Also, send copies of the menus from each place.

- The style of your wedding often sets the tone for the dinner—from a formal dinner with place cards and centerpieces to a simple, casual get-together.

- If it's being held the night before the wedding, schedule the dinner for an early hour, to allow everyone a good night's sleep.

- The following should be invited to the dinner: the bride and groom and their parents; all members of the bridal party, their spouses or fiancés; the parents of any children in the wedding party; and the officiant and his or her spouse or fiancé.

- Others to consider inviting are the organist and soloist(s) and their spouses or fiancés, the wedding coordinator and spouse or fiancé, out-of-town guests, and special friends.

PRE-CEREMONY BUFFET:

- A pre-ceremony buffet gives everyone an opportunity to relax, while also providing a nourishing boost for the remainder of the day. Too often everyone ends up eating take-out food from a fast-food restaurant because of a lack of time and planning.

- A friend might plan, prepare, and serve this special buffet for you.

- You might schedule the buffet at the bride's home or at the ceremony site, whichever is more convenient.

- The buffet could be served during the last 30 to 45 minutes prior to the ceremony, especially when you have arrived early for picture taking.

NEWSPAPER ANNOUNCEMENT

- Send your announcement to both yours and the groom's hometown newspapers.

- Most papers have a policy whereby only one announcement is printed—either the engagement or the wedding. Decide which announcement you prefer.

- Secure a submission form from the lifestyle editor (society editor) of the paper. An announcement will be written from the information you submit on the form. If a form is not available, study the announcements that appear in the paper and style yours accordingly.

- Before submitting a photograph with your announcement, check with the newspaper on their size preference. Many request a glossy 8" X 10" black-and-white print.

- Engagements are usually announced by the parents of the bride, a close relative, guardian, or friend.

- Designate a release date for the announcement if your engagement is to be announced at a surprise party.

- When the bride has been married before, it is better for her to forego an engagement announcement. She can, however, announce the wedding after it has occurred.

- Include your address and phone number in case the editor needs to verify any information you send.

- If the engagement is broken after it has been announced, you will need to send a notice to any newspaper that carried your formal announcement. Either of the following examples may be used to give notice to the paper.

  1. Mr. and Mrs. _____ announce that the marriage of their daughter, _____ , to Mr. _____ will not take place.

  2. The engagement of Ms. _____ and Mr. _____ will not take place.

SETTING UP HOUSE

WHERE TO LIVE:

- Questions to ask as you plan for setting up house include:
  — How much will you be able to afford in monthly payments?
  — Will a location you're considering be convenient to all your activities?

— Will it provide a sense of comfort and security—a feeling of being "at home?"

HOME FURNISHINGS:

- If buying major furnishings, buy the best you can afford.

- Consider multi-functional and modular pieces to avoid overcrowding your apartment or house.

- Shop for bargains as you accessorize your new home. You can create a pleasing atmosphere without spending a lot of money.

- When you buy, realize that you will probably live with whatever you purchase for a longer period of time than you may have planned —so be sure you like it.

MOVING:

- Your new address and apartment number are needed for acquiring utility services.

- Check with each utility several days before moving in, and pay required fees.

- You can either move yourself or hire professionals. It's better to hire professional movers if you are moving a great distance or have many possessions.

BRIDE'S MEDICAL

- Make an appointment with your doctor for a physical examination at least three months prior to your wedding.

- This would be a time to discuss the various forms of contraceptives with your physician.

- Your personal health, religious values, and length of intended use will all figure into the decision of which form of contraceptive to use.

- Your doctor can also answer other questions you may have about the marriage relationship.

MARRIAGE LICENSE

- All states require a marriage license. Regulations for obtaining a license vary from state to state.

- If your state requires blood tests to be taken, have verification of the results in hand when applying for your license.

- Proof of age or parental consent is necessary when making application for your license. Your driver's license, birth certificate, baptismal record, or adoption records can be used to show your age.

- If you need to show proof of citizenship, you may use your naturalization certificate, immigration record, adoption records, or passport.

- Find out if your state has a waiting period before the license is valid and you can marry; also check other timing requirements included in the license.

FINANCIAL/LEGAL

- Getting married means changes in your legal marital status on legal and financial documents, including changes in name, address, and beneficiaries.

- Although brides are not required legally to change their names to that of the husbands, this is a long established custom that is followed by the majority of women being married.

- Today, some women, because of already established professional names or to better maintain their own personal identity, are choosing not to follow this custom. They are retaining their former names, or using their former names professionally and their husbands' names socially, or using a hyphenated combination of both of their names.

- Whatever name you choose, be consistent to avoid confusion.

QUICK REFERENCE

NAMES & PHONE NUMBERS

❖ Ceremony / Reception Site ❖

_____ (___) _____
_____ (___) _____
_____ (___) _____

❖ Professional Services ❖

_____ (___) _____
_____ (___) _____
_____ (___) _____
_____ (___) _____
_____ (___) _____
_____ (___) _____
_____ (___) _____
_____ (___) _____
_____ (___) _____

❖ Party Hostesses ❖

_____ (___) _____
_____ (___) _____
_____ (___) _____
_____ (___) _____
_____ (___) _____
_____ (___) _____
_____ (___) _____

❖ Others ❖

_____ (___) _____
_____ (___) _____
_____ (___) _____

❖ Your Future Home ❖

_____ (___) _____

Our Wedding Keepsake

SOMETHING OLD: _____

    GIVEN BY: _____

SOMETHING NEW: _____

    GIVEN BY: _____

SOMETHING BORROWED: _____

    GIVEN BY: _____

SOMETHING BLUE: _____

    GIVEN BY: _____

BRIDAL BOUQUET CAUGHT BY: _____

_____

BRIDE'S GARTER CAUGHT BY: _____

_____

SPECIAL MEMORIES OF THE DAY: _____

_____

_____

_____

_____

_____

_____

_____

_____

_____

_____

_____

_____

_____

_____

_____

_____

_____

_____